Join a Cook's Tour of the World's Hottest Cuisines

From Mexico . . .
Holy Jalapeño Soup and Tacos with Salsa Fresca

From the Caribbean . . .
Jamaican Jerk-Spiced Tempeh and Rum and Lime-Laced Sweet Potatoes

From Italy . . .
Spicy Cavatelli Primavera and Stuffed Cherry Peppers

From the Middle East . . .
Red Chili Hummus and Vegetable Kebabs

From Africa . . .
Pumpkin Stew and Chickpea Patties

From Thailand . . .
Vegetable Spring Rolls and Spicy Peanut Sauce

. . . and many more spicy favorites from the United States, South America, Spain, India, China, Japan, Hungary, Korea, and other international hot spots.

Robin Robertson is a professional chef and cooking teacher. She was trained in French cuisine, but left the restaurant industry when she realized that the combination of long hours, rich sauces, and red meat was seriously affecting her health. Today, she cooks and teaches her own innovative, low-fat vegetarian cuisine. She is also the author of *366 Healthful Ways to Cook Tofu and Other Meat Alternatives*, *366 Simply Delicious Dairy-Free Recipes*, and *The Soy Gourmet*, all available from Plume.

Some Like It Hot

200 SPICY VEGETARIAN RECIPES FROM AROUND THE WORLD

Robin Robertson

A PLUME BOOK

Ed Blonz, Ph.D. is a nationally syndicated columnist and author of "Your Personal Nutritionist" Series (Signet, 1996). He is President of Nutrition Resource. Nutrition analysis was supplied using the Nutritionist IV™ software.

The information in this book is based upon the latest data made available by government agencies, food manufacturers and trade associations. It is important to note that all nutrient breakdowns for processed foods are subject to change by manufacturers without notice and may therefore vary from printing to printing.

PLUME
Published by the Penguin Group
Penguin Putnam Inc., 375 Hudson Street, New York, New York 10014, U.S.A.
Penguin Books Ltd, 27 Wrights Lane, London W8 5TZ, England
Penguin Books Australia Ltd, Ringwood, Victoria, Australia
Penguin Books Canada Ltd, 10 Alcorn Avenue, Toronto, Ontario, Canada M4V 3B2
Penguin Books (N.Z.) Ltd, 182–190 Wairau Road, Auckland 10, New Zealand

Penguin Books Ltd, Registered Offices: Harmondsworth, Middlesex, England

First published by Plume, an imprint of Dutton NAL, a member of Penguin Putnam Inc.

First Printing, September, 1998
10 9 8 7 6 5 4 3 2 1

 REGISTERED TRADEMARK—MARCA REGISTRADA

LIBRARY OF CONGRESS CATALOGING-IN-PUBLICATION DATA:

Robertson, Robin (Robin G.)
    Some like it hot : 200 spicy vegetarian recipes from around the world / Robin Robertson.
        p.   cm.
    Includes index.
    ISBN 0-452-27869-4
    1. Vegetarian cookery.   2. Spices.   3. Cookery, International.
I. Title.
TX837.R625   1998
641.5'636—dc21   98-10362
                                                                                              CIP

Printed in the United States of America
Set in Galliard
Designed by Eve L. Kirch

This book is dedicated to people throughout the world
who are helping to change our planet for the better
through the extended circle of compassion, respect for the environment,
and by eating a healthier diet.

CONTENTS

Introduction: A Culinary Passport   xi

One: The Americas

Recipe Mini-Index   3
Blazing Trails in the New World   5
The United States   7
Mexico   17
Caribbean   37
South America   45

Two: Mediterranean Europe

Recipe Mini-Index   53
Mediterranean Heat   55
Italy   57
Spain   73
Europe   83

Three: The Middle East and Africa

Recipe Mini-Index   97
Pungent Safaris and Fragrant Caravans   99

The Middle East   101
Africa   121

Four: India

Recipe Mini-Index   143
Fiery Bliss in India   145
India   147

Five: Asia

Recipe Mini-Index   179
Searing Asian Appetites   181
China   183
Thailand   203
Pan-Asia   217

Index   237

ACKNOWLEDGMENTS

Many thanks to my editor, Jennifer Moore, for her helpful insights during this project. I also wish to thank my agent, Arielle Eckstut, for her enthusiastic support, and my dear friends B. J. Atkinson, Pat Davis, Patty Gershanik, Lisa Lange, Marie Lange, and Marianne Swart, for sharing their resources and sampling my recipes. I'm also grateful to my sister, Carole Lazur, for our long-distance reminiscing of old family recipes and my husband, Jon Robertson, for his invaluable assistance, computer help, and tireless tasting of hot and spicy dishes throughout the writing of this book.

INTRODUCTION

A Culinary Passport

Heat Wave

Before the advent of refrigeration, spices were used not only to enhance the flavor of food but also to preserve it and keep it edible as long as possible. Spices were also used as money in arid or tropical countries such as India, Egypt, and the Middle East, where food spoiled quickly. The spicy traditions that arose from these practical beginnings have spread throughout the world, and spices are now valued above all for their ability to transform otherwise humble meals into exotic and aromatic delights. Spices lend themselves especially well to vegetarian cooking, which is becoming increasingly popular as people seek healthier lifestyles. Even people who still eat meat are now including meatless meals in their diets at least once or twice a week.

I have found that spicy international cooking is a great way to introduce people to vegetarian meals. While some family members or dinner guests may fear being served a naked slab of tofu instead of a juicy T-bone, they're not likely to complain when presented with a colorful international feast redolent with heady spices—a Moroccan tagine or an Indian curry, for example.

I learned to crave spicy food as a child growing up in an Italian household. Every Thursday I would anticipate my mother's rich, dark tomato sauce infused with fresh garlic, basil, and red wine, and sprinkled liberally with hot red pepper flakes. In our house "spicy" was synonymous with "hot." Early in life my dad taught me the art of snacking on scorching cherry peppers right from the jar.

During my childhood I thought that spicy foods belonged solely to the provinces of Italy, until I had my first taste of the Sichuan cooking of China. As a young adult, I began to explore spicy cuisines with regular trips to ethnic grocery stores and restaurants. Eventually I began talking to the chefs and shopkeepers in an effort to understand what gave a particular cuisine its identity. From Chinese to Mexican and Thai to

Indian, I was amazed at both the similarities and the differences among the spicy cuisines of the world. I became enamored of the exquisite flavors that spicy foods impart, and the fact that vegetarian ingredients are particularly well suited to spicy cooking which the mild flavors of grains and vegetables complement so well.

When I began working in restaurant kitchens in the 1970s, I incorporated global spices and cooking techniques into my recipes whenever possible. Throughout my cooking career, I have been fortunate to work with international chefs, picking up culinary tidbits along the way. I've also been blessed with friends from all over the world, whose cooking customs I'm always eager to absorb. In addition, each time I travel to a large city, I seek out the specialty grocery stores, the open-air markets, and of course, the ethnic restaurants that will excite my palate and transport me to regions of the world that, even without visiting, I have learned to know and love through food.

The two hundred recipes in this book will help you explore a wide spectrum of classic spicy international cuisines as well as some of my innovative fusion ideas. Along the way, you will discover many wonderful ways to enhance your personal recipe collection. There are recipes from the Middle East and Latin America, from Asia and the Mediterranean, and from many places in between. Most of these recipes are surprisingly easy to prepare, even though the spices give them an exotic and complex flavor. And they are not full of esoteric ingredients. Most simply combine common ingredients in exciting ways.

This book contains many familiar favorites, some reworked with healthful ingredients, and many recipes that may be new to you. Most feature beans, grains, and vegetables and are either indigenous to or inspired by a particular cuisine. In addition, I've reinterpreted some recipes traditionally made with meat, replacing the meat with tofu, tempeh, or other plant-based meat alternatives. Whatever your preferences, I am confident that you will enjoy exploring the flavors of the world using this book as your guide.

Chilies by Any Other Name

Chilies are the culinary world's most popular heat source. They are members of the capsicum family and are available whole, fresh, dried, canned, and jarred, and come in the form of oil, paste, powder, and flakes. Erroneously called chili "peppers," due to an error by Christopher Columbus, chilies are not peppers at all, but actually fruits.

With over a hundred varieties of chilies available, recipes calling for them can sometimes be confusing, especially since chilies range in heat from mildly sweet to searingly hot. To keep your spice life simple, you may want to pick a couple of chili varieties that you like and stick with them. Veteran aficionados of hot food, on the other hand, may enjoy experimenting with different varieties.

If a recipe calls for mild, dried chilies, anchos are a good choice. For hot dried chilies, try cayennes or serranos. Commercial chili powders, usually a blend of ground dried chilies combined with other spices, such as cumin and oregano, vary in quality. Experiment with a few different brands until you find one that you like. Paprika, the Hungarian word for "sweet pepper," refers to the powder made from ground sweet peppers. It can be labeled either "sweet" or "hot," depending on what parts of the pepper are used. When the seeds and membranes are included, or when hot varieties of chilies are also included, the result is a "hot" paprika.

Many hot condiments are made with chilies, such as chili oil, chili sauce, chili paste, hot bean sauce, salsas, and many chutneys. Tabasco is a brand of hot chili sauce that is in such wide use that it is known simply by its brand name.

The most commonly available fresh chilies are listed below along with their characteristics. (Lengths and widths are approximate.)

Anaheim (or California chili): Mild; light green; 6 inches long and 1 inch wide.
Cayenne: Very hot; bright red; usually dried and ground to produce "cayenne pepper"; 3 to 4 inches long and 1/2 inch wide.
Jalapeño: Very hot; medium to dark green; 2 inches long and 1/2 inch wide.
Habañero: Very hot; yellow to light green; 3 inches long and 1 inch wide.
Poblano: Mild to hot; dark green, resembles a bell pepper; called "ancho" when dried; 4 inches long and 3 inches wide.
Serrano: Very hot; deep green, bright red when ripe; 2 inches long and 3/8 inch wide.
Thai: Extremely hot; bright red; 2 1/2 inches long and 1/4 inch wide.

As anyone who has done direct "hand to chili" combat can tell you, the best way to handle hot chilies is very carefully. A hot variety of chili can actually cause your skin to burn on contact. It is wise to wear rubber or disposable gloves when handling chilies, and if that is not possible, try not to let your skin come in direct contact with them. If it does, wash the affected area immediately. Do not rub your eyes after handling chilies.

There are two schools of thought regarding chili identification. Chili purists would prefer to see specific names of chilies for particular uses. However, when you go to a supermarket, you may find a variety of chilies labeled simply "hot peppers." Those who don't know serranos from anchos need not be discouraged. While I do specify particular chilies in certain recipes, often I simply call for "hot" or "mild" chilies, and I promise that most recipes will work just fine when one chili is swapped for another. For those who avoid heat of any kind, simply substitute sweet red bell peppers for chilies, and you'll generally end up with a mild yet flavorful dish.

The Spices of Life

In addition to chilies, there are other sources of heat used in various cuisines throughout the world. The following are the most common.

Cumin: A component of both commercial chili powder and curry powder, cumin is used in Mexico, India, the Middle East, and North Africa. It has a strong, pungent, slightly bitter taste. Cumin seeds are yellowish brown and are sometimes confused with caraway seeds, though their flavors are completely different. Prior to using them, the seeds should be roasted and crushed to bring out their flavor. Cumin also comes in ground form.

Curry Powder and Paste: These blends of aromatic herbs and spices are sold premixed in the West but in places like India and Thailand, where curry dishes are quite common, they are almost always prepared fresh by the cook, who customizes his or her blend to the specific dish being prepared. Curry pastes often include chilies and herbs. Good-quality curry spice mixtures are available at ethnic grocery stores and specialty food shops. I have also included recipes for such spice mixtures in this book.

Ginger: Hot and pungent and used a lot in Asian cooking, this root adds a distinctive flavor and bite to both sweet and savory foods. When purchasing, look for firm, unblemished roots. Mature ginger needs to be peeled before using. It should be stored in a cool dry place. Powdered ginger, used mostly in baking and spice mixtures, doesn't compare in flavor or intensity to fresh ginger. The two are not interchangeable in recipes.

Horseradish: This herb is grown mainly for its large, white roots, which are sold fresh or preserved in vinegar or beet juice and bottled. Unlike the heat of chilies, which affects the tongue and lips, horseradish goes straight for the nose, clearing out the sinuses and bringing tears to the eyes. Horseradish is commonly used in Eastern European cooking. (Also see wasabi.)

Mustard: Available in the form of mustard seeds, mustard powder, or prepared mustard, this hot and spicy herb is used in many cuisines throughout the world. There are forty species of mustard, which belong to the crucifer (cabbage) family. Ground mustard is often mixed with water to form a paste. An especially hot variety is Chinese mustard. One of the most popular of the prepared mustards is Dijon, which is used in French cooking and has a rich depth of flavor. Like horseradish, mustard's pungency affects the nasal passages.

Peppercorns: Black, white, and green peppercorns are the same berry picked at different stages of ripeness and processed differently to produce varying degrees of heat. The black peppercorn is picked half-ripe and is the most hot and pungent. White pepper, the mildest, is made from berries that are picked very ripe and then soaked in saltwater to dissolve the dark outer shell. Green peppercorns, picked when underripe, are often pickled and sold in small jars. Their flavor is more piquant. Freshly ground pepper is generally added toward the end of cooking time, as it tends to lose its flavor and become bitter if cooked longer than an hour or so.

Wasabi: A member of the horseradish family, wasabi is served as a condiment with sushi in Japan. Available fresh or in a powder that is mixed with water, a little wasabi goes a long way. Be careful when you use it—too much can almost produce an altered state of consciousness.

Your International Pantry

In order to produce the spicy flavors of a particular cuisine, several ingredients are generally combined with chilies. For example, combine chilies with cumin and tomatoes, and you have the beginning of a Mexican recipe. Chilies coupled with soy sauce and sesame oil is a distinctly Asian combination. Pair chilies with coconut milk or lemongrass and you have transported yourself to Indonesia.

A well-stocked pantry allows you to prepare wholesome and delicious international meals on a moment's notice. Included in your inventory should be a variety of canned and dried beans, dried and canned chilies, capers, canned and sun-dried tomatoes, dried mushrooms, a variety of spices including good curry spice mixtures (both Indian and Thai varieties) and chili powder, plus dried fruits, oils, olives, whole grains, and pastas.

Following is a list of some of the other ingredients used often in the recipes in this book. Most are available in supermarkets, natural food stores, or ethnic grocery stores.

Basil: An aromatic herb that is used in Mediterranean, Thai, and Vietnamese cuisines. Sixty varieties of basil exist, and each has a distinctive subtle nuance, such as lemon, jasmine, or mint. Most basil varieties are interchangeable. Basil works especially well in tomato-based dishes, and is used both fresh and dried, though fresh basil is far superior in taste. A fragile and highly perishable plant, fresh basil leaves are best used raw, or added at the end of cooking time in a recipe.

Cilantro: The leaves (and sometimes even the roots and stems) of the coriander plant, also known as Chinese parsley, are widely used in Asian and Latin American cooking, imparting a strong perfumelike flavor and aroma. Cilantro is generally used fresh.

Coriander Seeds: One of the oldest spices known to humankind, coriander seeds are used whole or ground into powder in Indian, Asian, and Latin American dishes. They are an essential element in many Indian spice mixtures, including curry powder.

Couscous: A quick-cooking grain made from semolina, couscous is popular in countries of the Middle East and northern Africa. It can be served like rice or other grains to complement stewed dishes, soups, or salads, or it can be served as a hot cereal or even made into a dessert.

Garlic: This pungent edible bulb is used in cooking throughout the world, often in conjunction with chilies, herbs, and spices. Try to use fresh garlic whenever possible—garlic powder is a weak substitute.

Lemongrass: As the name implies, this aromatic grass has a pungent, lemony flavor. It is a key ingredient in Thai and Vietnamese cooking.

Olive Oil: This rich, fruity oil is commonly used in Mediterranean cooking. The best quality olive oils are labeled "extra-virgin."

Oregano: Used in Mexico and Europe, this pungent herb, of which there are over thirty varieties, is often used in tomato-based dishes such as pizza or pasta sauce. Oregano and marjoram are often used interchangeably.

Seitan: Called "wheat meat," seitan is made from wheat gluten and is used as a meat alternative in Asian cooking. It can be made from a dry mix or from scratch using whole-wheat flour. For convenience, I suggest using Seitan Quick Mix® by Arrowhead Mills or prepackaged seitan, which is available in the refrigerator or freezer section of many natural food stores.

Sesame Oil: This oil is available in light and dark varieties. The dark oil, made from toasted sesame seeds, has a rich nutty flavor and is used frequently in Asian cuisine. The light-colored oil is less flavorful but is more heat stable and is used for cooking at higher temperatures.

Tahini: A ground sesame seed paste widely used in Asian and Middle Eastern cooking.

Tamari: A high-quality soy sauce used in Asian cooking to impart a salty flavor. Low-sodium tamari can be used as a substitute for salt in many dishes.

Tempeh: An Indonesian meat alternative made from fermented soybeans that have been compressed into cakes. Firm in texture and high in protein, tempeh must always be cooked before eating. It can sometimes have a strong flavor, which can be mellowed by poaching it before using it in a recipe. Tempeh can be cubed, sliced, grated, or chopped and is especially good when marinated. It is available fresh or frozen in natural food stores.

Tofu: Soybean curd that has been pressed into white cakes. It is available in regular or silken varieties, both of which come in textures ranging from soft to extra-firm.

Tofu keeps for several days in the refrigerator when covered with water as long as the water is changed daily. It's best to use an opened package of tofu as soon as possible. Before using tofu, it should be pressed and blotted to remove excess water. Silken tofu is available in aseptic containers and may be stored without refrigeration until opened. Widely used in Asian cooking, tofu is high in protein and calcium, with no cholesterol, and can be used as a dairy or meat alternative. Since tofu absorbs the flavors of the foods with which it is cooked, it is highly versatile. Silken tofu is best used as a dairy substitute in sauces, soups, and desserts, whereas regular tofu, which is firmer and can be sautéed, braised, fried, or grilled, works well as a meat substitute.

Turmeric: An ingredient in many Indian curry mixtures, this spice adds a vivid yellow color and slightly peppery flavor to food and is often used as an economical substitute for saffron. Turmeric should be used sparingly so its flavor does not overpower other ingredients.

How the Book Is Organized

The recipes in this book are separated into the five main geographical sections where the world's spiciest cuisines are found: The Americas, Mediterranean Europe, The Middle East and Africa, India, and Asia. Within each main section, recipes are organized by particular countries or regions. For your convenience, each main section has its own mini-index to help you quickly find recipes for appetizers, soups, salads, main dishes, and condiments. This will help you put together your own great creative menus from the same cultural families.

The recipes are also thoroughly cross-indexed in the main index at the back, with listings for all the appetizers, soups and stews, main dishes, rice and noodle dishes, salads and side dishes, sauces, condiments, and main ingredients. This allows you the flexibility to either immerse yourself in a particular region's cuisine or look for an intriguing individual recipe for a less focused meal.

To further assist you in choosing recipes, super-hot dishes are marked with three flames (🔥🔥🔥), medium-hot dishes by two flames (🔥🔥), and mildly spicy dishes by a single flame (🔥). You can always alter the degree of heat by increasing or decreasing the quantity of chilies and other hot spices that you use, all according to individual preference. For example, if you like exotic flavors, but not too much heat, simply decrease the number of chilies or eliminate them entirely. While this may render some recipes less than "traditional," they will still be flavorful and delicious.

A Question of Dairy

Increasing numbers of medical experts agree that consumption of dairy products can be hazardous to your health. Fortunately, there are plenty of delicious alternatives now available at natural food stores. Made from soy, rice, oats, and other vegetable products, there are milks, cheeses, even vegan yogurt, cream cheese, and sour cream. A quarter cup of silken tofu can replace an egg in most recipes and other egg replacement products are also available. Soy milk, rice milk, and oat milk are interchangeable with dairy milk in most recipes.

Although I have eliminated dairy products from my cooking, in certain recipes in this book I give both dairy and dairy-free options.

Helpful Hints

Whenever available, buy fresh organic produce that is both firm and rich in color. Be sure to wash all produce well before using, rinsing leafy greens and scrubbing other vegetables and fruits. Fresh herbs, while a welcome addition to your cooking, can be expensive. Consider growing your own herbs in a window box, even if it's just a few of your favorites. You'll be rewarded with lovely plants, as well as lively seasonings at a fraction of the price of buying fresh herbs at the supermarket. Keep plenty of garlic, ginger, and onions on hand as they store well and are indispensable seasonings.

I generally recommend safflower oil, as it is among the lowest in saturated fat. However, many recipes require the special flavors of olive or sesame oil in order to succeed, and they are noted accordingly. If you wish to cut down on your intake of fats, you can substitute nonstick vegetable cooking spray, vegetable stock, or water in your cooking.

About Beans

From the tiny lentils to the meaty favas, beans are a major staple throughout the world. They are inexpensive, easy to store and prepare, and high in protein and other nutrients. In addition to grains, beans are a mainstay of the international vegetarian kitchen.

Many varieties of beans are available dried. When stored in airtight containers, they keep for several months. Be sure to pick through dried beans before using them to remove any small stones or other particles that may be hidden among them. They should also be rinsed well to free them from dust and other impurities. In order to shorten the cooking time, most dried beans require soaking before cooking, except for lentils and split peas, which cook relatively quickly. To soak beans, place them in a bowl with enough water to cover by two inches. Soak overnight, then drain before cooking.

To quick-soak beans, place them in a pot with enough water to cover by two inches. Bring to a boil for two minutes. Remove from the heat, cover, and let stand for two hours. Drain before cooking. Beans should be simmered on low heat in about two cups water per cup of beans, and cooked with the lid on, stirring occasionally. Salt should be added at the end of the cooking time, as salting too soon will toughen the beans and lengthen the cooking time. Generally, one cup dried beans will yield about two-and-a-half cups cooked beans. Cooking times may vary depending on the size and quality of the bean. Approximate cooking times for soaked beans are listed below.

Bean	Cooking time
Black beans	1 1/2 to 2 hours
Black-eyed peas	1 hour
Cannellini beans	2 hours
Chickpeas	2 to 3 hours
Great Northern beans	1 1/2 hours
Kidney beans	2 hours
Lentils	45 minutes
Pinto beans	2 hours
Split peas	45 minutes

When cooking dried beans, consider making a double batch and freezing the extra beans for future use. Otherwise, you can rely on one of my favorite convenience foods, canned beans. Available in many varieties, and ready to use after a quick rinsing and draining, thanks to them I have put together many meals in minutes. I generally list "cooked" beans when used as a recipe ingredient, thus allowing you to decide whether to prepare them ahead of time, or simply open a can.

Great Grains

Whole grains have been a dietary mainstay of most of the cultures in the world since ancient times. Although we often eat our grains in processed or refined forms such as breads and pastas, whole grains are more nutritious—they're high in protein, B vitamins, Vitamin E, iron, magnesium, and zinc. And nothing beats their nutty flavor!

To cook whole grains, rinse thoroughly to remove any particles or dust. After draining, most grains can be cooked in a pot with about two or three times as much water, depending on cooking time. Bring the water to a boil, cover, reduce the heat to low, and simmer until tender. The following is a list of cooking times for the most commonly used grains.

Grain (1 cup)	Water amount (in cups)	Cooking time	Yield (in cups)
Barley	3	1 hour	3½
Basmati rice	3	15 minutes	3
Brown rice	3	45 minutes	3
Bulgur	2	10 minutes	3
Couscous	2	10 minutes	2
Millet	3	30 minutes	3½
Quinoa	2	20 minutes	3½

Stock Answers

A basic vegetable stock is used in many of the recipes, mainly to enhance the flavor of the dish. While a homemade stock made with fresh vegetables is best, it is not always available. If you don't have your own vegetable stock on hand, use vegetable base or bouillon that has been reconstituted with water according to package directions. When choosing a commercial base, be sure to read the ingredient list to avoid products that contain monosodium glutamate or other additives. In a pinch, you can even substitute water seasoned with a little tamari or miso paste for stock. Canned vegetable broths are also available.

Basic Vegetable Stock

Amounts and types of vegetables may be varied, but avoid strong-flavored vegetables, such as cabbage, that might overpower the stock. For convenience, make this stock in advance and freeze it in easy-to-use portions.

1 tablespoon safflower oil
2 large onions, quartered
(including peel)
2 ribs celery, coarsely chopped
(including leaves)
2 carrots, coarsely chopped
1 potato (skin on), sliced

2 garlic cloves, unpeeled, crushed
1/2 cup chopped parsley (including
stems)
2 bay leaves
1 1/2 teaspoons salt
1/2 teaspoon black peppercorns

Heat the oil in a large stockpot over medium heat. Add the onions, celery, and carrots, cover and cook for 5 minutes. Add the potato, garlic, parsley, bay leaves, salt, and peppercorns. Cover the vegetables with twice the amount of water. Bring to a boil, then reduce the heat and simmer for an hour or more until a rich color and flavor are reached. Strain the stock through a colander into another pot. Stock can now be used in recipes or cooled, portioned, and stored in the freezer for future use.

Makes about 10 cups

Equipment

When you decide to journey into the realm of exotic cuisines, you shouldn't feel that you need to go out and buy special equipment. I feel that quality is better than quantity. I'd rather have a few good multipurpose pots and pans than collect a kitchen full of trendy gadgets.

Good-quality, heavy, stainless-steel pots and pans will get you through any recipe. You don't need a couscousière, a clay tagine pot, or a paella pan in order to make the correlating dishes because a good 12-inch skillet or a large saucepan will work fine. The same skillet can be used in place of a wok for stir-fries. However, lightweight aluminum pans spell disaster in any language because they distribute heat unevenly, which can cause food to cook unevenly or burn. Additionally, the aluminum can leach into the food.

A set of sharp high-carbon steel knives is a worthy kitchen investment, as is a sturdy, flat cutting board to use with the knives. A food processor, a blender, and a spice mill can cut labor time dramatically.

Cooling Down

Fiery food lovers can be made as well as born, since we are able to build up to a tolerance for heat in our food. However, even the most ardent fire-eater needs to know how to cool down after one chili too many. Whether it be with drink, a side dish, or a dessert, putting the fire out takes a bit of know-how.

While water may be the way to put out conventional fires, you can forget about using water to tame a fire in your mouth, since the capsaicin oil released from chilies is not water-soluble. Beers, wines, and creamy or fruity drinks are all more effective for cooling down the inside of your mouth. Some of the most natural foils for hot foods are bread, pasta, rice, or other grain-based starches, which cushion the assault of our favorite spicy dishes. Some cuisines, such as Italian, Indian, and Ethiopian, offer both grain and bread to soothe the tongue. Thai and other Asian cuisines rely on rice or noodles to soak up the heat. Many cultures include soothing dairy-based accompaniments in their cuisines, such as the Indian *raita*, which is made with yogurt. For those of us who don't eat dairy products, a puréed tofu-based or vegetable side dish can fill in. I find fresh fruit, a cooling sorbet, or a creamy pudding to be a perfect denouement to most spicy meals.

Ready for Departure

It's amazing to realize that in our very own kitchens, we can have the world at our fingertips. We can start with simple grains and fresh vegetables and with the mere grind of a spice mill finish with an astounding variety of international dishes. What better way to promote the true oneness of all people than by creating a fusion of various cuisines, a blending of flavors and customs to intrigue and delight the senses? This is one trip that never has to come to an end. The richness of varied cultures can be ours for the tasting anytime we desire. For those of us who enjoy feasting on dishes that are at once spicy, healthful, and delicious, what more could we ask?

ONE

The Americas

▼▼

The Americas Recipe Mini-Index

Appetizers

Jamaican Jerk-Spiced Tempeh Nuggets *38*   Smooth and Sassy Guacamole *17*

Spicy Plantain Fritters *37*   Texas Caviar *7*

Soups and Stews

Caribbean Vegetable Stew *39*   Chilled Avocado Soup *19*

Holy Jalapeño Soup with Tortilla Triangles *21*   Spicy Corn Soup *20*

Spicy Okra Gumbo *8*   Yucatán Potato Soup *18*

Salads

Avocado and Jicama Salad with Lime Dressing *23*   Island Rice Salad *40*

Lime-Marinated White Bean Salad *45*

Mexican Rice and Bean Salad with Cumin Vinaigrette *22*

Mexican Fruit Salad *24*

Sides

Cajun Coleslaw *9*   Quinoa-Stuffed Avocados *46*

Rum and Lime-Laced Sweet Potatoes *41*

Main Courses

Argentinean-Inspired Seitan Cutlets *47*   Baked Tempeh Enchiladas *32*

Barbados-Style Grilled Kebabs *42*   Brown Rice with Creole Sauce *12*

Chilean Stuffed Peppers *49*   Citrus-Marinated Tempeh with Sweet Potatoes *48*

Grilled Vegetable Fajitas *29*   Jamaican Baked Vegetables *43*

Jumpin' Jambalaya *11*   Mexican Seitan with Tomato-Orange Sauce *33*

Penne Pasta with Jalapeño Sauce *13*   Red Beans and Rice Casserole *31*

Red-Hot White Bean Chili *10*   Rice with Tomatillos and Chilies *34*

Spicy Bean and Spinach Burritos *27*   Tacos with Salsa Fresca *25*

Veggie Quesadillas *30*

Dressings, Sauces, and Condiments

Borracha Sauce *35*   Brazilian Lemon-Chili Sauce *50*

Cilantro-Chili Pesto *14*   Jamaican Jerk Sauce *44*   Mole Poblano *36*

Salsa Fresca *26*   Salsa Picante *28*   Texas Barbecue Sauce *15*

▲▲

Blazing Trails in the New World

The United States

Known as a melting pot of nationalities and customs, it has been argued that the United States doesn't have a national cuisine of its own. However, without exception, each region features a cuisine that has been influenced by the food and customs of other areas of the globe. While many international cuisines have become popular in the restaurants of its major cities, America's own spicy cuisines have sprung up mostly in the southern and southwestern states. In the states of Texas, New Mexico, and California, Mexican cuisine has had the most influence on regional cooking, with its use of chilies, cumin, and other spices, and has contributed greatly to what has come to be called Tex-Mex or Southwestern cooking.

It is said that chili con carne is not a Mexican dish, but rather an American invention, and there is no shortage of chili recipes throughout the United States. Another spicy, distinctly American favorite is barbecue sauce, which can be found in infinite variations.

Louisiana's spicy Cajun cuisine traces its origin to a number of sources and has been said to be the only cuisine actually invented in America. The word "Cajun" is a corruption of the word "Acadian," and the Acadians were French settlers from Nova Scotia who were exiled to Louisiana in the mid-1700s by the British. In addition to the European influence on their cooking, the Cajuns learned about filé (ground sassafras leaves) from the Indians and okra from the freed African slaves. They put it all together with the rice and chilies that proliferated in Louisiana. The liberal use of spices in the form of hot pepper sauce and ground cayenne, as well as a rich dark roux, are at the heart of many intoxicatingly pungent dishes of gumbo and jambalaya. Louisiana chefs also helped spicy blackened entrées find their place on restaurant menus throughout the country.

Mexico

Mexican cuisine is an exciting blend of ancient Indian cooking and that of the Spanish explorers and other Europeans. The Mexican Indians had long been making use of the abundance of native corn, tomatoes, beans, and squash. The Spanish brought wheat, olives, and rice, and introduced citrus fruits as a way to season food. The native Mexican Indian diet was largely vegetarian until the Spanish introduced the pig. Pork then became popular in Mexico, as did cooking with lard. Chilies have always abounded in Mexico, where they are said to have been first domesticated around 7000 B.C. In addition cumin, cilantro, oregano, garlic, and cinnamon are also used to flavor many Mexican dishes.

While many Mexican dishes have become fast food favorites in the United States, there is far more to Mexican cuisine than the ubiquitous tacos and enchiladas that come to us from the Chihuahua and Sonora regions. Beans, grains, and fresh vegetables are featured in many Mexican meals, and those dishes that are traditionally made with meat are easily adapted with meat alternatives. Mexico boasts many regional specialties, including such diverse sauces as *mole poblano*, the world-famous sauce from Puebla that combines chocolate and chilies, and the tangy *borracha* sauce, which blends chilies with tequila and fruit juices.

South America

Many of the countries of South America are known for their spicy cuisines, which have been influenced by their own ancient Indian civilizations, as well as by the Spanish and Portuguese explorers. While meat is widely used throughout South America, beans, corn, rice, and quinoa (a grain native to South America) are also staple foods. Potatoes are believed to have been first cultivated in Peru, and later transplanted to North America. Many South American dishes are highly seasoned with chilies, onions, garlic, and tomatoes.

The Caribbean

The Caribbean is home to a variety of cultures and traditions, ranging from African to Spanish, British, Dutch, French, and East Indian. The cuisine has been influenced by these varied cultures and also by the native fruits, vegetables, and spices, including allspice, cinnamon, ginger, nutmeg, peppercorns, chilies, and coconuts. Beans are called peas in the Caribbean, and black-eyed peas are a favorite. The use of rice and a colorful variety of tropical produce make island cooking vegetarian-friendly, and the abundance of some of the hottest chilies around helps to make it a spicy favorite as well.

The United States

Texas Caviar

This protein-packed spread is delicious on crackers or can be used as a dip for corn chips or raw vegetables. Black-eyed peas are popular throughout the southern United States, but they actually originated in Asia and are used widely in China, India, and Africa.

3 cups cooked black-eyed peas
1 small onion, quartered
2 tablespoons minced fresh parsley
1 garlic clove, quartered
$^1/_2$ teaspoon salt

$^1/_4$ teaspoon ground cumin
$^1/_8$ teaspoon cayenne
$^1/_8$ teaspoon dried oregano
2 tablespoons olive oil
$1^1/_2$ tablespoons red wine vinegar

In a food processor, combine the peas, onion, parsley, garlic, salt, cumin, cayenne, and oregano, and pulse until just mixed (but still retaining a coarse texture). Transfer the mixture to a bowl, add the oil and vinegar, and mix well. Taste and adjust seasoning. Set aside for an hour or so to allow flavors to develop.
Serves 6

Kilocalories 126 Kc • Protein 3 gm • Fat 5 gm • Percent of calories from fat 34% • Cholesterol 0 mg • Dietary fiber 4 gm • Sodium 198 mg • Calcium 113 mg

Spicy Okra Gumbo

The term gumbo originated from "gombo," the African word for okra, which was the original thickening agent for this robust soup. Sometimes filé powder, a seasoning made from ground sassafras leaves, is used instead of okra to help thicken the soup. I like to use them both! Either way, a rich brown roux is essential for a good gumbo. When serving, put a bottle of Louisiana hot sauce on the table for those who like a little extra kick.

2 tablespoons safflower oil	1/4 teaspoon Tabasco
2 tablespoons all-purpose flour	1/8 teaspoon dried thyme
1/2 cup chopped green bell pepper	1 28-ounce can peeled tomatoes, drained and chopped
1 small onion, chopped	3 cups Vegetable Stock (see page xxi)
1/4 cup chopped celery	Salt and freshly ground pepper
3/4 pound okra, cut into 1-inch pieces (about 3 cups)	2 cups hot cooked rice (white or brown)
1 teaspoon filé powder	1 tablespoon minced fresh parsley
1/8 teaspoon cayenne	

To make the roux, combine the oil and flour in a large saucepan over medium-high heat. Cook, stirring constantly, until the roux turns brown in color, about 10 minutes. Be careful not to burn. Lower the heat and add the bell pepper, onion, and celery. Cook, stirring, for about 2 minutes. Add the okra and cook an additional 2 minutes. Add the filé powder, cayenne, Tabasco, thyme, tomatoes, stock, and salt and pepper to taste. Bring to a boil, then lower the heat and simmer until the vegetables are tender, about 15 minutes. Taste and adjust seasoning. Divide the rice among 4 shallow soup bowls. Ladle the gumbo over the rice and sprinkle with the parsley.

Serves 4

Kilocalories 305 Kc • Protein 7 gm • Fat 7 gm • Percent of calories from fat 22% • Cholesterol 0 mg • Dietary fiber 8 gm • Sodium 111 mg • Calcium 167 mg

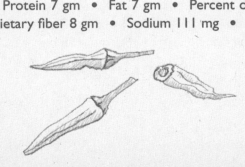

Cajun Coleslaw

This zesty slaw will wake up your taste buds. The flavor improves if you allow it to sit overnight, so plan to make it the day before you need it.

1 small cabbage, cored and shredded	1/4 cup red wine vinegar
1 medium carrot, grated	1 teaspoon sugar
1 garlic clove, chopped	1/2 teaspoon salt
1 jalapeño, halved and seeded	1/4 teaspoon Tabasco
2 tablespoons minced fresh parsley	1/3 cup olive oil

In a large bowl, combine the shredded cabbage and grated carrot and set aside. In a food processor, combine the garlic, jalapeño, parsley, vinegar, sugar, salt, and Tabasco, and process until well combined. With the machine running, slowly add the oil. Pour the dressing over the vegetables and mix well. Cover and refrigerate. Just before serving, drain the excess liquid and adjust the seasoning to taste.

Serves 8

Kilocalories 140 Kc • Protein 1 gm • Fat 14 gm • Percent of calories from fat 84% • Cholesterol 0 mg • Dietary fiber 2 gm • Sodium 232 mg • Calcium 30 mg

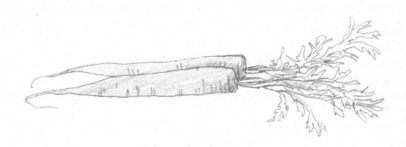

Red-Hot White Bean Chili

This quick and easy chili pulls together in a snap if you use a food processor to chop the vegetables. The optional topping, soy cheese flecked with jalapeños, is available at natural food stores.

1 tablespoon olive oil
1 medium onion, chopped
1 medium carrot, chopped
2 large garlic cloves, minced
1 jalapeño, seeded and minced
3 tablespoons chili powder
3/4 teaspoon salt
1/2 teaspoon ground cumin

1/2 teaspoon dried oregano
1/4 teaspoon cayenne
1/8 teaspoon freshly ground pepper
1 14 1/2-ounce can peeled tomatoes, drained and chopped
3 cups cooked cannellini beans
1/2 cup grated jalapeño soy cheese (optional)

Heat the oil in large saucepan over medium-low heat. Add the onion, carrot, garlic, and jalapeño, cover, and cook until tender, about 10 minutes. Blend in the chili powder, salt, cumin, oregano, cayenne, and pepper, and stir for 2 minutes.

Add 2 cups water and the tomatoes and bring to a boil. Reduce the heat, cover, and simmer until the vegetables are tender, stirring occasionally, approximately 20 minutes. Add the beans and cook 10 minutes longer to blend the flavors. Serve sprinkled with the soy cheese, if desired.

Serves 4

Kilocalories 249 Kc • Protein 14 gm • Fat 4 gm • Percent of calories from fat 15% • Cholesterol 0 mg • Dietary fiber 11 gm • Sodium 675 mg • Calcium 64 mg

Jumpin' Jambalaya

The term jambalaya is believed to derive from the French word jambon, *which means ham. Traditional jambalaya is a rice and tomato dish made with a selection of whatever meats happen to be on hand, such as chicken or sausage. This recipe demonstrates how well the tradition translates in a vegetarian kitchen. If you do not have seitan, double the amount of beans used.*

1¹/2 tablespoons safflower oil
1 medium onion, minced
1 green bell pepper, chopped
¹/2 cup chopped celery
1 teaspoon minced fresh garlic
2 teaspoons filé powder
³/4 teaspoon salt
¹/4 teaspoon cayenne
1 teaspoon Tabasco

¹/4 teaspoon dried thyme
3 cups canned tomatoes, drained
8 ounces soy sausage links, cut into
    1-inch pieces
8 ounces seitan, cut into 1-inch
    pieces
1 cup cooked kidney beans
Freshly cooked rice

Heat ¹/2 tablespoon of the oil in a large saucepan over medium heat. Add the onion, bell pepper, celery, and garlic, cover, and cook over medium heat, stirring occasionally, until softened, about 5 to 8 minutes. Remove the cover, add 1 cup water, the filé powder, salt, cayenne, Tabasco, and thyme. Chop the tomatoes and add them to the mixture. Bring to a boil, then reduce to a simmer. Continue to cook, stirring occasionally, for 15 minutes or until the sauce thickens.

Heat the remaining 1 tablespoon oil in a skillet over medium heat. Add the soy sausage and seitan, cook for 5 minutes or until lightly browned, then add to the tomato mixture. Adjust the seasoning to taste and simmer an additional 5 minutes. Serve over rice.

Serves 4 to 6

Kilocalories 296 Kc • Protein 32 gm • Fat 6 gm • Percent of calories from fat 16% • Cholesterol 0 mg • Dietary fiber 7 gm • Sodium 770 mg • Calcium 50 mg

Brown Rice with Creole Sauce

The versatile sauce is also delicious on pasta, baked potatoes, or even as your "special sauce" on veggie burgers. I use whole-grain brown rice instead of the usual white rice because it is more nutritious and imparts a nutty flavor.

2 cups brown rice, rinsed
1 tablespoon olive oil
1 green bell pepper, chopped
1 medium onion, chopped
1/4 cup minced celery
1 garlic clove, minced
1 cup chopped fresh or canned
    tomatoes
1 tablespoon tomato paste

1/8 teaspoon filé powder
1 tablespoon light brown sugar
1 tablespoon freshly squeezed lemon
    juice
1 tablespoon cider vinegar
1 teaspoon prepared brown mustard
1/4 teaspoon cayenne
Salt and freshly ground pepper
2 tablespoons minced fresh parsley

Bring 4 cups lightly salted water to a boil. Add the rice, reduce the heat to low, cover, and simmer for 45 minutes.

While the rice is cooking, heat the oil in a skillet over medium heat. Add the bell pepper, onion, celery, and garlic. Cover and cook until softened, stirring frequently, about 5 minutes. Add the tomatoes, tomato paste, filé powder, brown sugar, lemon juice, vinegar, mustard, and cayenne, and bring to a boil. Reduce the heat, add the salt and pepper to taste, and simmer, stirring occasionally, until the sauce thickens, about 10 minutes. Transfer the cooked rice to a shallow bowl, top with the sauce, and sprinkle with the parsley.

Serves 4

Kilocalories 424 Kc • Protein 9 gm • Fat 6 gm • Percent of calories from fat 13% • Cholesterol 0 mg • Dietary fiber 5 gm • Sodium 27 mg • Calcium 56 mg

Penne Pasta with Jalapeño Sauce

Fusion food never had it so good—a favorite Italian pasta shape linked with this zesty Southwestern jalapeño sauce thickened with silken tofu and soy milk instead of heavy cream.

2 tablespoons olive oil
2 jalapeños, seeded and minced
1 garlic clove, minced
1 tablespoon minced scallion
1/2 cup dry white wine
1/4 teaspoon minced fresh ginger
1/4 teaspoon chili powder, or to taste
1 10-ounce package silken tofu, quartered

1 cup soy milk
1 pound penne
1 large red bell pepper, cut into thin julienne strips
2 medium zucchini, halved lengthwise and cut into 1/2-inch slices
1 cup sliced fresh mushrooms

Heat 1 tablespoon of the oil in a large saucepan over medium heat. Add the chilies, garlic, and scallion, and cook, stirring, for 3 minutes or until soft. Add 1 cup water, the wine, ginger, and chili powder, bring to a boil, and simmer, stirring occasionally, for 15 minutes or until it is reduced by a third.

Transfer the mixture to a blender, add the tofu and soy milk and blend until smooth. Return the mixture to the saucepan, cover, and keep warm.

Meanwhile, bring a large pot of salted water to a boil, add the pasta, and cook for 8 to 10 minutes or until just tender. While the pasta is cooking, heat the remaining oil in a large skillet over medium heat. Add the bell pepper, zucchini, and mushrooms to the skillet and cook, stirring, for 5 minutes or until softened. When the pasta is cooked, drain well, and transfer to a serving bowl. Add the vegetables and sauce and toss well. Taste, adjust seasonings, and serve.

Serves 6

Kilocalories 388 Kc • Protein 14 gm • Fat 8 gm • Percent of calories from fat 18% • Cholesterol 0 mg • Dietary fiber 3 gm • Sodium 29 mg • Calcium 54 mg

Cilantro-Chili Pesto

A profusion of cilantro and dinner guests with a taste for Southwestern flavors prompted me to create this pesto variation, which can be used to enliven a bowl of Texas chili, punctuate a salad dressing, or jazz up a baked potato. Tossed with pasta, it creates a tasty fusion dish.

3 mild or hot fresh chilies, according
   to taste
1/4 cup olive oil
1/3 cup pine nuts

2 large garlic cloves
1/2 cup (packed) fresh cilantro
1/2 cup (packed) fresh parsley
Salt and freshly ground pepper

Place the chilies over a gas flame or under a broiler until their skins blacken. Place in paper bag and let stand 10 minutes to steam. Peel, seed, and pat dry. Place the chilies, oil, pine nuts, garlic, cilantro, and parsley in a food processor and process until smooth. Season with salt and pepper. Transfer to a container, cover tightly, and refrigerate until ready to use.

Serves 4 to 6 (makes about 1¹/₂ cups)

Kilocalories 205 Kc • Protein 4 gm • Fat 20 gm • Percent of calories from fat 83% • Cholesterol 0 mg • Dietary fiber 1 gm • Sodium 9 mg • Calcium 28 mg

Texas Barbecue Sauce

Although this sauce will keep well in the refrigerator for several weeks, it rarely lasts that long at my house. I use it to spice up everything from pinto beans to tofu, and it also tastes great on veggie burgers. Liquid smoke flavoring is available in most supermarkets.

2 large onions, chopped
1 large bell pepper, seeded and
  chopped
3 garlic cloves, minced
3 small fresh hot chilies, minced
1 1/2 cups ketchup

1/2 cup light brown sugar
1/2 cup cider vinegar
1 teaspoon salt
1/4 teaspoon oregano
1/2 teaspoon liquid smoke flavoring

Combine the onions, bell pepper, garlic, and chilies in a food processor or blender and process until puréed. Add the ketchup, brown sugar, vinegar, salt, oregano, and smoke flavoring, and process until smooth. Transfer the mixture to a saucepan and bring to a boil. Reduce the heat to a simmer and cook, stirring frequently, for about 20 to 30 minutes or until thick. Use immediately or allow to cool before covering and refrigerating. Sauce will keep for several weeks in the refrigerator.

Serves 8 to 12 (makes about 3 1/2 cups)

Kilocalories 131 Kc • Protein 1 gm • Fat .1 gm • Percent of calories from fat 0% • Cholesterol 0 mg • Dietary fiber 1 gm • Sodium 601 mg • Calcium 61 mg

Mexico

Smooth and Sassy Guacamole

Tortilla chips are the usual accompaniment to guacamole, but raw vegetables and pita or bagel chips make a welcome change. Avocados were originally introduced to Mexico in the 15th century by the Incas who brought them from Ecuador.

2 ripe avocados, peeled and pitted
2 teaspoons freshly squeezed lime
   juice
1/2 teaspoon salt
1/4 cup chopped fresh tomato

1/4 cup minced fresh onion
2 tablespoons minced canned
   jalapeños
1 teaspoon minced fresh garlic
1/8 teaspoon ground cumin

Purée the avocados, lime juice, and salt in a food processor. Add the tomato, onion, jalapeños, garlic, and cumin, and blend with short on and off bursts. Transfer to a serving bowl.
Serves 4

Kilocalories 166 Kc • Protein 2 gm • Fat 15 gm • Percent of calories from fat 75% • Cholesterol 0 mg • Dietary fiber 5 gm • Sodium 403 mg • Calcium 30 mg

Yucatán Potato Soup

The cuisine of the Yucatán varies from the other regions of Mexico because of influences from Europe and the Caribbean. This flavorful soup combines potatoes and garlic with the typically Mexican flavors of cumin and tomato.

4 medium round white potatoes
1 tablespoon safflower oil
1 large onion, chopped
1 garlic clove, minced
1/2 teaspoon ground cumin
4 medium tomatoes, peeled and
  chopped

4 cups Vegetable Stock (see page xxi)
1 jalapeño, seeded and minced
Salt and freshly ground pepper
3/4 cup soy milk or light cream

Place the potatoes in a medium saucepan, cover with water, and boil until tender, about 40 minutes. Cool the potatoes slightly, then peel and chop and set aside.

Heat the oil in a medium skillet over medium heat. Add onion and garlic and cook, covered, until softened, about 5 minutes. Add the cumin and tomatoes and continue to simmer for 5 minutes. Allow to cool slightly.

Working in batches, combine the potatoes, tomato mixture, stock, and jalapeño in a blender or food processor and purée until smooth. Transfer to a saucepan and add salt and pepper to taste. Bring to a boil, then reduce the heat and simmer, stirring constantly, for 2 minutes. Stir in the soy milk, adjust the seasonings to taste, and serve hot.

Serves 6

Kilocalories 163 Kc • Protein 4 gm • Fat 3 gm • Percent of calories from fat 16% • Cholesterol 0 mg • Dietary fiber 3 gm • Sodium 79 mg • Calcium 27 mg

Chilled Avocado Soup

The lime juice enhances the flavor of the avocado and ensures that the soup will hold its green color for up to two hours. Haas avocados are my favorite variety because of their rich flavor and creamy texture.

1 avocado, peeled and pitted
1 cup silken tofu or sour cream
2 tablespoons chopped fresh cilantro
1 tablespoon chopped scallion
1 tablespoon freshly squeezed lime juice

1 teaspoon chopped fresh garlic
2 cups Vegetable Stock (see page xxi)
3/4 teaspoon salt
1/8 teaspoon hot pepper sauce
Sunflower seeds

Combine the avocado, tofu, cilantro, scallion, lime juice, garlic, stock, salt, and hot pepper sauce in a blender or food processor and purée until smooth, about 2 minutes. Refrigerate, covered, for up to 2 hours, until chilled. Garnish with sunflower seeds and serve.

Serves 4

Kilocalories 129 Kc • Protein 5 gm • Fat 9 gm • Percent of calories from fat 59% • Cholesterol 0 mg • Dietary fiber 2 gm • Sodium 490 mg • Calcium 47 mg

Spicy Corn Soup

I like to garnish this soup with minced, canned chilies to give it an extra bite.

1 tablespoon olive oil
1 medium onion, chopped
1 garlic clove, minced
1/4 teaspoon cayenne
1/4 teaspoon ground cumin
1 medium potato, peeled and cut
    into 1/4-inch dice

3 cups fresh or frozen corn kernels
1 cup soy milk
1/2 teaspoon salt
1/4 teaspoon freshly ground pepper
Minced canned green chilies
    (optional)

Heat the oil in a large saucepan over medium heat. Add the onion, garlic, cayenne, and cumin and cover. Reduce the heat to low and cook until the onion is softened, about 5 minutes. Add the potato and 4 cups water. Bring to a boil over high heat. Add the corn, reduce the heat, and simmer until the potato is tender, about 20 minutes.

In a food processor, purée 2 cups of the soup. Combine the puréed soup with the rest of the soup and let cool to room temperature. Just before serving, stir in the soy milk and salt and pepper. Ladle the soup into bowls and sprinkle each serving with the minced chilies, if using.

Serves 4 to 6

Kilocalories 220 Kc • Protein 6 gm • Fat 5 gm • Percent of calories from fat 18% • Cholesterol 0 mg • Dietary fiber 4 gm • Sodium 324 mg • Calcium 40 mg

Holy Jalapeño Soup with Tortilla Triangles

The crunchy tortilla triangles provide some relief from the spiciness of the soup.

1 tablespoon safflower oil
1 large onion, chopped
2 large garlic cloves, minced
2 jalapeños, seeded and finely
    chopped
3 cups Vegetable Stock (see page xxi)
1 28-ounce can plum tomatoes,
    chopped (liquid reserved)
1/2 cup tomato sauce
2 teaspoons chili powder

1/2 teaspoon ground cumin
1/2 teaspoon minced fresh oregano
    or 1/8 teaspoon dried
3/4 teaspoon salt
1/8 teaspoon cayenne
4 8-inch flour tortillas, each one cut
    into 6 triangles
1/2 cup grated soy cheese alternative
    or Monterey Jack cheese
Minced fresh parsley or cilantro

Heat the oil in a large skillet over low heat. Add the onion and garlic, cover, and cook, stirring occasionally, until softened, about 5 minutes. Add the jalapeños and cook, stirring occasionally, until tender, about 4 minutes. Transfer to a large pot. Add the stock, tomatoes with liquid, tomato sauce, chili powder, cumin, oregano, salt, and cayenne, and bring to a boil. Reduce the heat and simmer 20 minutes to blend the flavors.

Place the tortilla triangles on a baking sheet and sprinkle with the grated cheese alternative. Bake in a preheated 400°F. oven for 5 minutes or until the cheese is melted. Ladle the soup into bowls and garnish with 3 of the tortilla triangles and parsley or cilantro. Serve immediately, with any remaining tortilla triangles on the side.

Serves 6 to 8

Kilocalories 149 Kc • Protein 6 gm • Fat 3 gm • Percent of calories from fat 16% • Cholesterol 0 mg • Dietary fiber 7 gm • Sodium 610 mg • Calcium 140 mg

Mexican Rice and Bean Salad with Cumin Vinaigrette

This colorful salad is one of my favorites because it can be made ahead of time, and is hearty enough to stand as a meal in itself. Although the recipe calls for romaine, you can use whatever salad greens you prefer. The rice and lime juice in this salad reflect the Spanish influence on Mexican cuisine. Brown rice is used because it is more healthful, but white rice can be used instead.

4 cups cooked brown rice, cooled
2 cups cooked pinto beans
1 cup cooked fresh or frozen corn
  kernels
1/2 medium-sized red onion,
  chopped
1 4-ounce can minced jalapeños
1/2 teaspoon minced fresh garlic
3 tablespoons cider vinegar
2 tablespoons freshly squeezed lime
  juice

1 teaspoon light brown sugar
1/2 teaspoon chili powder
1/2 teaspoon ground cumin
3/4 teaspoon salt
1/8 teaspoon cayenne
1/4 cup olive oil
6 cups torn romaine lettuce leaves
12 to 16 cherry tomatoes, halved

Combine the rice, beans, corn, onion, jalapeños, and garlic in a large bowl and set aside.

In a small bowl, combine the vinegar, lime juice, brown sugar, chili powder, cumin, salt, and cayenne. Whisk in the oil and adjust seasonings to taste. Pour the dressing over the salad and toss to coat. Set aside for 30 minutes at room temperature to allow the flavors to mingle.

Line the serving plates with the lettuce and top with the salad mixture. Garnish with the cherry tomatoes and serve.

Serves 6 to 8

Kilocalories 356 Kc • Protein 10 gm • Fat 11 gm • Percent of calories from fat 27% •
Cholesterol 0 mg • Dietary fiber 10 gm • Sodium 380 mg • Calcium 76 mg

Avocado and Jicama Salad with Lime Dressing

The jicama, also known as the Mexican potato, is a tuber related to the sweet potato and is now widely available in the produce section of most supermarkets. Jicamas can be eaten raw or cooked and taste similar to water chestnuts. Avocados and olive oil are both high in fat— but it's the "good" kind of fat—monounsaturated fatty acids. Still, if you prefer a lower fat version, you can reduce the oil by 1 tablespoon and use only 1 avocado instead of 2.

5 tablespoons freshly squeezed lime juice
1 tablespoon orange marmalade
1 teaspoon minced lime zest
1/2 teaspoon salt
1/8 teaspoon hot pepper sauce
5 tablespoons olive oil

8 cups torn butter lettuce
1 large jicama, halved lengthwise and peeled
2 avocados, peeled, pitted, and sliced
12 cherry tomatoes, halved
12 brine-cured black olives

Combine the lime juice, marmalade, lime zest, salt, and hot pepper sauce in a small bowl and mix well. Whisk in the oil in a thin stream.

Line 6 plates with the lettuce. Cut the jicama lengthwise into 1/8-inch-thick slices. Arrange the jicama and avocado slices alternately on top of the lettuce. Top with the cherry tomatoes and olives. Stir the dressing and pour over the salads.

Serves 6

Kilocalories 222 Kc • Protein 3 gm • Fat 17 gm • Percent of calories from fat 65% • Cholesterol 0 mg • Dietary fiber 7 gm • Sodium 370 mg • Calcium 52 mg

Mexican Fruit Salad

This colorful salad is traditionally served on Christmas Eve. While the main components of the salad need to be prepared in advance and allowed to marinate, the finished salad should be served immediately. The jicama, lime juice, and pomegranate seeds make it typically Mexican. If pomegranates are unavailable, substitute dry-roasted peanuts for added texture.

3 navel oranges, peeled and cut into 1-inch chunks

1 pineapple, peeled, cored, and cut into 1-inch chunks

1 jicama, peeled and cut into 3/4-inch chunks

1/2 cup freshly squeezed orange juice

1/4 cup freshly squeezed lime juice

1 large head red leaf lettuce

2 pears, cored and cut into 1-inch chunks

2 bananas, peeled and sliced

Seeds from 1 pomegranate

1 1/2 tablespoons chopped fresh mint

3 tablespoons cider vinegar

1/4 teaspoon chili powder

1/8 teaspoon cayenne

1 tablespoon minced scallions

1/4 cup safflower oil

Combine the orange, pineapple, jicama, orange juice, and lime juice in a large bowl and refrigerate for several hours to marinate. Line a shallow bowl or large platter with lettuce leaves. Drain the marinated fruit and jicama, reserving the juice. Combine the marinated ingredients with the pears and bananas and spoon over the lettuce. Sprinkle the salad with the pomegranate seeds and mint and set aside.

Combine 1/2 cup of the reserved juice, the vinegar, chili powder, cayenne, and scallions in a small bowl. Slowly whisk in the oil in a thin stream. Drizzle the vinaigrette over the salad. Serve immediately.

Serves 8

Kilocalories 222 Kc • Protein 2 gm • Fat 8 gm • Percent of calories from fat 28% • Cholesterol 0 mg • Dietary fiber 7 gm • Sodium 7 mg • Calcium 49 mg

Tacos with Salsa Fresca

The pinto beans can be chopped by pulsing them in your food processor, but be careful not to overprocess or you'll end up with bean dip!

1 tablespoon safflower oil
2 cups cooked pinto beans, coarsely
    chopped
1 teaspoon ground cumin
1/2 teaspoon cayenne
1/2 teaspoon salt

1/4 teaspoon freshly ground pepper
8 taco shells
2 cups shredded romaine lettuce
Salsa Fresca (see page 26)
1 cup shredded soy cheddar cheese
1/2 cup pitted and sliced black olives

Preheat the oven to 375°F. Heat the oil in a large skillet over medium heat. Add the beans, cumin, cayenne, salt, and pepper, and cook for 5 minutes, stirring occasionally. Reduce the heat to low and allow the bean mixture to simmer while the taco shells are heating.

Heat the taco shells in the oven for 1 to 2 minutes. Place about 1/2 cup shredded lettuce in each taco shell and top with about 1/4 cup of the bean mixture. Garnish with Salsa Fresca, shredded cheese, and black olives, as desired. Serve immediately.

Serves 4

Kilocalories 295 Kc • Protein 9 gm • Fat 13 gm • Percent of calories from fat 40% •
Cholesterol 0 mg • Dietary fiber 10 gm • Sodium 495 mg • Calcium 85 mg

Salsa Fresca

Salsa adds an extra-spicy touch to Mexican foods, and is a standard feature on virtually all Mexican tables. Substitute mild chilies if you prefer a less fiery salsa.

4 large ripe tomatoes, chopped
2 small fresh hot chilies, seeded and chopped
2 garlic cloves, minced
1 large onion, finely chopped

1/4 cup minced fresh cilantro
1/4 teaspoon freshly ground pepper
1 teaspoon sugar
Salt

Combine the tomatoes, chilies, and garlic in a blender or food processor until just blended. Pour into a bowl and add the onion, cilantro, pepper, sugar, and salt to taste. Cover and refrigerate for at least 1 hour before serving.

Serves 12 (makes about 4 cups)

Kilocalories 17 Kc • Protein 1 gm • Fat .2 gm • Percent of calories from fat 8% • Cholesterol 0 mg • Dietary fiber 1 gm • Sodium 5 mg • Calcium 8 mg

Spicy Bean and Spinach Burritos

2 cups cooked pinto beans
1 tablespoon olive oil
1 small onion, minced
1 teaspoon minced fresh garlic
2 jalapeños or other chilies, seeded
    and minced
1/2 teaspoon salt
1 teaspoon chili powder

1/4 teaspoon freshly ground pepper
1 10-ounce package frozen chopped
    spinach, thawed and well drained
1 cup shredded soy cheese
    alternative or Monterey Jack
    cheese
8 8-inch flour tortillas, warmed
Salsa Picante (see page 28)

Place the cooked beans in a food processor and chop coarsely with short on and off bursts. Set aside.

Heat the oil in a large skillet over medium heat. Add the onion and garlic, cover, and cook 5 minutes or until softened, stirring occasionally. Add the jalapeños, salt, chili powder, and pepper. Stir in the spinach and reserved beans and heat through, about 2 minutes. Remove from the heat and add the soy cheese, stirring to combine well.

To serve, spoon equal amounts of the filling mixture into the center of each tortilla. Top with a spoonful of salsa, to taste. Fold the bottom edge up over the filling, then fold the right and left sides toward the center, overlapping the edges.

Serves 4 to 6

Kilocalories 320 Kc • Protein 21 gm • Fat 2 gm • Percent of calories from fat 5% •
Cholesterol 0 mg • Dietary fiber 22 gm • Sodium 953 mg • Calcium 364 mg

Salsa Picante

Save time by letting your food processor do all the chopping, but be careful not to over-process.

2 large ripe tomatoes, chopped	1 tablespoon chopped fresh cilantro
1 small red onion, chopped	1 tablespoon chopped fresh parsley
1 serrano or jalapeño chili, halved, seeded, and chopped	2 tablespoons tomato paste
	1 teaspoon red wine vinegar
1 garlic clove, chopped	1/2 teaspoon salt

Combine the chopped tomatoes, onion, chili, garlic, cilantro, and parsley in a food processor using short on and off bursts. Add the tomato paste, vinegar, and salt, and mix with short on and off bursts until just blended but still chunky. Transfer the salsa to a small bowl. Cover and refrigerate for at least 1 hour before using.

Serves 6 to 8 (makes about 2 1/4 cups)

Kilocalories 21 Kc • Protein 1 gm • Fat .3 gm • Percent of calories from fat 10% • Cholesterol 0 mg • Dietary fiber 1 gm • Sodium 200 mg • Calcium 11 mg

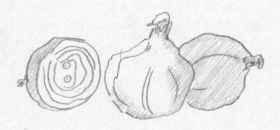

Grilled Vegetable Fajitas

I like the meaty texture of the portobello mushrooms in these fajitas. The grilled vegetables are wrapped in soft flour tortillas, and can be topped with guacamole (page 17), salsa (pages 26 or 28), or borracha sauce (page 35).

4 portobello mushroom caps	1 teaspoon salt
Juice of 3 limes (about 1/2 cup)	1 red onion, quartered
3 garlic cloves, chopped	1 red bell pepper, seeded and
1 hot green chili, chopped	quartered
2 tablespoons minced fresh cilantro	12 8-inch flour tortillas

In a shallow bowl, combine the mushrooms, lime juice, garlic, chili, cilantro, and salt. Cover and let marinate in the refrigerator for at least 1 hour.

Meanwhile, steam the onion over boiling water until slightly softened, about 3 minutes. Steam the red bell pepper over boiling water for 1 minute. Drain the mushrooms, reserving the marinade. Place the mushrooms, onion, and bell pepper on a grill or on a baking sheet in a 475°F oven. Grill the vegetables for about 2 minutes on each side or until browned, basting with the reserved marinade.

Slice the vegetables into thin strips and wrap up in the tortillas. Serve with bowls of guacamole, salsa, or borracha sauce and invite each diner to garnish their fajitas as desired.

Serves 4 to 6

Kilocalories 228 Kc • Protein 8 gm • Fat .2 gm • Percent of calories from fat 1% • Cholesterol 0 mg • Dietary fiber 20 gm • Sodium 859 mg • Calcium 97 mg

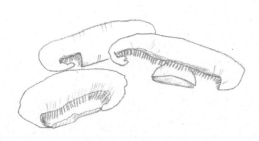

Veggie Quesadillas

Quesadillas are spicy south-of-the-border open-face sandwiches. Instead of traditional dairy sour cream, this version calls for the healthier tofu sour cream, which is every bit as delicious.

1 cup shredded soy cheddar cheese
    alternative
4 scallions, chopped
1 serrano or jalapeño chili, halved
    and seeded
$1/2$ cup tofu sour cream
1 tablespoon red wine vinegar
$1/2$ teaspoon salt

Freshly ground pepper
4 8-inch flour tortillas
1 green bell pepper, cored, seeded,
    and cut into thin strips
2 cups shredded romaine lettuce
1 avocado, peeled, pitted, and sliced
$1/2$ cup salsa, commercial or
    homemade (see pages 26 or 28)

Combine the soy cheese, scallions, chili, $1/4$ cup of the tofu sour cream, vinegar, salt, and pepper in a food processor and process until well combined.

Preheat the broiler and position an oven rack 6 inches from the heat source. Arrange the tortillas on a baking sheet. Divide the bell pepper strips among the tortillas. Cover each with an equal amount of the cheese mixture, spreading it to the edges. Broil until puffed and lightly browned, about 3 minutes. Top each quesadilla with lettuce, then with avocado, salsa, and the remaining tofu sour cream.

Serves 4

Kilocalories 247 Kc • Protein 12 gm • Fat 13 gm • Percent of calories from fat 45% • Cholesterol 0 mg • Dietary fiber 9 gm • Sodium 815 mg • Calcium 248 mg

Red Beans and Rice Casserole

If tofu sour cream is unavailable, substitute either silken tofu combined with a splash of lemon juice or dairy sour cream.

1 tablespoon olive oil
1 cup chopped onion
1/2 cup chopped red bell pepper
4 cups cooked brown rice
2 cups cooked kidney beans
1 4-ounce can chopped green chilies, drained

2 cups tofu sour cream
3/4 teaspoon salt
1/8 teaspoon cayenne
1/2 cup shredded soy cheese alternative
1/4 cup fine dry bread crumbs

Preheat the oven to 375°F. Coat a 2 1/2-quart baking dish with nonstick vegetable cooking spray. Heat the oil in a large skillet over medium heat. Add the onion and bell pepper, cover, and cook 5 minutes or until softened. Transfer the onion mixture to a large bowl. Add the cooked rice, kidney beans, and chilies to the onion mixture.

In a small bowl, combine the tofu sour cream, salt, and cayenne, and blend well. Fold the tofu sour cream mixture into the rice and bean mixture and mix well. Taste and adjust seasonings. Transfer the mixture to the prepared baking dish, cover, and bake 30 minutes or until heated through. Uncover during the last 5 minutes of baking and sprinkle with the soy cheese and bread crumbs. Continue baking just to melt the cheese and brown the crumbs, about 5 minutes.

Serves 6 to 8

Kilocalories 306 Kc • Protein 11 gm • Fat 13 gm • Percent of calories from fat 36% • Cholesterol 0 mg • Dietary fiber 6 gm • Sodium 737 mg • Calcium 90 mg

Baked Tempeh Enchiladas

Tempeh is used instead of the traditional ground meat in these delicious enchiladas. Coarsely chopped pinto beans are another vegetarian option.

1 tablespoon safflower oil
1/2 cup minced fresh onion
1/4 cup chopped green bell pepper
1 teaspoon minced fresh garlic
1 1/2 teaspoons chili powder

1 1/2 cups salsa, commercial or homemade (see pages 26 or 28)
1 cup tofu sour cream
3 cups chopped poached tempeh
8 8-inch flour tortillas

Preheat the oven to 350°F. Coat a 9×13-inch baking dish with nonstick vegetable cooking spray.

Heat the oil in a large saucepan over medium heat. Add onion, bell pepper, and garlic. Cover and cook 5 minutes or until softened. Stir in the chili powder, 1/2 cup water, and the salsa, and cook, stirring, until slightly thickened. Remove from the heat and add the tofu sour cream.

Combine 2 cups sauce and the tempeh. Spoon about 1/3 cup tempeh mixture onto each tortilla and roll up. Arrange the tortillas in the prepared dish, top with the remaining sauce, cover, and bake 25 minutes. Uncover and bake 5 minutes longer until browned and bubbly.

Serves 8

Kilocalories 266 Kc • Protein 15 gm • Fat 12 gm • Percent of calories from fat 37% • Cholesterol 0 mg • Dietary fiber 11 gm • Sodium 315 mg • Calcium 87 mg

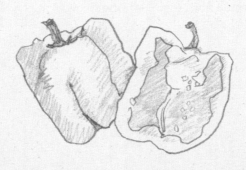

Mexican Seitan with Tomato-Orange Sauce

This dish traditionally features beef, but my vegetarian version made with "wheat meat" tastes great. I usually serve it over rice with a tossed salad.

2 tablespoons olive oil
1/4 cup minced scallion
2 teaspoons minced fresh garlic
1/2 teaspoon ground cumin
1/4 teaspoon hot red pepper flakes
2 cups drained, seeded, and chopped
    canned tomatoes

1/2 cup orange juice concentrate
1 teaspoon tomato paste
1 teaspoon salt
1/8 teaspoon freshly ground pepper
1 pound seitan, cut into 1/4-inch
    slices
1 cup Vegetable Stock (see page xxi)

Heat 1 tablespoon of the oil in a medium skillet over medium heat. Add the scallion, garlic, cumin, and hot red pepper flakes, and stir 30 seconds. Add the drained tomatoes, orange juice concentrate, tomato paste, 1/2 teaspoon of the salt, and the pepper, and cook 3 minutes, stirring occasionally. Adjust the seasonings and keep warm.

Meanwhile, heat the remaining 1 tablespoon oil in a large saucepan over medium-high heat. Add the seitan and cook until browned, about 5 minutes. Add the stock and the remaining 1/2 teaspoon salt, and bring to a boil. Cook until the liquid reduces by half, about 2 to 3 minutes. Transfer the seitan to a serving platter and spoon the reserved sauce on top.

Serves 6

Kilocalories 167 Kc • Protein 22 gm • Fat 5 gm • Percent of calories from fat 24% • Cholesterol 0 mg • Dietary fiber 2 gm • Sodium 570 mg • Calcium 12 mg

Rice with Tomatillos and Chilies

Tomatillos resemble a small green tomato and have a papery husk. They can be found in many supermarkets and specialty grocers. If unavailable, substitute green tomatoes or canned tomatillos, which are sold in ethnic markets.

6 tomatillos, chopped	1 tablespoon olive oil
2 small hot green chilies, seeded and chopped	$1/2$ cup minced scallions
	2 garlic cloves, chopped
2 tablespoons chopped fresh cilantro or parsley	3 cups long-grain white rice
	$3/4$ teaspoon salt

Combine the tomatillos, chilies, cilantro, and $1/2$ cup water in a blender or food processor and purée until smooth. In a large pot, heat the oil over medium heat. Add the scallions and garlic and cook 2 minutes to soften. Add the rice and stir constantly to coat, but do not allow it to brown. Add the purée and simmer, stirring, for 2 to 3 minutes. Add the salt and $4 1/2$ cups water, bring to a boil, and stir once with a fork. Reduce the heat to a simmer, cover, and simmer until the liquid is absorbed, about 20 minutes. If not quite tender, remove from the heat and allow to sit, covered, for several minutes. Fluff the rice and transfer to a serving bowl.

Serves 8

Kilocalories 281 Kc • Protein 5 gm • Fat 2 gm • Percent of calories from fat 8% • Cholesterol 0 mg • Dietary fiber 2 gm • Sodium 301 mg • Calcium 32 mg

Borracha Sauce

Borracha *means drunken, a reference to the tequila used to flavor this sauce, which can also be used as a table condiment or marinade.*

1 tablespoon olive oil
4 to 6 hot or mild green chilies,
    seeded and chopped
1 small onion, chopped
1 garlic clove, chopped
3/4 cup freshly squeezed orange juice

1/4 cup freshly squeezed lime juice
1 tablespoon honey or other natural
    sweetener
1/8 teaspoon salt
1/4 cup tequila

Heat the oil in a skillet over medium heat. Add the chilies, onion, and garlic, cover, and cook for 10 minutes or until soft. Transfer the mixture to a blender and purée with the orange juice, lime juice, honey, and salt. Return the mixture to the saucepan and cook for 10 minutes longer over medium heat or until sauce thickens slightly. Just before serving, add the tequila.

Serves 6 to 8 (makes 2 1/2 cups)

Kilocalories 82 Kc • Protein 1 gm • Fat 2 gm • Percent of calories from fat 35% • Cholesterol 0 mg • Dietary fiber 1 gm • Sodium 50 mg • Calcium 10 mg

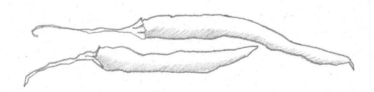

Mole Poblano

Perhaps the most famous and flavorful sauce of Mexico, mole (pronounced "mo-lay") poblano is a sublime blending of ingredients including chilies and chocolate. It is traditionally served with turkey, but I like to use it as a barbecue sauce with pinto beans or tofu. I've also used it as a dipping sauce for tempura vegetables and have even served it over pasta.

4 dried ancho chilies, stemmed and
    seeded
4 pasilla chilies, stemmed and seeded
    (see Note)
1/4 cup raisins
1 tablespoon safflower oil
1 medium onion, chopped
1 garlic clove, chopped
2 large ripe tomatoes, chopped
1/2 cup dry-roasted peanuts

1/2 cup tortilla chips
1 tablespoon white vinegar
1 tablespoon sesame seeds
1/4 teaspoon ground cinnamon
1/4 teaspoon ground coriander
1/8 teaspoon ground cloves
1 cup Vegetable Stock (see page xxi)
1 ounce bittersweet chocolate,
    chopped
Salt

Soak the chilies and raisins in a large bowl of boiling water for 1 hour or until softened. While the chilies and raisins are soaking, heat the oil in a skillet over medium heat. Add the onion and garlic, cover, and cook for 5 minutes or until softened.

In a blender, purée the chilies, raisins, and 1 cup of the soaking liquid until smooth. Add the onion mixture, tomatoes, peanuts, tortilla chips, vinegar, sesame seeds, cinnamon, coriander, and cloves, and purée until well blended. The mixture should be thick.

Transfer the puréed mixture to a saucepan, add the stock, chocolate, and salt to taste, and cook over low heat, stirring occasionally, for about 40 minutes or until thick but pourable. If the sauce is too thick, add a little more stock. Taste and adjust the seasonings.

Serves 8 to 10 (makes 4 cups)

NOTE: Traditional mole sauces include both ancho and pasilla chilies, but if you have difficulty finding the pasilla, simply increase the number of anchos by two.

Kilocalories 168 Kc • Protein 5 gm • Fat 9 gm • Percent of calories from fat 45% • Cholesterol 0 mg • Dietary fiber 3 gm • Sodium 127 mg • Calcium 37 mg

Caribbean

Spicy Plantain Fritters

Plantains are synonymous with island cooking and are available in most supermarkets. I like to serve these fritters with a bit of mango chutney on the side.

2 tablespoons margarine, softened
1 garlic clove, mashed to a paste
1/4 teaspoon brown sugar
1/8 teaspoon cayenne

1/8 teaspoon ground allspice
Pinch of salt
2 medium plantains, peeled
2 tablespoons safflower oil

Combine the margarine, garlic, brown sugar, cayenne, allspice, and salt in a bowl and stir until smooth. Coarsely grate the plantains and combine with the margarine mixture until well blended. Using about 1/4 cup at a time, press the mixture firmly between your palms to form tight flat patties.

Heat the oil in a large skillet over medium-high heat. Gently place the fritters in the hot oil without crowding. Fry, turning once, until golden brown and crisp, about 3 minutes total. Place on paper towels to drain, then transfer to a heat-resistant platter and place in a warm oven while cooking the remaining fritters.

Serves 4

Kilocalories 197 Kc • Protein I gm • Fat 10 gm • Percent of calories from fat 42% • Cholesterol 0 mg • Dietary fiber 2 gm • Sodium 71 mg • Calcium 5 mg

Jamaican Jerk-Spiced Tempeh Nuggets

This simple and easy hors d'oeuvre also makes a great main course. The jerk spice mixture is a popular flavor sensation in Jamaica, where it is commonly used to season meats.

1 teaspoon puréed garlic
3/4 teaspoon salt
1/2 teaspoon allspice
1/4 teaspoon freshly ground pepper
1/8 teaspoon cayenne

1/8 teaspoon nutmeg
1/8 teaspoon dried oregano, crumbled
1 pound tempeh, quartered
1 tablespoon safflower oil

Combine the garlic, salt, allspice, pepper, cayenne, nutmeg, and oregano in a small bowl and set aside.

Place the tempeh in a saucepan of boiling water. Reduce the heat to low and simmer for 10 minutes. Drain the tempeh, pat it dry, and cut into 1-inch cubes.

Heat the oil in a large skillet over medium-high heat. Add the tempeh and cook, turning frequently, until browned on all sides, about 10 minutes. Sprinkle the spice mixture over the tempeh cubes in the skillet and toss until fragrant and evenly distributed, about 20 seconds. Serve hot.

Serves 4

Kilocalories 259 Kc • Protein 22 gm • Fat 12 gm • Percent of calories from fat 40% • Cholesterol 0 mg • Dietary fiber 8 gm • Sodium 443 mg • Calcium 110 mg

Caribbean Vegetable Stew

Stews are popular throughout the islands and usually contain a wide variety of ingredients, such as, in this version, sweet potatoes, pineapple, and olives. Serve this flavorful stew over freshly cooked rice, millet, or quinoa.

1 tablespoon safflower oil
1 large onion, chopped
1 green bell pepper, chopped
1 red bell pepper, chopped
2 sweet potatoes, peeled and
    cut into $1/2$-inch dice
1 teaspoon minced fresh garlic
$1/2$ teaspoon ground cumin
$1/2$ teaspoon ground cinnamon
$1/2$ teaspoon salt
$1/8$ teaspoon cayenne

2 cups canned plum tomatoes,
    drained and chopped
$1/2$ cup salsa, commercial or
    homemade (see pages 26 or 28)
2 cups canned pineapple chunks,
    with juice reserved
2 teaspoons cornstarch
2 cups cooked pinto beans
$1/2$ cup pitted ripe olives
$1/2$ cup pimiento-stuffed olives

Heat the oil in a large saucepan over medium heat. Add the onion, bell peppers, sweet potatoes, and garlic, cover, and cook for 5 minutes or until vegetables begin to soften. Sprinkle with the cumin, cinnamon, salt, and cayenne. Add the tomatoes, salsa, and pineapple juice. Cover and simmer 20 minutes or until vegetables are tender. Combine the cornstarch with 2 tablespoons water and stir into the mixture. Cook, stirring, until the mixture boils and thickens, about 2 minutes. Add the pineapple, beans, and olives, and heat through.

Serves 4 to 6

Kilocalories 388 Kc • Protein 11 gm • Fat 8 gm • Percent of calories from fat 18% •
Cholesterol 0 mg • Dietary fiber 15 gm • Sodium 861 mg • Calcium 148 mg

Island Rice Salad

My friend Mary Woods Batson lived in Puerto Rico for many years. Her description of "life in paradise" inspired me to create this easy one-dish meal. The colorful variety of fresh fruits and vegetables combined with the spicy-sweet chutney is especially welcome after a day in the sun.

1 cup chutney, commercial or homemade (see pages 173–175)

1/8 teaspoon ground allspice

1/8 teaspoon cayenne

4 cups cooked brown rice

1 large mango, peeled, seeded, and cut into 1/2-inch pieces

1 red bell pepper, cut into 1/2-inch pieces

1/2 cup minced celery

2 tablespoons minced scallion

Butter lettuce (or other salad greens)

Slices of mango and red bell pepper (optional)

Combine the chutney, allspice, and cayenne in medium bowl and stir until well blended. Set aside. In a large bowl, combine the rice, mango, bell pepper, celery, and scallion. Fold in the dressing to coat. Taste and adjust seasonings. To serve, line plates with equal amounts of lettuce, top with equal amounts of rice salad, and garnish with slices of mango and red bell pepper, if desired.

Serves 4

Kilocalories 419 Kc • Protein 5 gm • Fat 2 gm • Percent of calories from fat 4% • Cholesterol 0 mg • Dietary fiber 7 gm • Sodium 32 mg • Calcium 42 mg

Rum and Lime-Laced Sweet Potatoes

Though sweet potatoes and yams are from distinctly different plant species, they are interchangeable in cooking.

6 long slender sweet potatoes or
    yams (about 3 pounds)
1/2 cup light brown sugar
1/4 cup margarine or butter
1/4 cup freshly squeezed lime juice

1/4 teaspoon salt
1/8 teaspoon cayenne
3 tablespoons dark rum
2 tablespoons freshly grated
    lime zest

Place the sweet potatoes in a large saucepan with just enough water to cover, place over medium-high heat, and cook until just tender, about 15 minutes. Drain well and cool. Trim the ends of the sweet potatoes, peel, and cut crosswise into 1/2-inch slices.

Preheat the oven to 400°F. Coat a shallow 9×13-inch baking dish with non-stick vegetable cooking spray. Arrange the potatoes in the baking dish in slightly overlapping rows. Combine the sugar, margarine, lime juice, salt, and cayenne in a medium saucepan over low heat and stir until the margarine melts. Increase the heat to medium and bring to a simmer. Remove from the heat and stir in the rum. Pour the mixture over the top of the potatoes. Bake for 10 minutes, basting a few times. Sprinkle the lime zest over the potatoes and continue baking until soft, about 10 minutes more.

Turn oven setting to broil and broil the potatoes until browned on top, about 2 minutes. Serve hot.

Serves 8

Kilocalories 266 Kc • Protein 3 gm • Fat 3 gm • Percent of calories from fat 10% • Cholesterol 0 mg • Dietary fiber 5 gm • Sodium 163 mg • Calcium 62 mg

Barbados-Style Grilled Kebabs

Coconut milk can be found in the gourmet section of most supermarkets. Be sure to soak the bamboo skewers in water for 30 minutes before using to prevent burning.

1/4 cup safflower oil
1/4 cup unsweetened canned
    coconut milk
1/4 cup dark rum
1 teaspoon hot red pepper flakes
1 teaspoon minced fresh garlic
1/2 teaspoon grated fresh ginger
1 large Spanish onion, quartered

1 large red bell pepper, cut into
    2-inch pieces
8 ounces seitan, cut into 1 1/2-inch
    cubes
2 seedless oranges, peeled and
    quartered
8 to 12 bamboo skewers, soaked in
    water for 30 minutes

Combine the oil, coconut milk, rum, hot red pepper flakes, garlic, and ginger in a small bowl.

Place the onion quarters in a vegetable steamer and steam until slightly softened, about 3 minutes.

Put the onion, bell pepper, and seitan cubes in a shallow bowl and pour the coconut milk mixture on top. Cover and refrigerate for 2 hours, stirring occasionally.

Preheat a grill or broiler. Drain the seitan and vegetables, reserving the marinade. Thread the seitan, onion, orange, and bell pepper pieces onto skewers. Grill the kebabs over hot coals or broil for about 5 minutes total, turning frequently and brushing with the reserved marinade.

Serves 4

Kilocalories 338 Kc • Protein 17 gm • Fat 15 gm • Percent of calories from fat 39% •
Cholesterol 0 mg • Dietary fiber 2 gm • Sodium 129 mg • Calcium 32 mg

Jamaican Baked Vegetables

If you wish to add something "meaty" to this tropical vegetable feast, sauté chunks of seitan or tempeh at the end of the cooking time, and add to the vegetables.

1 large Spanish onion, cut into
    1-inch chunks
2 large red bell peppers, cut into
    1-inch strips
4 yams or sweet potatoes, peeled
    and cut into 2-inch chunks
2 pounds butternut squash, peeled,
    cut into 1-inch chunks
1/2 cup crushed canned pineapple
1/2 cup freshly squeezed orange juice

1/4 cup freshly squeezed lime juice
1/2 cup light brown sugar
4 garlic cloves, minced
1/2 tablespoon grated fresh ginger
1/8 teaspoon ground cloves
1 teaspoon grated orange zest
1 teaspoon hot red pepper flakes
1/2 teaspoon salt
1/4 teaspoon freshly ground pepper
1/3 cup dark Jamaican rum

Preheat the oven to 350°F. Coat a large roasting pan with nonstick vegetable cooking spray. Place the onion, bell peppers, yams, and squash in the pan, add 1/2 cup water, cover, and bake for 30 minutes.

In a blender or food processor, combine the pineapple, orange juice, lime juice, brown sugar, garlic, ginger, cloves, orange zest, hot red pepper flakes, salt, and pepper and purée. Pour the purée over the top of the vegetables, return to the oven and bake, uncovered, for another 45 minutes, until soft and lightly browned, basting occasionally with the liquid in the pan.

Transfer the vegetables to a heated serving platter and keep warm. Transfer the liquid in the pan to a small saucepan and bring to a boil over high heat, stirring frequently. Add the rum and continue cooking, stirring constantly, for 2 minutes. Pour over the vegetables on the platter and serve.

Serves 6

Kilocalories 272 Kc • Protein 5 gm • Fat .6 gm • Percent of calories from fat 2% • Cholesterol 0 mg • Dietary fiber 6 gm • Sodium 221 mg • Calcium 103 mg

Jamaican Jerk Sauce

Jamaican jerk spices are generally used to season grilled meats, but I enjoy using this aromatic sauce on everything from veggie burgers to grilled vegetables. It also makes a great marinade for tofu or tempeh, or dipping sauce for vegetable fritters or tempura.

1 small onion, chopped	2 tablespoons cider vinegar
2 small hot chilies, seeded and chopped	2 tablespoons molasses
1 garlic clove, chopped	1 tablespoon dark Jamaican rum
2 tablespoons olive oil	1 tablespoon ground allspice
2 tablespoons low-sodium tamari	1/4 teaspoon dried thyme
	1/4 teaspoon nutmeg

Combine the onion, chilies, garlic, oil, tamari, vinegar, molasses, rum, allspice, thyme, and nutmeg in a food processor or blender and purée until well blended. Transfer to a saucepan and heat to boiling. Reduce the heat to low and simmer 10 minutes, stirring occasionally until sauce thickens slightly.
Serves 8

Kilocalories 59 Kc • Protein 1 gm • Fat 3 gm • Percent of calories from fat 52% • Cholesterol 0 mg • Dietary fiber 1 gm • Sodium 155 mg • Calcium 55 mg

South America

Lime-Marinated White Bean Salad

Known as seviche *or* ceviche, *this lime-marinated salad from Peru is traditionally made with raw fish or scallops, but cannellini or other white beans also work well.*

3 cups cooked white beans
1/4 cup plus 2 tablespoons freshly
    squeezed lime juice
1/4 teaspoon salt
1/4 teaspoon cayenne
1 large ripe tomato, chopped

2 teaspoons minced fresh parsley
1 scallion, minced
2 teaspoons chopped capers
1/4 cup olive oil
4 cups torn salad greens

Place the cooked beans in a shallow bowl with 1/4 cup of the lime juice, the salt, and 1/8 teaspoon of the cayenne, and toss gently to coat. Refrigerate, covered, for 1 hour.

Meanwhile, in a small bowl, combine the tomato, parsley, scallion, capers, olive oil, the remaining 2 tablespoons lime juice, and the remaining 1/8 teaspoon cayenne until well blended. Arrange the salad greens on individual plates. Place the bean mixture on top of the lettuce and drizzle with dressing.

Serves 4

Kilocalories 329 Kc • Protein 14 gm • Fat 14 gm • Percent of calories from fat 37% • Cholesterol 0 mg • Dietary fiber 10 gm • Sodium 214 mg • Calcium 155 mg

Quinoa-Stuffed Avocados

Quinoa is an ancient grain native only to Bolivia and a mainstay of the Bolivian diet, along with potatoes and corn. Quinoa is available in natural food stores and makes an interesting, nutritious replacement for rice. Avocados are also plentiful in Bolivia and are often included in holiday feasts.

2 tablespoons olive oil
1 small onion, minced
1 cup cooked quinoa
1 ripe medium tomato, chopped
1 tablespoon minced fresh parsley
1/4 teaspoon salt

1/4 teaspoon freshly ground pepper
2 ripe avocados
1 tablespoon freshly squeezed lemon juice
4 large butter lettuce leaves

Heat 1 tablespoon of the oil in skillet over medium heat, add the onion, cover, and cook for 5 to 7 minutes to soften. Transfer the onion to a medium bowl. Add the quinoa, tomato, parsley, salt, and pepper, and mix until well combined.

Carefully halve the avocados lengthwise and remove the pits. Run a small knife between the avocado skin and flesh and remove the pulp, keeping the shells intact. Cut the pulp into 1/2-inch dice and add to the quinoa mixture. Add the lemon juice and remaining 1 tablespoon oil and toss gently to combine. Taste and adjust seasonings. Spoon the mixture into the reserved avocado shells and serve immediately on salad plates lined with lettuce leaves.

Serves 4

Kilocalories 273 Kc • Protein 4 gm • Fat 23 gm • Percent of calories from fat 70% • Cholesterol 0 mg • Dietary fiber 6 gm • Sodium 163 mg • Calcium 28 mg

Argentinean-Inspired Seitan Cutlets

My friend Patty Gershanik is from Argentina and her description of the ubiquitous grilled beef dishes in her native land inspired this vegetarian alternative. The Argentineans use lemons on everything from salads to meats, and much of their cuisine has been influenced by Italian and Spanish immigrants.

$1/3$ cup freshly squeezed lemon juice
$1/2$ teaspoon hot red pepper flakes
1 bay leaf
$1/8$ teaspoon salt
$1/4$ cup olive oil

1 pound seitan, cut into $1/2$-inch
    cutlets
1 cup dried bread crumbs
Lemon wedges

To make the marinade, combine the lemon juice, hot red pepper flakes, bay leaf, salt, and olive oil in a small bowl. Arrange the seitan cutlets in a baking dish without overlapping them and pour the marinade over them. Marinate the seitan for 1 hour at room temperature, or several hours in the refrigerator, turning once or twice to spread the seasoning mixture evenly.

Remove the seitan from the marinade and dredge in the bread crumbs, pressing the crumbs into the cutlets with your hands. Broil under a preheated broiler or sauté in a skillet for 2 minutes on each side or until browned. Serve with lemon wedges.

Serves 4

Kilocalories 183 Kc • Protein 32 gm • Fat 1 gm • Percent of calories from fat 6% • Cholesterol 0 mg • Dietary fiber 1 gm • Sodium 370 mg • Calcium 16 mg

Citrus-Marinated Tempeh
with Sweet Potatoes

This recipe was inspired by the Peruvian roasted pig dish called Chancho Adobado. *I make my version with tempeh that is marinated for several hours. Serve with hot steamed flour tortillas.*

1/4 cup freshly squeezed lemon juice
1/3 cup freshly squeezed orange juice
1/4 cup chopped onion
1 teaspoon minced fresh garlic
1/2 teaspoon salt
1/4 teaspoon cayenne

1 pound tempeh, cut into 1/2-inch strips
2 large sweet potatoes
2 tablespoons safflower oil
1 tablespoon chopped fresh parsley

In a food processor or blender, combine the lemon juice, orange juice, onion, garlic, salt, and cayenne, and process until blended. Transfer the marinade to a shallow bowl, add the tempeh, and refrigerate for several hours.

Boil the sweet potatoes until tender, about 25 minutes. Allow to cool slightly, then peel and cut into 1/2-inch-thick slices. Set aside.

Heat the oil in a large skillet over medium-high heat, add the tempeh, and cook until browned on all sides, about 5 minutes. Reduce the heat to low and add the marinade. Cover and simmer, stirring occasionally, to heat through, about 5 minutes. Spoon the tempeh onto a serving platter and keep warm. Add the sweet potato slices to the sauce and simmer until heated through. Arrange the sweet potatoes around the tempeh on the serving platter. Pour the sauce over everything and sprinkle with the parsley.

Serves 4

Kilocalories 358 Kc • Protein 23 gm • Fat 16 gm • Percent of calories from fat 37% • Cholesterol 0 mg • Dietary fiber 10 gm • Sodium 306 mg • Calcium 127 mg

Chilean Stuffed Peppers

Stuffing vegetables is popular throughout the world, and Chile is no exception. In this recipe bell peppers are stuffed with a spicy tomato-corn mixture.

6 large green bell peppers
2 tablespoons safflower oil
1 large onion, chopped
1/4 teaspoon nutmeg
1/4 teaspoon ground cumin
1/4 teaspoon cayenne
4 medium tomatoes, peeled and
    chopped

2 cups fresh or frozen corn kernels
1/2 cup fresh bread crumbs
1/2 cup soy milk
1 teaspoon sugar
1/8 teaspoon salt
2 tablespoons dry bread crumbs

Preheat the oven to 350°F.

Slice the tops off the peppers and remove the seeds. Heat 1 tablespoon of the oil in a skillet over medium heat. Add the onion, cover, and cook, stirring occasionally, for 5 minutes or until softened. Add the nutmeg, cumin, and cayenne, and cook, stirring, for 1 minute. Add the tomatoes to the skillet and cook until the mixture thickens, about 3 minutes. Add the corn and mix well.

Combine the fresh bread crumbs and soy milk in a small bowl and mix well. Add the bread crumb mixture, sugar, and salt to the corn mixture in the skillet. Fill the peppers with the corn mixture and arrange in a baking dish. Sprinkle the dry bread crumbs over the tops. Drizzle the remaining tablespoon oil over the bread crumbs and add 1 cup water to the pan. Cover and bake for 30 minutes or until the peppers are tender and the stuffing is lightly browned (but still moist).

6 servings

Kilocalories 167 Kc • Protein 4 gm • Fat 6 gm • Percent of calories from fat 29% • Cholesterol 0 mg • Dietary fiber 4 gm • Sodium 101 mg • Calcium 35 mg

Brazilian Lemon-Chili Sauce

This tangy and refreshing sauce from Brazil adds a new dimension to anything from steamed vegetables to tofu.

3 hot chilies, fresh or dried, seeded
    and chopped
1/2 cup chopped onion
2 garlic cloves, minced

1/2 cup freshly squeezed lemon juice
2 tablespoons chopped fresh parsley
Salt

In a food processor or blender, combine the chilies, onion, garlic, lemon juice, parsley, and salt to taste, and process until blended. Let stand 1 hour at room temperature or 2 hours in the refrigerator before using.

Serves 4 to 6 (makes 1 cup)

Kilocalories 23 Kc • Protein 1 gm • Fat .1 gm • Percent of calories from fat 2% • Cholesterol 0 mg • Dietary fiber 1 gm • Sodium 3 mg • Calcium 13 mg

TWO

Mediterranean Europe

▼▼

Mediterranean Europe Recipe Mini-Index

Appetizers
Chili Alioli *73*   Peperonata *58*   Stuffed Cherry Peppers *57*
Tapenade on French Bread Rounds *83*

Soups and Stews
Basque Chickpea Stew *85*   Escarole Soup *59*   Garlic Soup *74*
Italian Vegetable Ragout *61*   Portuguese Spicy Kale Soup *84*
Ratatouille *86*   Tuscan White Bean Soup *60*   White Gazpacho *75*

Salads
Arugula Potato Salad *65*   Basque Eggplant Salad *87*
Basque Chicory Salad *88*   Farfalle Salad with Roasted Peppers *63*
Red Pepper and Mushroom Salad with Walnuts *76*   Sicilian Orange Salad *62*
Spicy Cavatelli Primavera *64*

Sides
Cauliflower with Mustard-Dill Sauce *90*   Roasted Catalan-Style Vegetables *79*
Roasted Potatoes and Peppers *67*   Spanish Lentils *77*
Spicy Spanish Potatoes *78*   Svikla *91*
Sweet and Sour Onions and Zucchini *66*

Main Courses
Farsia Intchauspe *92*   Italian Easter Pie *69*   Majorcan Baked Vegetables *89*
Pasta alla Putanesca *72*   Penne with Uncooked Tomato Sauce and Olives *70*
Rice with Fava Beans and Vegetables *81*   Tempeh Cacciatore *68*
Tofu Piperade *93*   Tofu with Romesco Sauce *82*   Vegetarian Paella *80*
Ziti with Spicy Tomato Sauce *71*

▲▲

Mediterranean Heat

It is said that the closer to the equator a country is, the spicier the cuisine. Accordingly, there are only a few European cuisines that are well known for their spiciness. These are found primarily around the rim of the Mediterranean, especially in Italy and Spain.

Italy

Historically, Italy's various regions have been known for their own specialties, with many of the spicier dishes hailing from the southern regions. In central Italy, beans are widely used, especially the chickpea, kidney bean, and cannellini bean. The cuisine of northern Italy shows influences from its European neighbors, incorporating potatoes and lighter sauces in many of its dishes.

In Italy, chilies are frequently used fresh as well as dried, along with garlic, basil, oregano, and olives, to create irresistible classic dishes. The abundant use of fresh produce, herbs, and spices, along with pasta, rice (risotto), and cornmeal (polenta), make Italian cooking a treasure trove for vegetarians. Meat is often used merely to flavor soups or sauces or as a side dish in Italy, and the recipes are easily adapted by using meat alternatives. While cheeses are a very important part of Italian cooking, there are many delicious low-fat and dairy-free cheese alternatives now available. In recipes such as lasagne, tofu makes a low-fat high-protein alternative to cholesterol-laden ricotta cheese.

Italy is home to a seemingly limitless variety of pasta, many of which are included in the recipes in this book. Have fun experimenting with different pasta shapes, from the tiny pastina to the curly fusili or the sturdy ziti. Generally, the thicker pastas are used with the more robust sauces, while the thinner pastas are paired with lighter sauces. If you are fortunate enough to have fresh pasta, you will find that it cooks quickly and is quite tender. Dried pasta takes longer to cook, depending on the shape, and should be cooked al dente, or firm to the bite. Always cook pasta in a large pot of lightly salted boiling water, stirring frequently so it doesn't stick. The best way to test for doneness is to retrieve a piece of pasta from the pot, run it under cold water, and bite into it.

Spain

The food of Spain is often erroneously compared to Mexican food, when in fact it is much closer to Italian. While Spaniards use the Mediterranean ingredients of tomatoes, garlic, chilies, and olive oil, their cooking was also influenced by the Moors, hence their use of cumin, almonds, rice, and saffron. Although meat and fish are eaten liberally throughout Spain, many of the dishes are equally good when made meatless, using fresh produce, herbs, and spices. Some of the spiciest dishes of Spain come from Majorca and the Catalan region.

The Rest of Europe

The occasional spiciness sometimes present in French cuisine generally comes from peppercorns, mustard, garlic, and herbs, rather than chilies. Delightful vegetable dishes, such as ratatouille and tapenade, redolent of garlic and herbs, are world-famous. Great Britain and much of Eastern Europe favor horseradish and mustard, while Hungary and other middle European countries enjoy a pungent paprika (ground sweet red peppers) in many of their recipes.

While Greek cooking incorporates an exotic blending of herbs and spices, it's generally considered mild in terms of heat. Greek cuisine is similar in some ways to that of Italy and Spain, with its abundant use of olives, eggplant, oregano, bell peppers, tomatoes, and zucchini. However, Greece has more striking similarities to Middle Eastern cuisines, with its use of grape leaves, phyllo dough, and pita bread, as well as lemons, artichokes, mint, cinnamon, and rice.

The Basque people who live in a region bordered by Spain and France have their own cuisine that is similar in some ways to French and Spanish cooking in its use of mustard and peppercorns as well as olive oil, tomatoes, garlic, and numerous spices.

Italy

Stuffed Cherry Peppers

My childhood was well spiced with hot appetizers like these, which my Italian grand-mother used to make at holiday time. Now I make them year-round, especially when I'm expecting company.

2 12-ounce jars hot cherry peppers,
   drained and rinsed (about
   20 peppers)
1 tablespoon olive oil

2 cups fresh bread crumbs
2 tablespoons sugar
1 cup raisins
1/2 cup chopped figs

Preheat the oven to 400°F.

With a small sharp knife, remove the caps and seeds from the peppers and set aside. Heat the oil in a medium skillet over medium heat. Add the bread crumbs, sugar, raisins, and figs, and sauté for 2 minutes to combine flavors. Press the stuffing mixture inside each of the peppers and arrange on a baking pan. Sprinkle the peppers with additional sugar and oil if desired. Bake for 10 minutes or until the peppers are softened and the crumbs are browned.

Serves 6 to 8

Kilocalories 274 Kc • Protein 2 gm • Fat 31 gm • Percent of calories from fat 35% • Cholesterol 0 mg • Dietary fiber 19 gm • Sodium 202 mg • Calcium 43 mg

(Cherry pepper sodium values are Progresso—drained 30 mg/oz)

Peperonata

This simple Italian dish of stewed bell peppers is best when prepared several hours in advance so the flavors have time to develop. Similar to the French ratatouille, it can be served as a first course, with crackers, or as a side dish.

1/4 cup olive oil
1 medium onion, finely chopped
2 red bell peppers, cut into 1/2-inch pieces (about 2 cups)
2 green bell peppers, cut into 1/2-inch pieces (about 2 cups)

1 teaspoon minced fresh garlic
1 28-ounce can whole peeled tomatoes, drained and chopped
1/2 teaspoon salt
1/4 teaspoon freshly ground pepper

Heat the oil in a medium saucepan over medium heat. Add the onion, bell peppers, and garlic and cook, covered, for 10 minutes to soften. Add the tomatoes and cook, uncovered, until the tomato liquid has evaporated, about 15 minutes. Remove from the heat and add the salt and pepper. Allow to cool slightly before serving.

Serves 4 to 6

Kilocalories 77 Kc • Protein 5 gm • Fat 1 gm • Percent of calories from fat 11% • Cholesterol 0 mg • Dietary fiber 4 gm • Sodium 309 mg • Calcium 17 mg

Escarole Soup

My mother learned to make this soup from my grandmother, who came from the Abruzzi region of Italy, and then passed the recipe on to me. The mellow cannellini beans provide the perfect balance to the flavorful broth and peppery greens.

1 tablespoon olive oil
1 medium onion, chopped
2 carrots, diced
1 garlic clove, minced
1/4 teaspoon hot red pepper flakes
1 head escarole, chopped
1/4 cup small dried pasta, such as
    pastina or orzo

2 cups cooked cannellini beans
2 bay leaves
1/2 teaspoon dried marjoram
2 tablespoons minced fresh parsley
1 teaspoon salt
1/8 teaspoon freshly ground pepper

Heat the oil in a large saucepan over medium heat. Add the onion, carrots, and garlic, and cook, covered, for 5 minutes or until softened. Add the hot red pepper flakes and 6 cups water and bring to a boil. Add the escarole and simmer 10 minutes. Add the pasta and cook until tender, about 10 minutes. Add the beans, bay leaves, marjoram, parsley, salt, and pepper and cook until just heated through, about 5 minutes. Remove the bay leaves before serving.

Serves 4

Kilocalories 233 Kc • Protein 11 gm • Fat 4 gm • Percent of calories from fat 16% • Cholesterol 0 mg • Dietary fiber 9 gm • Sodium 618 mg • Calcium 76 mg

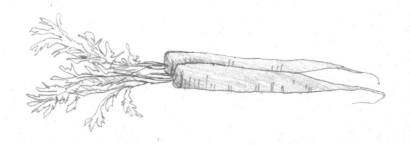

Tuscan White Bean Soup

Add some cooked pasta elbows for a delicious version of pasta e fagioli. *Serve with crusty bread and a tossed green salad for a satisfying and economical meal. Place the hot red pepper flakes on the table for those who want to add more heat to the soup.*

1 tablespoon olive oil	2¹/₂ cups cooked Great
1 medium onion, chopped	Northern beans
1 carrot, thinly sliced	1 tablespoon tomato paste
¹/₄ cup minced celery	¹/₂ teaspoon hot red pepper flakes
2 garlic cloves, minced	1 teaspoon freshly squeezed
2 28-ounce cans plum tomatoes,	lemon juice
drained and chopped	Salt and freshly ground pepper
1 bay leaf	¹/₄ cup minced fresh basil

Heat the oil in a large saucepan over medium heat. Add the onion, carrot, celery, and garlic. Cover and cook until softened, about 5 minutes. Stir in 4 cups water, the tomatoes, and bay leaf, and bring to a boil. Reduce the heat, and simmer, covered, stirring occasionally, for about 20 minutes. Blend in the beans, tomato paste, hot red pepper flakes, and lemon juice. Season to taste with salt and pepper, then simmer uncovered 10 minutes longer. Remove the bay leaf, add the basil, and serve.

Serves 8

Kilocalories 153 Kc • Protein 7 gm • Fat 2 gm • Percent of calories from fat 12% • Cholesterol 0 mg • Dietary fiber 8 gm • Sodium 36 mg • Calcium 116 mg

Italian Vegetable Ragout

I make this hearty dish when summer's harvest is plentiful. Tomatoes, zucchini, basil, and parsley fresh from the garden make this an especially flavorful and comforting treat. Serve it with crusty Italian bread, warm from the oven.

2 tablespoons olive oil
1 medium onion, thinly sliced
1/2 cup dry white wine
2 zucchini, halved lengthwise and
    cut into 1/2-inch slices
2 pounds ripe plum tomatoes,
    chopped

1/8 teaspoon hot red pepper flakes
2 cups cooked fava beans
1/4 cup chopped fresh parsley
1/4 cup chopped fresh basil
Salt and freshly ground pepper

Heat the olive oil over medium heat in a large skillet. Add the onion, cover, and cook until softened, about 5 minutes. Uncover, add the wine, and cook until it evaporates. Add the zucchini, tomatoes, hot red pepper flakes, fava beans, and parsley. Cover and cook over medium-low heat for 15 to 20 minutes or until the vegetables are tender. Add the basil and season to taste with salt and pepper.

4 servings

Kilocalories 242 Kc • Protein 9 gm • Fat 8 gm • Percent of calories from fat 28% • Cholesterol 0 mg • Dietary fiber 8 gm • Sodium 47 mg • Calcium 67 mg

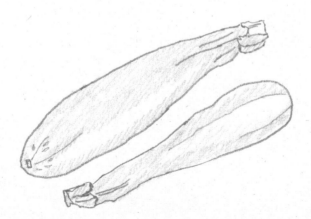

Sicilian Orange Salad

This vibrant and colorful salad adds a refreshing accent to a rich pasta dinner. It gets its bite from the freshly ground black peppercorns, which bring out the sweetness of the oranges.

4 medium navel oranges, peeled and cut into 1/4-inch rounds

3 tablespoons olive oil

1 tablespoon freshly squeezed orange juice

1 teaspoon freshly squeezed lemon juice

1 teaspoon minced fresh garlic

1/2 teaspoon sugar

1/8 teaspoon salt

1 teaspoon black peppercorns, coarsely cracked

8 oil-cured olives, halved and pitted

2 tablespoons minced fresh parsley

Arrange the orange slices on a serving platter. In a small bowl, combine the oil, orange juice, lemon juice, garlic, sugar, and salt, and whisk until blended. Drizzle the dressing over the orange slices. Sprinkle with the cracked peppercorns, olives, and parsley. Cover the plate with plastic wrap and set aside at room temperature for at least 1 hour before serving.

Serves 6

Kilocalories 122 Kc • Protein 1 gm • Fat 9 gm • Percent of calories from fat 60% • Cholesterol 0 mg • Dietary fiber 3 gm • Sodium 127 mg • Calcium 39 mg

Farfalle Salad with Roasted Peppers

The flavor of this salad improves if allowed to sit overnight. If farfalle, or bow ties, are unavailable, substitute any small-shaped pasta, such as rotini or penne.

1 large red bell pepper	2 tablespoons red wine vinegar
1 large yellow bell pepper	3/4 teaspoon salt
1 medium-sized red onion, chopped	1/8 teaspoon hot red pepper flakes
1/2 cup fresh basil leaves	8 ounces farfalle, freshly cooked
1/4 cup olive oil	2 cups cooked chickpeas

Char the bell peppers over a gas flame or in a broiler about 4 inches from the heat, turning, until blackened on all sides. Transfer the peppers to a paper bag, fold the top of the bag over a few times to close, and steam for about 10 minutes to loosen the skin. Peel and seed the peppers, then cut into 1/4-inch julienne.

In a food processor, combine the onion, basil, oil, vinegar, salt, and hot red pepper flakes until well blended. Combine the bell pepper julienne, farfalle, and chickpeas in a shallow bowl. Add the vinaigrette and toss gently. Taste and adjust the seasonings. Cool. Cover and refrigerate several hours before serving.

Serves 4

Kilocalories 491 Kc • Protein 15 gm • Fat 15 gm • Percent of calories from fat 27% • Cholesterol 0 mg • Dietary fiber 7 gm • Sodium 448 mg • Calcium 71 mg

Spicy Cavatelli Primavera

I find the frozen cavatelli available in Italian specialty stores to be superior in flavor and texture to the dried variety, though not as good as homemade.

1 pound cavatelli, preferably frozen
1/3 cup plus 1 tablespoon olive oil
3 tablespoons white wine vinegar
1/2 teaspoon salt
1/8 teaspoon cayenne
1/2 pound green beans, cut into
    1-inch lengths, steamed
2 small zucchini, halved lengthwise,
    cut into 1/2-inch pieces, steamed
2 cups thinly sliced mushrooms
    (about 3/4 pound)

1 teaspoon minced seeded fresh hot
    red or green chili
1/4 cup plus 2 tablespoons minced
    fresh parsley
2 teaspoons minced fresh garlic
8 ripe plum tomatoes, chopped
2 tablespoons chopped fresh basil or
    1 teaspoon dried
Salt and freshly ground pepper

Cook the cavatelli in a pot of boiling salted water until al dente, about 12 minutes. Drain and rinse under cold running water. Drain well and set aside in a large bowl.

Whisk 1/3 cup of the olive oil, the vinegar, 1/2 teaspoon salt, and the cayenne in a small bowl and set aside. Place the steamed green beans and zucchini in a large serving bowl and set aside.

Heat the remaining 1 tablespoon oil in a large skillet over medium heat. Add the mushrooms, chili, 1/4 cup of the parsley, the garlic, and tomatoes, and cook, stirring occasionally, for 5 minutes. Add to the green beans and zucchini. Stir in the basil. Add the vinaigrette to the vegetables in the serving bowl and toss well. Let the vegetables marinate at room temperature for 5 minutes. Add the cooked pasta and salt and pepper to taste. Toss to mix well. Garnish with the remaining 2 tablespoons parsley and serve at room temperature.

Serves 8 to 10

Kilocalories 341 Kc • Protein 10 gm • Fat 11 gm • Percent of calories from fat 29% • Cholesterol 0 mg • Dietary fiber 4 gm • Sodium 161 mg • Calcium 44 mg

Arugula Potato Salad

Arugula, also known as rocket cress or rocket lettuce, can be eaten raw or cooked, and in Italy it is often served braised. In this recipe, arugula's piquant flavor is enhanced by the capers and cayenne in the dressing, making it a perfect complement to the potatoes. Whenever arugula is unavailable, watercress is an excellent substitute.

1¹/₂ pounds small red potatoes, halved and cut into ¹/₂-inch slices
1 teaspoon salt
2 large red bell peppers
1 garlic clove
1 tablespoon capers, rinsed and drained
2 teaspoons freshly squeezed lemon juice

¹/₄ cup balsamic vinegar
¹/₈ teaspoon cayenne
¹/₂ cup olive oil
1¹/₂ cups lightly packed arugula (1 large bunch), coarsely chopped

Place the potatoes and ¹/₂ teaspoon of the salt in a medium saucepan with enough cold water to cover by 1 inch. Bring to a boil, reduce the heat to a simmer, and cook, uncovered, until the potatoes are just tender, about 10 minutes. Drain and rinse under cold water and drain again.

Char the bell peppers over a gas flame or in a broiler about 4 inches from the heat, turning, until blackened on all sides. Put the charred peppers in a paper bag, fold the top of the bag over a few times to close, and let the peppers steam for about 10 minutes to loosen the skins. Scrape off the blackened skin and remove the seeds and stems. Chop the peppers into ¹/₂-inch dice and set aside.

Purée the garlic and capers in a food processor or blender. Add the lemon juice, vinegar, cayenne, and remaining ¹/₂ teaspoon salt, and process until well blended. Slowly begin to add the olive oil to emulsify. When the emulsion thickens (after about half of the oil has been added), add in the remaining oil in a thin stream. Toss the potatoes, arugula, and reserved chopped peppers with the dressing until coated. Serve.

Serves 6

Kilocalories 371 Kc • Protein 3 gm • Fat 27 gm • Percent of calories from fat 64% • Cholesterol 0 mg • Dietary fiber 3 gm • Sodium 451 mg • Calcium 23 mg

Sweet and Sour Onions and Zucchini

I like to use the delicately sweet cipollini onions, when I can find them in the gourmet produce section of the supermarket. If unavailable, I use small Vidalia or other sweet onions. This dish can be served hot or at room temperature.

1 pound small yellow onions, preferably cipollini, about 1 1/2 inches in diameter	Salt
	3 large garlic cloves, sliced
	1 bay leaf
2 tablespoons olive oil	1/4 cup red wine vinegar
4 small zucchini, halved lengthwise and cut into 1/2-inch slices	1/4 teaspoon hot red pepper flakes
	1 teaspoon sugar

Bring a large pot of water to a boil. Add the onions in their skins, bring back to a boil, and cook for 5 minutes. Remove from the heat, allow to cool, then remove the skins, leaving the onions whole.

Heat the oil in a skillet over medium heat. Add the zucchini, season with salt to taste, and cook until crisp-tender, about 3 minutes. Transfer the zucchini to a bowl. Add the onions, garlic, and bay leaf to the skillet. Cover and cook over medium heat for 15 minutes or until the onions are tender and lightly browned. Stir in the vinegar, hot red pepper flakes, and sugar. Increase the heat to medium-high and cook, stirring, until the sugar dissolves, about 2 minutes. Pour the onion mixture over the zucchini and marinate at least 1 hour before serving. Taste and adjust seasonings. Remove the bay leaf and serve.

Serves 8 to 10

Kilocalories 60 Kc • Protein 1 gm • Fat 4 gm • Percent of calories from fat 50% • Cholesterol 0 mg • Dietary fiber 1gm • Sodium 3 mg • Calcium 18 mg

Roasted Potatoes and Peppers

This is a typical way to prepare potatoes in Italy.

3 medium potatoes, peeled and cut
    into 1/2-inch slices
2 medium onions, cut into eighths
4 medium-sized red bell peppers, cut
    lengthwise into 1-inch-wide
    slices

1/2 teaspoon salt
1/4 teaspoon freshly ground pepper
1/4 cup extra-virgin olive oil
1 teaspoon finely chopped fresh basil
    or 1/2 teaspoon dried
1 tablespoon balsamic vinegar

Preheat the oven to 400°F. Place the potatoes, onions, and bell peppers in a large roasting pan. Add the salt, pepper, and oil, and toss to coat the vegetables. Bake, stirring occasionally, for about 45 minutes or until the potatoes are tender. Sprinkle on the basil and vinegar, toss to combine, and serve.

Serves 6

Kilocalories 175 Kc • Protein 2 gm • Fat 9 gm • Percent of calories from fat 46% •
Cholesterol 0 mg • Dietary fiber 3 gm • Sodium 200 mg • Calcium 22 mg

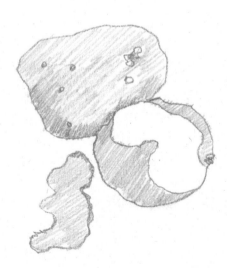

Tempeh Cacciatore

Tempeh is the perfect vegetarian alternative to the traditional chicken in this zesty tomato-based main course.

2 tablespoons olive oil
1 pound tempeh, cut into 2-inch
    pieces
Salt and freshly ground pepper
1 onion, finely chopped
1 carrot, cut into 1/8-inch slices
1 celery rib, cut into 1/8-inch slices
1 green bell pepper, cut into 1/2-inch
    pieces

3 garlic cloves, minced
1/2 teaspoon hot red pepper flakes
1 16-ounce can tomatoes, drained
    and chopped, reserving the juice
1/2 cup dry white wine
1/2 teaspoon dried oregano
2 tablespoons minced fresh parsley

Heat the oil in a large saucepan over medium-high heat. Add the tempeh and brown lightly on all sides, about 5 minutes. Season with salt and pepper to taste, then transfer to a plate and set aside.

In the same saucepan, combine the onion, carrot, celery, and bell pepper. Cover and cook the vegetables over medium-low heat, stirring occasionally, until softened, about 5 to 7 minutes. Add the garlic and the hot red pepper flakes and cook, stirring, for 1 minute. Add the chopped tomatoes and cook over medium-high heat, stirring, until the liquid has evaporated, about 2 to 3 minutes. Add the wine and boil the mixture, stirring, until it is reduced by half, about 5 minutes. Stir in the reserved tomato juice and the oregano, add the tempeh, and bring the liquid to a boil. Cover the saucepan, reduce heat to medium, and cook for 20 minutes until sauce thickens. Transfer the tempeh to a platter and keep it warm. Bring the liquid to a boil, stirring, to reduce. Stir in the parsley and salt and pepper to taste and spoon the sauce over the tempeh.

Serves 6

Kilocalories 241 Kc • Protein 16 gm • Fat 11 gm • Percent of calories from fat 37% • Cholesterol 0 mg • Dietary fiber 7 gm • Sodium 25 mg • Calcium 92 mg

Italian Easter Pie

Traditionally this savory pie, which has many different names in Italy, features hot sausage, ricotta cheese, and eggs. My meatless version, made with vegetarian sausage and tofu, has the same great flavor but is healthier. My family has always called this Easter Pie because we only make it at Easter time.

2 cups all-purpose flour
1 cup (2 sticks) margarine
1/4 teaspoon sugar
1 1/4 teaspoons salt
1 pound vegetarian sausage, crumbled
2 pounds firm tofu, crumbled

1/4 cup soy Parmesan cheese alternative
1/4 cup minced fresh parsley
1/2 teaspoon freshly ground pepper
1/4 teaspoon cayenne
1/4 teaspoon paprika
1/4 teaspoon ground fennel seeds

Preheat the oven to 350°F.

Place the flour, margarine, sugar, and 1/4 teaspoon of the salt in a food processor. With the machine running, add enough water (approximately 1/4 cup) for a dough ball to form. Divide the dough into 2 equal balls and set aside.

In a large bowl, combine the vegetarian sausage, tofu, soy Parmesan, parsley, the remaining 1 teaspoon salt, the pepper, cayenne, paprika, and fennel seeds. Taste and adjust seasonings.

Roll out the dough into 2 11-inch rounds. Place the bottom crust in a 10-inch pie plate and spread the filling mixture over it. Cover with the top crust, pinch the edges, and prick with the tines of a fork. Bake for 1 hour or until golden brown.

Serves 8

Kilocalories 386 Kc • Protein 25 gm • Fat 16 gm • Percent of calories from fat 38% • Cholesterol 0 mg • Dietary fiber 2 gm • Sodium 893 mg • Calcium 262 mg

Penne with Uncooked Tomato Sauce and Olives

This sauce is a summertime favorite for two reasons: It's a delicious way to feature the season's fresh ripe tomato crop and making it doesn't heat up the kitchen. Another plus is that it's equally delicious served with hot or cold pasta.

2 pounds ripe tomatoes, chopped (about 4 cups)
1 cup black oil-cured olives, halved and pitted
1/4 cup olive oil
1/4 cup chopped fresh basil
1 tablespoon minced fresh garlic
1 tablespoon minced fresh parsley
1/2 teaspoon salt
1/4 teaspoon hot red pepper flakes
1 pound penne or other tubular pasta, cooked

Combine the tomatoes, olives, oil, basil, garlic, parsley, salt, and hot red pepper flakes in a large bowl. Cover and let stand at room temperature for 30 minutes, stirring occasionally. Add the cooked pasta and toss gently to combine. Serve immediately or cover and refrigerate to serve cold later on.

Serves 6

Kilocalories 474 Kc • Protein 11 gm • Fat 19 gm • Percent of calories from fat 35% • Cholesterol 0 mg • Dietary fiber 6 gm • Sodium 573 mg • Calcium 28 mg

Ziti with Spicy Tomato Sauce

This quick, hearty sauce was handed down from my grandmother, a wonderful Italian cook. Grandma's version was made with ground beef or, sometimes, sausage. I now enjoy it with chopped mushrooms or cannellini beans.

2 tablespoons olive oil
1/2 pound chopped mushrooms
2 large garlic cloves, minced
1 35-ounce can plum tomatoes, with
    their juice, chopped
1/2 teaspoon hot red pepper flakes

Salt and freshly ground pepper
1 pound ziti or other tubular pasta
2 tablespoons grated soy Parmesan
    cheese alternative
2 tablespoons minced fresh basil

Heat the oil in a large skillet over medium heat. Add the mushrooms and garlic and sauté until softened, about 5 minutes. Add the tomatoes with their juice, hot red pepper flakes, and salt and pepper to taste. Bring to a boil, reduce the heat to medium-low, and simmer, uncovered, for 15 minutes.

Cook the pasta in boiling salted water according to the package directions. Drain well. In a large serving bowl, toss the pasta with the sauce, soy Parmesan cheese, and basil, then serve.

Serves 6

Kilocalories 386 Kc • Protein 13 gm • Fat 6 gm • Percent of calories from fat 14% •
Cholesterol 0 mg • Dietary fiber 5 gm • Sodium 68 mg • Calcium 103 mg

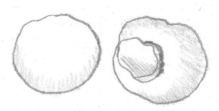

Pasta alla Puttanesca

This dish is said to have gotten its name—"whore's pasta" in English—because the sauce is too good to resist. The classic version contains anchovies but I think my interpretation without them is even more irresistible.

2 tablespoons olive oil
4 garlic cloves, finely chopped
1 28-ounce can plum tomatoes,
    drained and chopped
1/2 teaspoon hot red pepper flakes
1/2 teaspoon dried basil
1/2 teaspoon dried oregano
Salt and freshly ground pepper

1 cup black olives, pitted and sliced
3 tablespoons capers, rinsed and
    drained
1/2 teaspoon hot pepper sauce
1/4 cup dry white wine
1 pound spaghetti
2 tablespoons minced fresh parsley

In a medium saucepan, heat the olive oil over medium heat. Add the garlic and when it becomes fragrant, add the tomatoes, hot red pepper flakes, basil, oregano, and salt and pepper to taste. Bring the sauce to a boil, stirring continuously to help break up the tomatoes. Reduce the heat to low and simmer for 20 minutes, stirring continuously, until the tomatoes make a thick sauce. Add the olives, capers, hot pepper sauce, and wine to the sauce and keep warm.

Meanwhile, bring a pot of salted water to a boil. Add the spaghetti to the water and cook according to the package directions until al dente. Drain and transfer to a large serving bowl. Taste the sauce and adjust seasonings. Add the sauce to the pasta and toss to combine. Serve immediately, sprinkled with the minced parsley.

Serves 6

Kilocalories 402 Kc • Protein 11 gm • Fat 9 gm • Percent of calories from fat 21% • Cholesterol 0 mg • Dietary fiber 4 gm • Sodium 329 mg • Calcium 67 mg

Spain

Chili Alioli

A popular alternative to butter, alioli is placed alongside the bread basket in many Spanish restaurants. This especially fiery version is also good served as a dip with raw sliced vegetables, or added as a final flourish to a steaming bowl of soup.

1 small dried hot chili
4 garlic cloves
1 teaspoon salt
1 teaspoon red wine vinegar

1/8 teaspoon cayenne
1/8 teaspoon chili powder
3/4 cup extra-virgin olive oil

Place the dried chili in a bowl, pour boiling water over it, and soak until softened, about 15 minutes. Drain, place in a food processor, and purée. Add the garlic and the salt to the food processor and purée to form a smooth paste. Blend in the vinegar, cayenne, and chili powder. With the machine running, slowly drizzle in the oil, almost by the drop, until it begins to emulsify. Do not overprocess. Transfer to a bowl and allow to sit at room temperature until serving time.

Serves 8 to 10

Kilocalories 245 Kc • Protein 0 gm • Fat 27 gm • Percent of calories from fat 97% •
Cholesterol 0 mg • Dietary fiber 1 gm • Sodium 291 mg • Calcium 6 mg

Garlic Soup

I find this Spanish classic with its rich full-bodied flavor to be an amazing restorative.
Try some the next time you have a cold—you'll wonder what all the fuss is about chicken soup.

2 tablespoons olive oil
6 garlic cloves, minced
4 garlic cloves, crushed
5 cups Vegetable Stock (see page xxi)
1/4 teaspoon freshly ground pepper

1/8 teaspoon cayenne
1/8 teaspoon dried sage (optional)
1 cup cubed French bread
1 tablespoon dry sherry

Heat 1 tablespoon of the oil in a large saucepan. Add the garlic and cook over medium heat until softened, about 5 minutes, being careful not to brown. Add the stock, pepper, cayenne, and sage (if using). Bring to boil and simmer 15 minutes or until the garlic is soft and sweet-flavored. While the soup is cooking, sauté the bread cubes in the remaining 1 tablespoon oil until toasted. Set aside. Add the sherry to the soup and serve immediately, topped with the reserved croutons.

Serves 4

Kilocalories 145 Kc • Protein 2 gm • Fat 7 gm • Percent of calories from fat 44% •
Cholesterol 0 mg • Dietary fiber 1 gm • Sodium 160 mg • Calcium 24 mg

White Gazpacho

This unusual and delicious soup should be served very cold. The grapes and almonds reflect the Moorish influence on Spanish cooking.

$1/2$ pound seedless white grapes
3 garlic cloves, halved
$1/3$ cup blanched almonds, coarsely
   chopped
$1/2$ teaspoon salt
$1/4$ teaspoon white pepper

$1/8$ teaspoon cayenne
4 slices dry white bread, crusts
   removed
$1/4$ cup extra-virgin olive oil
2 tablespoons white vinegar
$3^1/2$ cups ice water

Pour boiling water over the grapes to loosen the skins, then drain and peel them. Place the peeled grapes in a small bowl and refrigerate.

In a food processor, purée the garlic, chopped almonds, salt, white pepper, and cayenne to a fine paste. Soak the bread in cold water for 5 minutes, then squeeze it dry. Add the bread to the almond and garlic paste, then process again until smooth. With the processor running, slowly drizzle the oil into the mixture, followed by the vinegar. Add the ice water. Taste and adjust seasonings, then refrigerate to chill thoroughly. Just before serving, garnish the chilled soup with the peeled grapes.

Serves 4

Kilocalories 276 Kc • Protein 5 gm • Fat 19 gm • Percent of calories from fat 58% •
Cholesterol 0 mg • Dietary fiber 2 gm • Sodium 427 mg • Calcium 72 mg

Red Pepper and Mushroom Salad
with Walnuts

This salad is a wonderful combination of color, texture, and flavor. It is delicious by itself, though I sometimes serve it over salad greens that have been tossed lightly with oil and vinegar.

1 teaspoon minced fresh garlic	1/4 cup olive oil
2 tablespoons red wine vinegar	3 cups sliced mushrooms
1/8 teaspoon salt	1/2 cup finely chopped walnuts
1/8 teaspoon cayenne	1/4 cup chopped red bell pepper
1/8 teaspoon dry mustard	1 tablespoon minced fresh parsley

In a food processor or bowl, combine the garlic, vinegar, salt, cayenne, and dry mustard, and mix well. With the machine running, slowly stream in the olive oil, then set aside. In a large bowl, combine the mushrooms, walnuts, bell pepper, and parsley. Pour the salad dressing over the mushroom mixture and toss lightly to coat evenly. Allow the salad to sit for about 30 minutes before serving so the flavors can mingle.

Serves 4 to 6

Kilocalories 189 Kc • Protein 3 gm • Fat 18 gm • Percent of calories from fat 83% • Cholesterol 0 mg • Dietary fiber 1 gm • Sodium 76 mg • Calcium 14 mg

Spanish Lentils

Whether served as a side dish or in a soup or stew, lentils always add flavorful richness to a meal.

1 tablespoon olive oil
1/2 cup minced onion
1/2 cup minced celery
2 tablespoons chopped sun-dried
   tomatoes

1 garlic clove, minced
1 jalapeño, seeded and minced
1/2 cup chopped fresh parsley
3/4 cup dried lentils
Salt and freshly ground pepper

In a medium saucepan, heat the oil over medium heat. Add the onion, celery, sun-dried tomatoes, garlic, jalapeño, and parsley. Sauté, stirring occasionally, until the onion and celery are softened but not browned, about 5 minutes. Stir in the lentils and 3 cups water. Bring to a boil, cover, reduce the heat, and add salt and pepper to taste. Simmer until the lentils are tender and most of the liquid has been absorbed, about 45 minutes.

Serves 4

Kilocalories 171 Kc • Protein 11 gm • Fat 4 gm • Percent of calories from fat 19% • Cholesterol 0 mg • Dietary fiber 12 gm • Sodium 62 mg • Calcium 46 mg

Spicy Spanish Potatoes

Called Patatas Bravas, *these potatoes are recommended only for those with no fear of fire. Many versions of this dish exist in Spain, where they are served with meat and vegetables, or with eggs. The potatoes themselves help temper the heat of the sauce, but you'll want to be sure to serve them with a mild entrée. Since we don't eat eggs at my house, I usually serve these potatoes with scrambled tofu and toast for a Sunday brunch or light supper.*

1¹/2 pounds small potatoes
2 tablespoons olive oil
Salt and freshly ground pepper
2 teaspoons sweet paprika

¹/2 teaspoon cayenne
2 tablespoons red wine vinegar
2 teaspoons tomato paste

Peel the potatoes and cut them into bite-sized chunks. Heat the oil in a large skillet over medium heat. Add the potatoes and cook, turning frequently, for about 5 minutes, until they are lightly browned. Season with salt and pepper, reduce the heat to low, and cover the pan. Cook the potatoes for 20 minutes, stirring occasionally. Turn the heat up to medium, sprinkle the potatoes with the paprika and cayenne, and stir well to coat. Blend the vinegar and tomato paste and carefully add to the pan. Cook for 2 minutes, stirring constantly, until the potatoes are well coated with a thick sauce. There should be no liquid left in the pan.

Serves 6

Kilocalories 141 Kc • Protein 2 gm • Fat 5 gm • Percent of calories from fat 29% • Cholesterol 0 mg • Dietary fiber 2 gm • Sodium 6 mg • Calcium 11 mg

Roasted Catalan-Style Vegetables

When weather permits, try grilling the vegetables over hot coals.

1 pound red bell peppers	1 head garlic, in its skin
1 pound eggplant	¼ cup extra-virgin olive oil
1 pound onions, in their skins	Salt

Preheat the oven to 375°F. Place the bell peppers, eggplant, onions, and garlic on a baking sheet and bake for 1 hour or until tender. Remove from the oven and cover the vegetables with a dish towel or transfer the vegetables to a paper bag and keep closed for 10 minutes.

Remove the charred skin of the peppers and scrape out the seeds. Cut the flesh into strips. Remove the skin of the eggplant and cut the flesh lengthwise into strips. Peel and chop the onions.

Arrange the roasted vegetables in a serving dish. Separate the baked garlic cloves from the papery skins and place in a food processor. With the machine running, slowly add the olive oil to make a paste, adding a pinch of salt. Drizzle the garlic purée on the vegetables and sprinkle with salt to taste.

Serves 6

Kilocalories 157 Kc • Protein 3 gm • Fat 9 gm • Percent of calories from fat 51% • Cholesterol 0 mg • Dietary fiber 5 gm • Sodium 7 mg • Calcium 38 mg

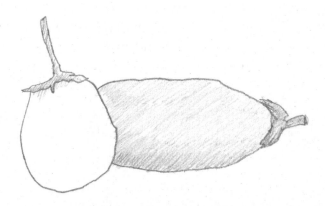

Vegetarian Paella

While the many variations of paella generally feature chicken, sausage, and shellfish, I think there's room for a vegetarian version as well. The meat alternatives are well suited to the flavorful sauce.

2 tablespoons olive oil
1 pound vegetarian sausage, cut into
   1-inch pieces
8 ounces seitan, cut into 1½-inch
   pieces
8 ounces tempeh, cut into
   1-inch dice
½ pound green beans, cut into
   1-inch pieces
2 28-ounce cans plum tomatoes,
   drained and chopped

2 garlic cloves, finely chopped
4 cups Vegetable Stock (see page xxi)
½ teaspoon hot red pepper flakes
¼ teaspoon saffron
¼ teaspoon ground fennel seeds
3 cups short-grain rice, such as
   Arborio
1 teaspoon salt
½ cup frozen peas

Heat the oil in a large skillet or saucepan. Add the vegetarian sausage, seitan, and tempeh, and cook for 5 minutes, turning occasionally to brown on all sides. Remove from the pan with a slotted spoon and set aside.

Add the green beans, chopped tomatoes, garlic, and stock to the pan. Bring to a boil, then stir in the hot red pepper flakes, saffron, and fennel seeds. Reduce the heat, cover, and simmer for 10 minutes. Add the rice and salt to taste, stir well to combine, and return to a boil. Lower the heat, cover, and simmer for 10 minutes. Add the peas, cover, and cook for 10 minutes longer, until the rice has absorbed all the liquid. Add the reserved meat alternatives and toss to heat through. Remove from the heat and let stand for 10 minutes before serving.

Serves 8

Kilocalories 550 Kc • Protein 30 gm • Fat 6 gm • Percent of calories from fat 10% • Cholesterol 0 mg • Dietary fiber 10 gm • Sodium 468 mg • Calcium 130 mg

Rice with Fava Beans and Vegetables

In this vegetarian interpretation of Arroz con Pollo, *firm meaty fava beans replace the chicken, or* pollo. *Seitan, tempeh, or firm tofu work well too. Accompany this hearty one-dish meal with salsa and crusty bread.*

1 tablespoon olive oil
1 medium onion, chopped
1 red bell pepper, chopped
1 small carrot, chopped
3 garlic cloves, chopped
1/2 teaspoon dried oregano
1/2 teaspoon ground cumin
1 1/2 cups white rice
1 cup drained and chopped canned
    tomatoes

1/2 cup green beans, cut into 1-inch
    lengths
Salt
2 cups cooked fava beans
1/4 cup salsa, commercial or
    homemade (see pages 26 or 28)
1/2 cup pimiento-stuffed green olives
1/2 cup frozen peas, thawed
Freshly ground pepper

Heat the oil in a large saucepan over medium heat. Add the onion, bell pepper, and carrot, cover, and cook for 5 minutes or until softened. Add the garlic, oregano, and cumin, and sauté for 1 to 2 minutes longer. Stir in the rice. Add the tomatoes, 2 1/2 cups water, green beans, and salt to taste. Cover and simmer for 15 to 20 minutes, until tender. Add the fava beans, salsa, olives, and peas, and season with salt and pepper to taste. Cook about 5 minutes to heat through. Taste and adjust seasonings before serving.

Serves 4

Kilocalories 514 Kc • Protein 14 gm • Fat 9 gm • Percent of calories from fat 16% •
Cholesterol 0 mg • Dietary fiber 11 gm • Sodium 221 mg • Calcium 94 mg

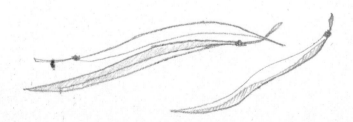

Tofu with Romesco Sauce

The traditional Spanish Romesco sauce uses a large amount of olive oil. I have pared it down considerably and it still tastes great. The Spanish use this sauce on broiled fish, chicken, or cooked vegetables, but I like to serve it over tofu, accompanied by a rice pilaf and a green vegetable.

2 tablespoons olive oil
1 small red chili, seeded and minced
1 red bell pepper, chopped
2 tablespoons chopped onion
1 tablespoon chopped garlic
1 14$^{1}/_{2}$-ounce can peeled tomatoes, drained and halved

2 tablespoons red wine vinegar
$^{1}/_{3}$ cup blanched almonds, toasted
1 pound extra-firm tofu, cut into $^{1}/_{4}$-inch slices
Salt

Heat 1 tablespoon of the oil in a large skillet over medium heat. Add the chili, bell pepper, onion, and garlic, and cook, covered, until soft, about 15 minutes. Stir in the tomatoes and vinegar and cook 15 minutes longer to achieve a thick sauce. Transfer the mixture to a food processor or blender and purée with the almonds, until the sauce is thick and creamy. Set aside.

Place the tofu slices on a baking sheet lined with paper towels to remove excess liquid. Season the tofu with salt to taste. Heat the remaining tablespoon oil in a large skillet, add the tofu, and sauté until golden, about 5 minutes on each side. While the tofu is cooking, gently reheat the sauce. Transfer the tofu to a serving platter and spoon the sauce over it to serve.

Serves 4

Kilocalories 262 Kc • Protein 19 gm • Fat 18 gm • Percent of calories from fat 59% • Cholesterol 0 mg • Dietary fiber 2 gm • Sodium 22 mg • Calcium 90 mg

Europe

Tapenade on French Bread Rounds

This piquant spread from Provence gets its depth of flavor from the blending of olives, capers, garlic, herbs, and spices. To turn up the heat, be generous with the freshly ground black pepper or add a dash of cayenne.

³/₄ cup pitted small black olives
¹/₄ cup capers, rinsed and drained
1 small garlic clove
2 tablespoons minced fresh parsley
¹/₈ teaspoon dried thyme
1 tablespoon red wine vinegar

1 tablespoon freshly squeezed lemon juice
¹/₄ cup extra-virgin olive oil
Salt and freshly ground pepper
1 12-inch baguette

Purée the olives, capers, garlic, parsley, and thyme in a food processor. Add the vinegar, lemon juice, olive oil, and salt and pepper to taste, and blend to a smooth paste. Cut the baguette into ³/₄-inch slices. Toast both sides until golden brown, spread one side with the paste, and serve. Cover the remaining tapenade with a thin layer of oil to store in the refrigerator.

Serves 6 to 8

Kilocalories 204 Kc • Protein 3 gm • Fat 15 gm • Percent of calories from fat 66% • Cholesterol 0 mg • Dietary fiber 2 gm • Sodium 635 mg • Calcium 3 mg

Portuguese Spicy Kale Soup

A healthful interpretation of a Portuguese classic that's traditionally made with sausage. This soup is even better made a day ahead and reheated.

1 tablespoon olive oil
1 large Spanish onion, chopped
1 large carrot, chopped
2 garlic cloves, minced
1 pound red potatoes, cut into
   1-inch cubes

1 teaspoon salt
1 bay leaf
1 pound kale, trimmed, leaves torn
   into 1-inch pieces
1/2 teaspoon hot red pepper flakes
3 cups cooked red kidney beans

Heat the oil over medium heat in a large saucepan. Add the onion and carrot and cook, covered, stirring frequently, until softened, 5 to 7 minutes. Add the garlic, potatoes, salt, bay leaf, and enough cold water to cover by 1 inch. Simmer for 30 minutes. Add the kale and hot red pepper flakes. Cook for 30 minutes longer. Add the kidney beans to the soup and simmer 5 minutes. Taste and adjust seasonings. Remove the bay leaf before serving.

Serves 8

Kilocalories 192 Kc • Protein 9 gm • Fat 2 gm • Percent of calories from fat 11% • Cholesterol 0 mg • Dietary fiber 7 gm • Sodium 314 mg • Calcium 73 mg

Basque Chickpea Stew

The Basques call their homeland Euskadi. Little is known of the origin of the people or their language—but, happily, some of their cooking traditions lean to the spicy side.

1 tablespoon safflower oil
1 large onion, chopped
1 28-ounce can peeled tomatoes,
 drained and chopped
1 tablespoon tomato paste
2 cups Vegetable Stock (see page xxi)
2 tablespoons minced fresh garlic

1 tablespoon minced fresh rosemary
 or 1 teaspoon dried, crumbled
1 serrano chili, seeded and minced
Salt
1 pound zucchini, cut into 1/2-inch
 pieces
2 1/2 cups cooked chickpeas

Heat the oil in a large saucepan over medium heat. Add the onion, cover, and cook until softened, stirring occasionally, about 5 minutes. Add the tomatoes, tomato paste, and stock. Add the garlic, rosemary, chili, and salt to taste, and bring to a boil. Reduce the heat to low and simmer, covered, for 30 minutes, stirring occasionally until slightly thickened. Add the zucchini and chickpeas and simmer 8 to 10 minutes or until zucchini is tender. Taste and adjust seasonings.
Serves 4

Kilocalories 293 Kc • Protein 15 gm • Fat 4 gm • Percent of calories from fat 12% • Cholesterol 0 mg • Dietary fiber 9 gm • Sodium 72 mg • Calcium 90 mg

Ratatouille

A touch of cayenne brings out the flavor of the fresh vegetables in this version of the classic vegetable stew from Provence. Ratatouille is best served the day after it is made.

2 tablespoons olive oil
1 large onion, diced
1 small eggplant, cut into 1/2-inch
    cubes
1 red bell pepper, cut into 1/2-inch
    pieces
4 garlic cloves, chopped
1 pound zucchini, halved lengthwise
    and cut into 1/2-inch slices

2 pounds plum tomatoes, peeled,
    seeded, and chopped
1 tablespoon chopped fresh parsley
2 tablespoons chopped fresh basil
1 teaspoon minced fresh thyme
1 teaspoon salt
1/8 teaspoon cayenne

Heat the oil in a large saucepan over medium heat. Add the onion, cover, and cook for 5 minutes, until softened. Add the eggplant, bell pepper, and garlic, cover, and cook 5 minutes longer, stirring occasionally. Add the zucchini, tomatoes, parsley, basil, thyme, salt, and cayenne, and cook for 10 minutes or until all the vegetables are tender. Taste and adjust seasonings.

Serves 8 to 10

Kilocalories 82 Kc • Protein 2 gm • Fat 4 gm • Percent of calories from fat 40% • Cholesterol 0 mg • Dietary fiber 3 gm • Sodium 305 mg • Calcium 27 mg

Basque Eggplant Salad

The mustard in this Basque recipe reflects a distinct French influence.

1 large eggplant
1/3 cup olive oil
1/4 cup red wine vinegar
1 tablespoon Dijon mustard
1 tablespoon chopped fresh parsley

1 teaspoon minced fresh garlic
1/2 teaspoon salt
1/4 teaspoon freshly ground pepper
Butter lettuce

Preheat the oven to 375°F. Cut the eggplant in half lengthwise and place, cut side down, on a lightly oiled baking pan. Bake for 30 minutes or until tender. Allow to cool slightly, then peel and dice into 1-inch cubes. In a small bowl, combine the oil, vinegar, mustard, parsley, garlic, salt, and pepper. Place the eggplant in a shallow bowl and combine with the marinade. Refrigerate 1 hour. Serve over butter lettuce.

Serves 4 to 6

Kilocalories 196 Kc • Protein 2 gm • Fat 18 gm • Percent of calories from fat 81% • Cholesterol 0 mg • Dietary fiber 3 gm • Sodium 316 mg • Calcium 17 mg

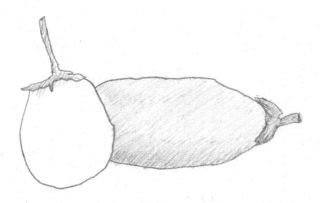

Basque Chicory Salad

An unusual salad of cooked greens given to me by my friend Marie Lange from her col-lection of Basque family recipes. The chicory, also called curly endive, can be replaced with other crisp bitter greens, such as escarole.

1 head chicory	1 teaspoon freshly squeezed lemon
3 tablespoons olive oil	juice
2 medium onions, sliced	6 whole black peppercorns
2 medium tomatoes, diced	3/4 teaspoon salt

Cut the end off the chicory and remove any damaged outer leaves. Wash the chicory well, then boil in salted water for 5 minutes. Drain well.

Heat the oil in a large saucepan over medium heat. Add the onions, chicory, toma-toes, lemon juice, peppercorns, and salt. Cover and simmer over low heat for about 30 minutes or until vegetables are tender. Transfer to a bowl to cool. Serve cold or at room temperature.

Serves 4 to 6

Kilocalories 210 Kc • Protein 7 gm • Fat 12 gm • Percent of calories from fat 44% • Cholesterol 0 mg • Dietary fiber 14 gm • Sodium 576 mg • Calcium 296 mg

Majorcan Baked Vegetables

This Majorcan dish, known as tumbet, *makes a substantial main course, and needs little more than a salad and some crusty bread for accompaniments.*

1 large eggplant, cut into ¼-inch
   slices
Salt
¼ cup olive oil
1 pound new potatoes, sliced
2 large green bell peppers, cut into
   ½-inch strips

4 garlic cloves
1½ pounds plum tomatoes,
   chopped
¼ teaspoon freshly ground pepper
⅛ teaspoon cayenne

Sprinkle the eggplant slices with salt and blot with paper towels to remove excess liquid.

Heat the oil in a large skillet over medium heat. Add the potato slices and cook for 5 minutes, turning frequently, until lightly browned. Remove with a slotted spoon and drain on paper towels. Add the peppers to the oil and cook for 2 minutes, until just softened. Remove with a slotted spoon and blot on paper towels. Rinse and drain the eggplant and cook in batches in the oil approximately 2 minutes or until golden on both sides. Remove and drain on paper towels.

Preheat the oven to 375°F. Coat a large baking dish with nonstick vegetable cooking spray and set aside. Add the garlic to the skillet, cook 1 minute, then add the tomatoes and cook, stirring, for 5 minutes to thicken. Season with salt, pepper, and cayenne. Arrange the cooked vegetables in the prepared baking dish in layers, seasoning each layer. Pour the tomato sauce over the top, cover, and bake for 30 minutes until vegetables are tender. Let stand 10 minutes before serving.

Serves 6

Kilocalories 209 Kc • Protein 4 gm • Fat 10 gm • Percent of calories from fat 39% • Cholesterol 0 mg • Dietary fiber 5 gm • Sodium 16 mg • Calcium 23 mg

Cauliflower with Mustard-Dill Sauce

The rich yellow-orange sauce flecked with dill is a lovely contrast to the creamy white cauliflower in this traditional Hungarian dish.

$^1/_2$ cup tofu sour cream or dairy sour
    cream
2 garlic cloves, minced
1 tablespoon Dijon mustard
1 tablespoon minced fresh dill or 1
    teaspoon dried dill
1 tablespoon freshly squeezed
    lemon juice

1 teaspoon olive oil
1 teaspoon dry mustard
$^1/_2$ teaspoon sugar
$^1/_2$ teaspoon Hungarian paprika
$^3/_4$ teaspoon salt
1 medium head cauliflower

Combine the tofu sour cream, garlic, Dijon mustard, dill, lemon juice, oil, dry mustard, sugar, paprika, and $^1/_2$ teaspoon of the salt in a food processor or blender and purée to form a smooth sauce.

Meanwhile, trim the cauliflower of its leaves and center core, leaving the head intact. Place the cauliflower head on a steamer rack in a saucepan. Add enough water to touch the cauliflower, sprinkle with the remaining $^1/_4$ teaspoon salt, cover, and steam for 10 to 12 minutes or until just tender. Remove the cauliflower to a serving bowl and top with the mustard sauce. Serve immediately.

Serves 6

Kilocalories 71 Kc • Protein 3 gm • Fat 5 gm • Percent of calories from fat 58% •
Cholesterol 0 mg • Dietary fiber 2 gm • Sodium 398 mg • Calcium 23 mg

Svikla

No collection of spicy recipes would be complete without this horseradish and red beet relish from Eastern Europe. I've adapted my sister's recipe, which she makes every year at Easter time—a family tradition passed down from her husband's Slovak ancestors.

3 pounds fresh red beets
1 root fresh horseradish (or 1 jar
   prepared white horseradish)
2 tablespoons sugar

$^{1}/_{4}$ cup white vinegar
$^{1}/_{4}$ cup water
Pinch salt

Cook the beets whole in a pot of boiling water until just tender, but not soft, about 30 minutes. Cut off the root ends and tops and slip off the skin. Grate the beets by hand or in a food processor. Grate the horseradish root and add to the grated beets (or add the prepared horseradish).

In a small saucepan, combine the sugar, vinegar, water, and salt, over medium heat stirring well to dissolve the salt and sugar. Add to the beet mixture and mix well. Transfer the beet relish to sterilized jars or other containers with tight-fitting lids. The relish will keep for several weeks in the refrigerator.

Serves 12

Kilocalories 67 Kc • Protein 2 gm • Fat .2 gm • Percent of calories from fat 2% •
Cholesterol 0 mg • Dietary fiber 4 gm • Sodium 83 mg • Calcium 32 mg

Farcia Intchauspe

This spicy stuffing is named for Marie Intchauspe, the Basque grandmother of my friend Lisa Lange. Traditionally made with chorizo sausage and used to stuff poultry, Lisa and Marie, her mom, both vegetarians, have adapted their favorite family recipe with tofu, and enjoy it as their main course for holiday meals. I've also made it using soy sausage instead of tofu. Either way, it's great baked in a pan by itself, or stuffed into a large winter squash for a spectacular centerpiece. Save time by using a food processor to chop the vegetables.

2 tablespoons olive oil
2 large Spanish onions, chopped
4 ribs celery, including leaves, chopped
2 green bell peppers, chopped
2 garlic cloves, chopped
1 pound firm tofu or soy sausage, crumbled
2 large Granny Smith apples, peeled and chopped
1 cup chopped fresh parsley
1 teaspoon salt

3/4 teaspoon freshly ground pepper
1/4 teaspoon ground cumin
1/2 teaspoon dried thyme
1 teaspoon sugar
1/4 teaspoon ground sage
1/4 teaspoon ground cloves
1/4 teaspoon ground nutmeg
1/4 teaspoon dried oregano
1/4 teaspoon cayenne
1/4 teaspoon ground turmeric
4 cups cubed white or wheat bread

Preheat the oven to 350°F. Lightly oil a 9×13-inch baking pan.

Heat the oil in a large saucepan over medium heat. Add the onions, celery, bell peppers, and garlic, cover, and cook until softened, about 10 minutes. Add the tofu sausage, apples, parsley, salt, pepper, cumin, thyme, sugar, sage, cloves, nutmeg, oregano, cayenne, and turmeric, and cook 10 minutes longer, until mixture is softened. Add the cubed bread and mix well to combine, adding a little water or stock if too dry. Taste and adjust seasonings. Transfer the mixture to the prepared baking pan. Cover and bake for 1 hour until firm and lightly browned.

Serves 12

Kilocalories 123 Kc • Protein 5 gm • Fat 4 gm • Percent of calories from fat 31% • Cholesterol 0 mg • Dietary fiber 3 gm • Sodium 265 mg • Calcium 97 mg

Tofu Piperade

Tofu replaces eggs in this classic Basque dish. Serve with plenty of warm crusty bread.

2 tablespoons olive oil
1/4 cup chopped tempeh bacon
1 large onion, diced
1 teaspoon minced fresh garlic
2 large ripe tomatoes, cored, seeded,
    and diced
1 green bell pepper, diced
1 red bell pepper, diced

1 small hot chili, seeded and minced
1/2 teaspoon salt
1/4 teaspoon sugar
1/4 teaspoon freshly ground pepper
1 pound firm tofu, liquid
    pressed out
1/8 teaspoon ground turmeric
1 tablespoon chopped fresh parsley

Heat 1 tablespoon of the olive oil in a large skillet over medium heat. Add the tempeh bacon and cook until browned, about 5 minutes. Remove with a slotted spoon and keep warm.

Heat the remaining tablespoon oil in the skillet, add the onion and garlic, and sauté until the onion is softened, about 5 minutes. Stir in the tomatoes, bell peppers, chili, salt, sugar, and pepper. Cook, covered, over low heat until the vegetables are soft and the mixture has thickened, about 20 minutes. Uncover, increase the heat, and continue to cook until the liquid evaporates, about 3 to 5 minutes.

Meanwhile, crumble the tofu in a bowl, pressing and blotting excess liquid. Stir in the turmeric to give the tofu a pale yellow color. Add the crumbled tofu to the skillet with the tomato mixture. Simmer over low heat, stirring, to heat through. Stop stirring and let the tofu set about 2 minutes. Spoon onto serving plates. Top with the warm tempeh bacon and sprinkle with the parsley.

Serves 4 to 6

Kilocalories 217 Kc • Protein 14 gm • Fat 12 gm • Percent of calories from fat 50% • Cholesterol 0 mg • Dietary fiber 3 gm • Sodium 344 mg • Calcium 214 mg

THREE

The Middle East and Africa

▼▼▼▼▼▼▼▼▼▼▼▼▼▼▼▼▼▼▼▼▼▼▼▼▼▼▼▼▼▼▼▼▼▼▼▼▼▼

The Middle East and Africa Recipe Mini-Index

Appetizers

Baba Ghanouj *102*   Egyptian Chickpea Patties *121*   Red Chili Hummus *101*

Soups and Stews

Ethiopian Wat *129*   Middle Eastern Chickpea Soup *103*
Moroccan Chickpea and Lentil Soup *126*
Moroccan Vegetable Tagine with Apricots *128*   Nigerian Peanut Soup *122*
North African Pumpkin Stew *124*   Senegalese Soup *125*
West African Yam and Groundnut Stew *123*

Salads

African Yam Salad *130*   Middle Eastern Rice Salad *106*
Moroccan Couscous Salad *131*   Syrian Beet Salad *104*
Turkish Spiced Orange and Onion Salad *105*

Sides

Chickpeas and Sweet Potatoes *107*   Egyptian Fava Beans *132*
Moroccan Spiced Carrots *133*   South African Green Beans *134*

Main Courses

Broiled Vegetables Tekka *112*   Cameroon-Style Seitan and Spinach *136*
Couscous with Spiced Vegetables *139*   Middle Eastern Bulgur-Stuffed Peppers *117*
Moroccan Rice with Apricots and Pine Nuts *135*
Persian Orange Rice with Pistachios *113*
Persian Pilaf with Almonds and Golden Raisins *115*
Rice with Lentils and Onions *110*   Seven Vegetable Couscous *140*
South African Bobotie *138*   Spicy Skewered Vegetable Kebabs *108*
Stuffed Tomatoes with Currants and Pine Nuts *111*
Tahini Vegetables with Pita Bread *116*   Tunisian Couscous *137*
Turkish Bulgur Pilaf *114*   Turkish Stuffed Eggplant *109*

Dressings, Sauces, and Condiments

Harissa Sauce *127*   Middle Eastern Garlic-Mint Sauce *118*
Orange Ginger Dressing *119*

▲▲▲▲▲▲▲▲▲▲▲▲▲▲▲▲▲▲▲▲▲▲▲▲▲▲▲▲▲▲▲▲▲▲▲▲▲▲

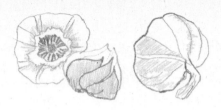

Pungent Safaris and Fragrant Caravans

The Middle East

The countries of the Middle East abound with spicy gastronomic pleasures. In Iran, Syria, Lebanon, and Turkey, chilies are used along with garlic, cumin, mint, fennel, saffron, and cinnamon. Traditional dishes are made with eggplant, tomatoes, artichokes, rice, couscous, and lentils, among other staples.

The warm climate of the Middle East supports a wide variety of fresh produce that includes figs, grapes, apricots, and pomegranates. Fruit is generally served with most meals, and dried fruits are a popular snack food.

Northern Africa

The northern African countries that frame the southern rim of the Mediterranean Sea, such as Morocco, Tunisia, Algeria, and Egypt, enjoy foods that are different from the rest of Africa. In fact, North Africa has two distinct cuisines, one in the East and one in the West. In western North African countries such as Morocco, the heady spice mixtures used to season food can be likened to Indian food with its wide use of cinnamon, ginger, turmeric, and coriander. There is also a tradition of using fruit in cooking and long, slow cooking methods. A prime example of these traditions is the *tagine*, which is the name of both a Moroccan stew and the clay pot it is cooked in.

In contrast, the foods of eastern North Africa more closely resemble the Middle East because of their use of cumin, garlic, mint, and parsley.

Africa

This book includes some of the delightful offerings of Ethiopia, Senegal, Sierra Leone, and other countries all the way down to South Africa, where both European and Indian influences are evident.

Grains, such as rice, bulgur, millet, barley, and couscous, are plentiful throughout the continent. Beans such as chickpeas, lentils, split peas, and fava beans are used throughout Africa and the Middle East in a variety of ways to make everything from breakfast to dessert.

Because grains, beans, vegetables, and fruits are such an important part of the diet in these regions, many of the dishes are natural choices for a vegetarian table. I have also adapted many of the native meat and seafood recipes with vegetarian alternatives.

The Middle East

Red Chili Hummus

The traditional chickpea and sesame dip enlivened with chilies.

2 cups cooked chickpeas
1/4 cup freshly squeezed lemon juice
2/3 cup tahini (sesame paste)
2 garlic cloves

1 hot red chili, seeded and chopped
1/4 teaspoon salt
1/8 teaspoon sweet paprika
1 tablespoon chopped fresh parsley

Place the chickpeas, lemon juice, tahini, garlic, chili, and salt in a food processor and purée until smooth. Taste to check the seasonings, adding more lemon juice or salt, if necessary. Transfer the hummus to a small bowl. When ready to serve, sprinkle with the paprika and chopped parsley.
Serves 6 to 8

Kilocalories 292 Kc • Protein 13 gm • Fat 18 gm • Percent of calories from fat 56% • Cholesterol 0 mg • Dietary fiber 4 gm • Sodium 102 mg • Calcium 84 mg

Baba Ghanouj

This Lebanese purée of grilled eggplant is a great party food, served with crackers or pita triangles. I've seen people who swear they hate eggplant come back for seconds of this luscious spread.

2 large eggplants	3/4 teaspoon salt
2 garlic cloves, crushed	1/2 teaspoon ground cumin
1/3 cup freshly squeezed lemon juice	1/4 cup chopped fresh parsley
2/3 cup tahini (sesame paste)	

Place the eggplants under a hot broiler for 20 minutes, turning them regularly until the skin is blistered all over. Place the eggplants in a closed paper bag or cover with a clean towel for 10 minutes. Peel off the charred skin. Squeeze the eggplants to remove the bitter juices. Transfer the eggplant pulp to a food processor or blender and purée with the garlic, lemon juice, tahini, salt, cumin, and parsley. Taste and adjust seasonings, adding more lemon juice or salt, if necessary. Serve at room temperature.

Serves 6 to 8

Kilocalories 231 Kc • Protein 9 gm • Fat 18 gm • Percent of calories from fat 67% • Cholesterol 0 mg • Dietary fiber 4 gm • Sodium 296 mg • Calcium 69 mg

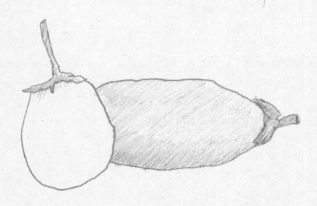

Middle Eastern Chickpea Soup

The combination of chickpeas, garlic, parsley, mint, and lemon juice is typically Middle Eastern, and makes this velvety soup uncommonly delicious.

1 tablespoon olive oil
1 large onion, chopped
2 large garlic cloves, chopped
1 bay leaf
1 teaspoon grated fresh lemon zest
1/2 teaspoon ground cumin
1/4 teaspoon ground coriander
1/8 teaspoon ground turmeric

3 cups Vegetable Stock (see page xxi)
2 cups cooked chickpeas
1/2 teaspoon salt
1/8 teaspoon cayenne
Approximately 2 tablespoons freshly squeezed lemon juice
2 tablespoons minced fresh parsley
2 tablespoons minced fresh mint

Heat the oil in a large saucepan over low heat. Add the onion, garlic, bay leaf, lemon zest, cumin, and coriander. Cover and cook, stirring occasionally, until the onion softens, about 5 minutes. Stir in the turmeric. Cover and cook, stirring occasionally, for 10 minutes. Add the stock and chickpeas. Cover partially and simmer 10 minutes. Cool. Discard the bay leaf. Purée the soup in a blender or food processor until smooth. Return the soup to the saucepan and season with the salt and cayenne. Add lemon juice to taste. Ladle the soup into bowls. Garnish with the parsley and mint.

Serves 4

Kilocalories 215 Kc • Protein 9 gm • Fat 4 gm • Percent of calories from fat 16% • Cholesterol 0 mg • Dietary fiber 5 gm • Sodium 362 mg • Calcium 64 mg

Syrian Beet Salad

I use small young beets in this recipe because they take less time to cook and are more fla-vorful than the larger ones.

1 pound raw young beets
3 scallions, white parts only, minced
1 garlic clove, minced
2 tablespoons chopped fresh parsley
1 tablespoon freshly squeezed lemon
  juice

1½ tablespoons freshly squeezed
  orange juice
3 tablespoons olive oil
Salt and freshly ground pepper

Place the beets in a saucepan, cover with water, and boil until tender, about 30 minutes. When cool enough to handle, peel and dice the beets. In a medium bowl, combine the beets, scallions, garlic, and parsley.

In a small bowl, combine the lemon juice, orange juice, and oil, and season with salt and pepper to taste. Pour the dressing over the beets while still warm, and allow to cool before serving.

Serves 4

Kilocalories 146 Kc • Protein 2 gm • Fat 10 gm • Percent of calories from fat 61% • Cholesterol 0 mg • Dietary fiber 4 gm • Sodium 84 mg • Calcium 26 mg

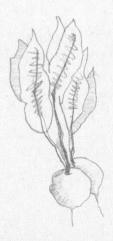

Turkish Spiced Orange and Onion Salad

Spiced orange salads are enjoyed in many parts of the world, including the Middle East. In this recipe the sweetness of the oranges balances perfectly with the pungency of the onion and the salty black olives, all of which are accentuated with a gentle jolt of cayenne.

Romaine lettuce leaves
3 seedless oranges, peeled
1 red onion, cut into thin rings
8 brine-cured black olives

3 tablespoons olive oil
2 tablespoons freshly squeezed
   lemon juice
1/8 teaspoon cayenne

Line a serving plate with the lettuce leaves. Cut the peeled oranges crosswise into 1/4-inch slices and arrange on the plate. Scatter the onion rings over the orange slices and scatter the olives on top. In a small bowl, whisk together the olive oil, lemon juice, and cayenne, and drizzle over the salad.
Serves 4

Kilocalories 180 Kc • Protein 1 gm • Fat 13 gm • Percent of calories from fat 61% • Cholesterol 0 mg • Dietary fiber 4 gm • Sodium 157 mg • Calcium 48 mg

Middle Eastern Rice Salad

This colorful mélange is a feast for all the senses.

3 cups cooked long-grain brown rice
1 medium-sized red onion, diced
1/2 cup chopped celery
4 scallions, minced
2 tablespoons slivered blanched
    almonds
2 tablespoons chopped fresh mint
2 tablespoons minced crystallized
    ginger
1 tablespoon sesame seeds
1 tablespoon minced fresh parsley

2 seedless oranges, separated into
    segments and cut into bite-sized
    pieces
1/2 teaspoon hot red pepper flakes
1/4 cup freshly squeezed orange juice
2 tablespoons freshly squeezed
    lemon juice
3 tablespoons olive oil
1/2 teaspoon salt
1/8 teaspoon freshly ground pepper
6 cups torn romaine lettuce

In a large bowl, mix together the rice, red onion, celery, scallions, almonds, mint, ginger, sesame seeds, parsley, orange segments, and hot red pepper flakes. Set aside. In a small bowl, combine the orange juice, lemon juice, oil, salt, and pepper, and whisk until well blended. Pour the dressing over the rice mixture and toss gently to combine. Line plates with the lettuce and spoon the rice mixture on top.

Serves 4 to 6

Kilocalories 370 Kc • Protein 8 gm • Fat 15 gm • Percent of calories from fat 34% •
Cholesterol 0 mg • Dietary fiber 8 gm • Sodium 329 mg • Calcium 124 mg

Chickpeas and Sweet Potatoes

This vibrantly colored dish is delicious and easy to prepare. I often serve it with couscous or rice and a dark green vegetable for a well-balanced and satisfying meal.

2 small sweet potatoes, peeled and
   cubed
1 tablespoon safflower oil
1/2 teaspoon ground turmeric
1/4 teaspoon ground cumin
1/8 teaspoon ground cinnamon

1/8 teaspoon cayenne
1 medium onion, diced
2 cups cooked chickpeas
2 medium tomatoes, diced
1/4 teaspoon salt

Steam the sweet potatoes for 20 minutes until just tender.

In a large skillet, heat the oil over medium heat. Add the turmeric, cumin, cinnamon, cayenne, and onion, cover, and cook for 5 minutes, stirring occasionally, until onions are softened. Add 1/2 cup water, the sweet potatoes, chickpeas, tomatoes, and salt. Bring to a boil, then reduce the heat and simmer for 10 minutes until mixture thickens to a stewlike consistency.

Serves 6

Kilocalories 173 Kc • Protein 6 gm • Fat 3 gm • Percent of calories from fat 14% •
Cholesterol 0 mg • Dietary fiber 5 gm • Sodium 112 mg • Calcium 48 mg

Spicy Skewered Vegetable Kebabs

Grill these garlic-and-lime-infused kebabs outside for a delicious taste sensation. I accompany them with grilled bread that I have brushed with some of the marinade. Remember to soak the wooden skewers in water for 30 minutes before using to prevent burning.

3 garlic cloves, crushed
1/4 cup safflower oil
1/4 cup freshly squeezed lime juice
1/2 teaspoon ground cumin
1/2 teaspoon ground coriander
1/2 teaspoon salt
1/4 teaspoon cayenne
2 medium onions, quartered
2 bell peppers, cut into 1 1/2-inch
    pieces

2 medium zucchini, cut into
    1 1/2-inch chunks
2 cups whole mushrooms, trimmed
1 pint cherry tomatoes
Hot cooked basmati rice
Approximately 8 wooden skewers,
    soaked in water for 30 minutes

Combine the garlic, oil, lime juice, cumin, coriander, salt, and cayenne in a large bowl and whisk until well blended. Set aside.

Steam the onions over boiling water for 1 minute. Add the bell peppers and zucchini to the steamer and continue steaming 1 minute longer. Add the mushrooms to the steamer and continue steaming 1 minute longer. Transfer all of the lightly steamed vegetables to the bowl with the marinade and toss until coated. Let stand, covered, at room temperature for 30 minutes, tossing occasionally.

Preheat the broiler. Coat the broiler pan with oil and place 4 inches from the heat source. Remove the vegetables from the marinade and thread them onto the skewers, ending with a cherry tomato on each skewer. Brush with the marinade and broil 5 minutes, turning once or twice until browned. Serve over hot cooked rice.

Serves 4

Kilocalories 239 Kc • Protein 4 gm • Fat 17 gm • Percent of calories from fat 60% • Cholesterol 0 mg • Dietary fiber 5 gm • Sodium 309 mg • Calcium 51 mg

Turkish Stuffed Eggplant

This dish is called Imam Bayildi *in Arabic, or "the imam fainted," supposedly because the* imam, *the term for a Muslim religious leader, found it so delicious. If you can't find small eggplants, use 3 large ones and cut them in quarters. In the traditional dish, the eggplant is simmered in a generous amount of olive oil for several hours. This calorie-conscious version is significantly pared down but still delicious.*

6 small eggplants	2 garlic cloves, chopped
3 tablespoons olive oil	1 teaspoon tomato paste
1 large onion, chopped	1/2 teaspoon ground allspice
1 green bell pepper, chopped	1/2 teaspoon salt
1 28-ounce can plum tomatoes, drained and chopped	1/8 teaspoon cayenne
1/4 cup currants	2 tablespoons sliced almonds
	2 tablespoons minced fresh parsley

Preheat the oven to 350°F. Cut the eggplants in half lengthwise and bake for 10 minutes. Do not turn off the oven. Let the eggplants cool, then press out the juices.

Heat 2 tablespoons of the oil in a medium skillet over medium heat. Add the onion and bell pepper and sauté until softened, about 5 minutes. Add half of the tomatoes, the currants, garlic, tomato paste, allspice, salt, and cayenne. Cook for 5 minutes.

Cut a long slit to form a pocket in each eggplant half and stuff with the onion mixture. Sprinkle the remaining tomatoes on top of the stuffed eggplants. Scatter the almonds on top and sprinkle with the remaining tablespoon oil. Bake for 30 minutes or until the eggplants are tender. Allow to cool before serving. Serve garnished with the minced parsley.

Serves 6

Kilocalories 169 Kc • Protein 3 gm • Fat 9 gm • Percent of calories from fat 44% • Cholesterol 0 mg • Dietary fiber 6 gm • Sodium 215 mg • Calcium 73 mg

Rice with Lentils and Onions

This Lebanese dish is about as basic as it gets. Good simple food, delicious and economical. What could be better?

2 large onions
1¼ cups dried lentils
3 tablespoons olive oil
1 teaspoon ground cumin
1 teaspoon ground coriander

½ teaspoon sweet paprika
Salt and freshly ground pepper
1 cup long-grain white or
    brown rice

Finely mince 1 of the onions and set aside. Cut the remaining onion in half lengthwise, then slice each half crosswise very thinly, and set aside.

Bring a saucepan of water to a boil. Add the lentils and cook for 10 minutes. Heat 1 tablespoon of the oil in a large skillet over medium heat. Add the minced onion and cook, stirring frequently, until lightly browned, about 10 minutes. Drain the lentils and combine in the saucepan with the cooked onion. Add the cumin, coriander, paprika, and salt and pepper to taste. Add the rice and 3 cups cold water, bring to a boil, and cook, uncovered, for about 30 minutes, until the lentils and rice are cooked through. Reduce the heat to low, cover, and leave for 10 minutes.

Meanwhile, heat the remaining 2 tablespoons oil in a skillet over medium-high heat. Add the sliced onion and cook for 15 to 20 minutes, stirring frequently, until brown and caramelized. Put the rice and lentil mixture in a large bowl, sprinkle with the crispy fried onion, and serve.

Serves 4 to 6

Kilocalories 498 Kc • Protein 21 gm • Fat 11 gm • Percent of calories from fat 20% • Cholesterol 0 mg • Dietary fiber 21 gm • Sodium 12 mg • Calcium 70 mg

Stuffed Tomatoes with Currants and Pine Nuts

Although this recipe calls for tomatoes, you can use this typical Middle Eastern filling to stuff eggplant, squash, or grape leaves as well. This dish is known as yalanchi *in the Middle East.*

6 large, firm, ripe tomatoes
Salt
2 tablespoons olive oil
1 medium onion, chopped
1/2 cup currants or raisins, soaked in warm water for 10 minutes and drained
1/4 cup pine nuts
2 tablespoons minced fresh parsley
1/4 teaspoon ground allspice

1/4 teaspoon freshly ground pepper
1/4 teaspoon sweet paprika
1/8 teaspoon ground cinnamon
1/8 teaspoon cayenne
1 tablespoon freshly squeezed lemon juice
2 1/2 cups cooked white or brown rice
1/4 cup dry white wine

Preheat the oven to 350°F. Coat a baking pan with nonstick vegetable cooking spray. Slice off the tomato tops and scoop out the pulp. Lightly sprinkle the insides of the tomatoes with salt and invert onto paper towels to drain.

Heat 1 tablespoon of the oil in a large skillet over medium heat. Add the onion and cook, covered, over medium heat for 5 minutes or until softened. Add the currants, pine nuts, parsley, allspice, pepper, paprika, cinnamon, and cayenne, stirring to combine. Transfer the mixture to a large bowl, add the lemon juice and rice, and mix well.

Stuff the mixture into the tomatoes and place the tomatoes in the prepared baking pan. Drizzle with the remaining 1 tablespoon oil and the white wine. Bake for 30 minutes or until the tomatoes are tender and the stuffing is lightly browned.

Serves 6

Kilocalories 260 Kc • Protein 5 gm • Fat 11 gm • Percent of calories from fat 37% • Cholesterol 0 mg • Dietary fiber 5 gm • Sodium 15 mg • Calcium 35 mg

Broiled Vegetables Tekka

This vegetarian version of a Pakistani skewered chicken dish is made with "meaty" porto-bello mushrooms. It can also be prepared on the grill. Remember to soak the wooden skewers for 30 minutes to prevent burning.

1/2 cup soft silken tofu or low-fat yogurt

2 tablespoons olive oil

1 tablespoon ground coriander

1 1/2 tablespoons freshly squeezed lemon juice

2 teaspoons finely grated fresh ginger

1 teaspoon minced fresh garlic

1 teaspoon ground cinnamon

3/4 teaspoon salt

1/4 teaspoon cayenne

1/4 teaspoon ground cardamom

1 pound small portobello mushroom caps (see note)

1 large onion, quartered and separated

1 green bell pepper, cut into 2-inch pieces

Approximately 12 wooden skewers, soaked in water for 30 minutes

In a large bowl, combine the tofu, oil, coriander, lemon juice, ginger, garlic, cinnamon, salt, cayenne, and cardamom, and mix until well blended. Add the mushrooms, onion, and bell pepper pieces and toss to coat well. Cover the mixture and refrigerate for 1 hour.

Preheat the broiler. Thread the mushrooms, onion, and bell pepper pieces onto the wooden skewers. Broil until softened, about 5 to 7 minutes, brushing frequently with the remaining marinade and turning once. Serve immediately.

Serves 6

NOTE: Try to find mushrooms that are approximately 2 inches in diameter. If only the larger portobello mushrooms are available, they may be quartered.

Kilocalories 87 Kc • Protein 4 gm • Fat 5 gm • Percent of calories from fat 54% • Cholesterol 0 mg • Dietary fiber 4 gm • Sodium 301 mg • Calcium 55 mg

Persian Orange Rice with Pistachios

At once fruity and spicy, redolent of oranges, garlic, ginger, and cinnamon, this aromatic rice dish from Iran is a sublime blending of colors and flavors, and makes a lovely addition to a buffet table.

2 large seedless oranges	1 teaspoon sugar
2 garlic cloves, minced	1 tablespoon safflower oil
1 tablespoon grated fresh ginger	1/2 cup Vegetable Stock (see page xxi)
1/2 teaspoon hot red pepper flakes	
1/2 teaspoon ground turmeric	4 cups cooked brown rice
1/2 teaspoon ground cinnamon	1/3 cup chopped pistachios
1/4 cup frozen orange juice concentrate	1/2 cup minced fresh parsley
	Salt and freshly ground pepper

Grate the oranges to remove the zest (the colored part of the peel). Blanch the orange zest by plunging in boiling water and set aside. Peel and chop the oranges.

Combine the oranges, garlic, ginger, hot red pepper flakes, turmeric, cinnamon, orange juice, and sugar in a blender and purée. Heat the oil in a large skillet over low heat. Add the orange zest and gently sauté for 1 minute. Add the contents of the blender and the stock and simmer, stirring occasionally, for 5 minutes. Add the rice and stir gently to fluff. Add the pistachios and parsley and fluff again. Season to taste with salt and pepper. Transfer to a serving dish and serve hot.

Serves 4 to 6

Kilocalories 403 Kc • Protein 9 gm • Fat 10 gm • Percent of calories from fat 22% •
Cholesterol 0 mg • Dietary fiber 6 gm • Sodium 107 mg • Calcium 64 mg

Turkish Bulgur Pilaf

Made from wheat kernels, bulgur is said to have originated thousands of years ago in Syria, though it is eaten throughout the Middle East. It has a hearty, nutty flavor and, like couscous, takes only a few minutes to prepare.

³/4 cup medium bulgur (cracked wheat)
2 tablespoons safflower oil
2 medium carrots, cut into ¹/4-inch dice
1 medium onion, chopped

1 teaspoon salt
¹/8 teaspoon cayenne
1¹/2 cups Vegetable Stock (see page xxi)
1 tablespoon chopped fresh mint

Place the bulgur in a large bowl and cover with cold water. Drain the bulgur and set aside.

Heat the oil in a medium saucepan over medium heat. Add the carrots and onion, cover, and cook, stirring occasionally, until softened, about 5 minutes. Add the bulgur, salt, and cayenne, and stir until the bulgur is well coated with oil, about 1 minute. Add the stock and heat to boiling. Reduce the heat to low, cover, and simmer until the bulgur is tender and the liquid has been absorbed, about 10 minutes. Remove the bulgur to a warmed serving bowl, fluff with a fork, and sprinkle with the mint.

Serves 4

Kilocalories 170 Kc • Protein 4 gm • Fat 7 gm • Percent of calories from fat 37% • Cholesterol 0 mg • Dietary fiber 5 gm • Sodium 616 mg • Calcium 23 mg

Persian Pilaf with Almonds and Golden Raisins

I like to team up this pilaf with Broiled Vegetables Tekka (page 112) for a fabulous Middle Eastern treat.

2 tablespoons olive oil
1 medium onion, minced
2 tablespoons slivered almonds
1 cup basmati rice

2 tablespoons golden raisins
1 teaspoon sweet paprika
Salt and freshly ground pepper
1 tablespoon minced fresh parsley

Heat 1 tablespoon of the oil in a large skillet over low heat. Add the onion, cover, and cook gently for 5 to 7 minutes, or until soft. Raise the heat to medium-high and add the almonds. Cook for 5 minutes, stirring constantly, until the nuts are lightly browned. Remove from skillet and set aside. Heat the remaining tablespoon oil in the skillet and add the rice, raisins, and paprika. Cook gently for 3 minutes, stirring continuously to coat the rice in the oil. Bring 2½ cups water to a boil, pour over the rice, season with salt and pepper, stir once, and cover. Simmer gently for 15 minutes, or until the water is absorbed. Take the rice off the heat and stir in the nut mixture. Cover again and allow to stand for 15 minutes. Fluff the rice with a fork, sprinkle with the parsley, and serve.

Serves 4

Kilocalories 291 Kc • Protein 5 gm • Fat 11 gm • Percent of calories from fat 32% • Cholesterol 0 mg • Dietary fiber 3 gm • Sodium 5 mg • Calcium 43 mg

Tahini Vegetables with Pita Bread

This makes a tasty lunch or a nourishing supper when paired with Middle Eastern Chickpea Soup (page 103).

1/4 cup minced fresh parsley
2 tablespoons minced fresh cilantro
1 teaspoon chopped fresh garlic
3 tablespoons tahini (sesame seed paste)
2 tablespoons freshly squeezed lemon juice
2 tablespoons safflower oil
2 tablespoons water

1/2 teaspoon salt
1/4 teaspoon cayenne
1/2 large cucumber, halved lengthwise and seeded
1 large ripe tomato, chopped
1 small onion, minced
4 pita bread loaves
1/2 head lettuce, shredded

Preheat the oven to 350°F. In a food processor, combine the parsley, cilantro, garlic, tahini, lemon juice, oil, water, salt, and cayenne, and blend until well combined. Transfer to a mixing bowl and set aside. Cut the cucumber into thin slices and add to the mixing bowl. Add the chopped tomato and minced onion and toss to combine well. Taste and adjust seasonings.

Wrap the pita together in foil and heat in the oven for 15 minutes. Halve each loaf to form 2 pockets and gently open the pockets. Spoon about 2 tablespoons shredded lettuce and 3 tablespoons vegetable mixture into each pocket. Serve immediately.

Serves 4

Kilocalories 350 Kc • Protein 12 gm • Fat 16 gm • Percent of calories from fat 39% • Cholesterol 0 mg • Dietary fiber 7 gm • Sodium 643 mg • Calcium 76 mg

Middle Eastern Bulgur-Stuffed Peppers

6 large green bell peppers
2 tablespoons olive oil
1 large onion, chopped
1/2 cup chopped celery
2 garlic cloves, minced
2 small fresh hot chilies, seeded and
   minced
1/4 cup minced fresh parsley
1 tablespoon minced fresh dill or 1
   teaspoon dried dill

1/2 teaspoon ground cumin
2 tablespoons freshly squeezed
   lemon juice
1/4 cup pine nuts
1/4 cup currants
1 teaspoon sugar
1/2 teaspoon salt
1/8 teaspoon freshly ground pepper
2 cups cooked medium bulgur
   (cracked wheat)

Preheat the oven to 350°F. Cut tops off the bell peppers and remove the seeds. Blanch the peppers in a pot of boiling water for 5 minutes or until softened. Remove the peppers from the water and set aside to cool.

Heat the oil in a large skillet over medium heat. Add the onion, celery, garlic, and chilies, and cook 5 minutes or until softened. Add the parsley, dill, cumin, lemon juice, pine nuts, currants, sugar, salt, pepper, and bulgur, and mix well. Gently stuff the mixture into the peppers and arrange in a baking dish. Add 1/2 cup water to the bottom of the baking dish. Cover and bake for 30 minutes or until the peppers are tender.

Serves 6

Kilocalories 191 Kc • Protein 5 gm • Fat 8 gm • Percent of calories from fat 37% • Cholesterol 0 mg • Dietary fiber 6 gm • Sodium 213 mg • Calcium 36 mg

Middle Eastern Garlic-Mint Sauce

For a great fusion dish, toss this Middle Eastern "pesto" with cooked pasta. I often use this versatile sauce as a dipping sauce for steamed green beans or fried tofu cubes. I also like to toss it with rice, couscous, or potatoes for a refreshing change of pace.

2 cups fresh bread crumbs
5 medium garlic cloves
1/2 teaspoon salt
3/4 cup ground walnuts

1/4 cup chopped fresh mint
1/2 cup olive oil
1/2 cup white wine vinegar

Place the bread crumbs in a bowl with 1 cup cold water and let stand until absorbed, about 3 minutes. Squeeze any excess liquid from the crumbs. In a food processor, combine the garlic and salt and process to a paste. Add the walnuts and mint and process finely. Add the bread crumbs and blend until a paste forms. With the machine running, slowly add the oil and vinegar through feed tube and blend until smooth. Add enough warm water to form a thick sauce.

Serves 8 (makes about 3 1/2 cups)

Kilocalories 213 Kc • Protein 4 gm • Fat 20 gm • Percent of calories from fat 83% • Cholesterol 0 mg • Dietary fiber 1 gm • Sodium 181 mg • Calcium 26 mg

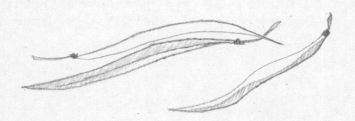

Orange Ginger Dressing

An exotic and creamy dressing perfect for a green salad served with Middle Eastern or Indian food.

¹/₃ cup frozen orange juice
    concentrate
¹/₂ cup soft silken tofu or low-fat
    yogurt
1 tablespoon freshly squeezed lemon
    juice

1 teaspoon finely grated fresh ginger
¹/₄ teaspoon ground cumin
¹/₈ teaspoon cayenne
¹/₈ teaspoon ground coriander
¹/₈ teaspoon ground cinnamon
¹/₈ teaspoon ground turmeric

In a blender, purée the orange juice concentrate, tofu, lemon juice, ginger, cumin, cayenne, coriander, cinnamon, and turmeric until creamy. Transfer to a small bowl and refrigerate until ready to use.

Serves 4 to 6 (makes about 1 cup)

Kilocalories 52 Kc • Protein 2 gm • Fat .9 gm • Percent of calories from fat 16% • Cholesterol 0 mg • Dietary fiber 1 gm • Sodium 3 mg • Calcium 18 mg

Africa

Egyptian Chickpea Patties

Chickpea patties, or falafel, are popular throughout the Middle East and are eaten as an appetizer, a snack, in pita bread sandwiches, and even as a main course.

2 tablespoons medium bulgur
  (cracked wheat)
2 tablespoons freshly squeezed
  lemon juice
2 cups cooked chickpeas, drained
1/2 teaspoon salt

1/4 teaspoon freshly ground pepper
1/8 teaspoon cayenne
1/8 teaspoon ground cumin
1/4 cup minced fresh parsley
1 tablespoon olive oil
Safflower oil, for frying

Combine the bulgur and lemon juice in a small bowl and let stand for 15 minutes. In a food processor, combine the chickpeas, salt, pepper, cayenne, cumin, parsley, bulgur mixture, and olive oil, blending thoroughly. Taste and adjust seasonings. Form the mixture into patties, using about 2 tablespoons of the mixture for each one.

Heat the safflower oil in a large skillet over medium-high heat using enough oil to cover the bottom of the pan. When hot, add 3 to 4 patties at a time and cook about 2 minutes on each side, until lightly browned. Drain the cooked patties on paper towels. Repeat until all of the patties are browned.

Serves 8

Kilocalories 66Kc • Protein 2 gm • Fat 3.5 gm • Percent of calories from fat 45% • Cholesterol 0 mg • Dietary fiber 2 gm • Sodium 213 mg • Calcium 13 mg

Nigerian Peanut Soup

Peanuts and okra are common cooking ingredients throughout Africa and are the main ingredients in this spicy soup.

4 cups Vegetable Stock (see page xxi)
1 large onion, chopped
1 cup cooked white or brown rice
1 small fresh hot chili, seeded and chopped
1 red bell pepper, seeded and chopped

1 cup roasted salted peanuts
1 cup fresh okra, cut into ¼-inch rings
Salt and freshly ground pepper

In a large saucepan over high heat, bring 3 cups of the stock and the onion to a boil, then reduce the heat to low and simmer until the onion is tender, about 15 minutes. Add the rice, chili, and bell pepper, and bring to a boil. Reduce the heat to a simmer and cook for 10 minutes.

Meanwhile, in a blender, purée the remaining 1 cup of stock and ¾ cup of the peanuts. Stir the purée into the soup in the saucepan and continue cooking for 10 minutes longer. Chop the remaining peanuts and set aside.

Boil the okra until tender, about 5 minutes. Drain thoroughly. Add the okra to the soup, stir, and remove from the heat. Season to taste with salt and pepper. To serve, ladle the soup into bowls and sprinkle with the reserved chopped peanuts.

Serves 6

Kilocalories 392 Kc • Protein 17 gm • Fat 23 gm • Percent of calories from fat 52% • Cholesterol 2 mg • Dietary fiber 6 gm • Sodium 240 mg • Calcium 67 mg

West African Yam and Groundnut Stew

The yam is a staple food of Africa and is often confused with the sweet potato in North America. Though the yam is less sweet than the sweet potato, they are generally interchangeable in recipes. Peanuts are called groundnuts in Africa.

1 tablespoon olive oil
1 medium onion, chopped
3 garlic cloves, minced
1 medium green or red bell pepper, seeded and chopped
2 pounds yams, peeled and cut into 1/2-inch chunks
3 small fresh mild chilies, seeded and chopped

2 large tomatoes, chopped
4 cups Vegetable Stock (see page xxi)
1 tablespoon brown sugar
3/4 teaspoon ground cinnamon
1 teaspoon chili powder
1 teaspoon salt
1/4 teaspoon freshly ground pepper
1/4 teaspoon hot red pepper flakes
1 cup chopped roasted peanuts

Heat the olive oil in a large saucepan over medium heat. Add the onion, garlic, bell pepper, yams, and chilies, cover and cook, stirring occasionally, until the vegetables begin to soften, about 5 minutes. Add the tomatoes, stock, brown sugar, cinnamon, chili powder, salt, pepper, and hot red pepper flakes, and bring to a boil. Reduce the heat, cover, and simmer until the vegetables are tender, about 20 minutes. Taste and adjust seasonings. Garnish with the chopped peanuts and serve.
Serves 8

Kilocalories 314 Kc • Protein 7 gm • Fat 13 gm • Percent of calories from fat 35% • Cholesterol 0 mg • Dietary fiber 7 gm • Sodium 494 mg • Calcium 40 mg

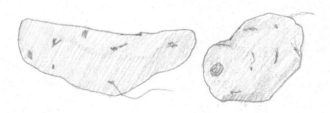

North African Pumpkin Stew

1 tablespoon safflower oil
1 large onion, cut into 1/2-inch dice
4 garlic cloves, finely minced
1 or 2 small, fresh hot chilies,
    seeded and chopped
1 teaspoon grated fresh ginger
1/2 teaspoon ground cinnamon
1/4 teaspoon ground cumin

1/4 teaspoon ground allspice
1/8 teaspoon ground cloves
2 pounds cooking pumpkin, seeded,
    peeled, and cut into bite-sized
    cubes (about 5 cups)
3 tablespoons dark brown sugar
Salt and freshly ground pepper
2 cups cooked kidney beans

Heat the oil in a large saucepan over medium heat. Add the onion, cover, and cook until tender but not browned, about 5 minutes. Add the garlic, chilies, ginger, cinnamon, cumin, allspice, and cloves, and cook, stirring, for about 2 minutes. Add the pumpkin and toss until evenly coated with the spices. Add 1 cup water, the brown sugar, and salt and pepper to taste. Bring to a boil, then reduce the heat to low. Cover and simmer until the vegetables are tender, about 30 minutes. Add the beans, and cook until heated through, about 10 minutes.

Serves 6

Kilocalories 214 Kc • Protein 8 gm • Fat 5 gm • Percent of calories from fat 21% •
Cholesterol 0 mg • Dietary fiber 7 gm • Sodium 13 mg • Calcium 84 mg

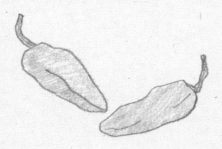

Senegalese Soup

1 tablespoon safflower oil
1 medium onion, chopped
2 ribs celery, chopped
1½ teaspoons curry powder
1 Granny Smith apple, peeled,
    cored, and chopped
1 cup apple cider

1½ cups silken tofu or low-fat
    yogurt
1 cup soy milk
½ teaspoon cayenne
½ teaspoon salt
2 tablespoons minced fresh parsley

Heat the oil in a medium saucepan over medium-low heat. Add the onion and celery, cover, and cook, stirring occasionally, until softened, about 5 minutes. Stir in the curry powder and apple and cook 2 minutes. Add the cider and simmer about 5 minutes. Remove from the heat. Spoon the onion mixture and the tofu into a blender or food processor and purée until smooth. Transfer the mixture to a large bowl and gradually whisk in the soy milk. Add the cayenne and salt and refrigerate for 2 hours or until cold. Serve chilled, garnished with the minced parsley.

Serves 6

Kilocalories 113 Kc • Protein 4 gm • Fat 5 gm • Percent of calories from fat 34% • Cholesterol 0 mg • Dietary fiber 2 gm • Sodium 228 mg • Calcium 49 mg

Moroccan Chickpea and Lentil Soup

Called harira *in Arabic, this thick spicy bean and vegetable soup is eaten in Morocco to break the fast of Ramadan. While there are many versions of this soup, chickpeas and lentils are usually included in all of them.*

2 tablespoons olive oil
1 medium onion, chopped
1/2 cup chopped celery
3 cloves garlic, chopped
1 16-ounce can plum tomatoes, drained and chopped
1/2 cup dried lentils
1/2 teaspoon ground turmeric
1/2 teaspoon ground cinnamon
1/4 teaspoon ground ginger
1/4 teaspoon ground cumin
3/4 teaspoon salt

1/4 teaspoon freshly ground pepper
1/4 teaspoon ground cardamom
6 cups Vegetable Stock (see page xxi)
1 teaspoon tomato paste
2 cups cooked chickpeas
2 tablespoons freshly squeezed lemon juice
2 teaspoons Harissa Sauce (see page 127) or commercial garlic-chili paste
2 tablespoons chopped fresh parsley or cilantro

Heat the oil in a large saucepan over medium heat. Add the onion, celery, and garlic, cover, and cook for 5 minutes or until softened. Add the tomatoes, lentils, turmeric, cinnamon, ginger, cumin, salt, pepper, and cardamom, and cook 5 minutes longer to bring out the flavor of the spices. Add the stock and tomato paste, cover, and cook for 45 minutes or until the lentils are tender. Add the cooked chickpeas and lemon juice and cook, uncovered, for 10 minutes to blend flavors. Stir the harissa into the hot soup and cook a minute longer. Sprinkle with the chopped parsley or cilantro and serve.

Serves 8

Kilocalories 262 Kc • Protein 11 gm • Fat 5 gm • Percent of calories from fat 18% • Cholesterol 0 mg • Dietary fiber 10 gm • Sodium 414 mg • Calcium 79 mg

Harissa Sauce

Use this classic—and fiery—North African condiment to season soups, stews, and grilled vegetables and tofu. If you prefer more flavor than heat, use ancho or other mild chilies instead of hot chilies.

1 teaspoon caraway seeds	4 garlic cloves
8 dried hot red chilies	1 teaspoon ground coriander
1 tablespoon olive oil	1/2 teaspoon salt

Grind caraway seeds in a spice mill. Stem and seed the chilies and break them into pieces. Soak the pieces in warm water for 5 minutes. Drain. Combine the chilies, oil, garlic, coriander, caraway, and salt in a food processor and purée to a paste. Blend in 3 tablespoons water to make a sauce.

Serves 8

Kilocalories 9 Kc • Protein 0 gm • Fat .7 gm • Percent of calories from fat 65% • Cholesterol 0 mg • Dietary fiber 0 gm • Sodium 51 mg • Calcium 3 mg

Moroccan Vegetable Tagine with Apricots

A tagine is a delicately spiced Moroccan stew, named after the earthenware pot in which it is cooked. It is traditionally made with meat, fruit, and fragrant spices. I use chickpeas instead of meat; seitan or tempeh are more meatlike options. Bread is the traditional accompaniment, but fresh cooked rice or couscous also complement it nicely.

1 tablespoon olive oil	1/4 teaspoon cayenne
1 large onion, chopped	2 tablespoons minced fresh cilantro
1 large carrot, chopped	2 tablespoons minced fresh parsley
1 teaspoon minced fresh garlic	4 cups Vegetable Stock (see page xxi)
1 teaspoon ground ginger	1 cup dried apricots, chopped
1/2 teaspoon ground cinnamon	2 1/2 cups cooked chickpeas
1/2 teaspoon ground turmeric	Salt and freshly ground pepper
1/2 teaspoon salt	

Heat the oil in a large saucepan over medium heat. Add the onion and carrot, cover, and cook for 5 minutes until softened. Add the garlic, ginger, cinnamon, turmeric, salt, cayenne, cilantro, parsley, and stock. Reduce the heat to low and simmer for 30 minutes until liquid reduces slightly.

While the onion mixture is cooking, soak the apricots for 30 minutes in hot water, then drain. Add the apricots to the onion mixture in the saucepan and cook for 10 minutes longer to blend flavors. Add the chickpeas, season with salt and pepper, and cook 10 minutes longer or until stew thickens. Taste and adjust seasonings before serving.

Serves 4 to 6

Kilocalories 339 Kc • Protein 12 gm • Fat 4 gm • Percent of calories from fat 10% •
Cholesterol 0 mg • Dietary fiber 10 gm • Sodium 393 mg • Calcium 89 mg

Ethiopian Wat

What's wat? *It's Ethiopian stew and is traditionally made with chicken. It's also very hot and spicy, so take care in adding the seasonings—you may want to cut back a little on the cayenne.*

2 tablespoons olive oil
2 cups finely chopped shallots
1 pound tempeh, cut into 1-inch
    slices
3/4 teaspoon or less cayenne,
    according to taste
1 tablespoon tomato paste
1/2 teaspoon salt

1/2 teaspoon ground cumin
1/2 teaspoon ground cinnamon
1/4 teaspoon ground cardamom
1/8 teaspoon ground nutmeg
1/8 teaspoon ground turmeric
Freshly cooked white rice
1/4 cup ground roasted peanuts

Heat 1 tablespoon of the oil in a large saucepan over medium heat. Add the shallots and cook until golden, about 5 minutes. Remove the shallots from the pan with a slotted spoon and set aside. In the same pan, heat the remaining tablespoon oil over medium-high heat. Add the tempeh pieces and cook 5 to 10 minutes, turning, until lightly browned on all sides. Remove from the heat. Add the reserved shallots, cayenne, tomato paste, salt, cumin, cinnamon, cardamom, nutmeg, and turmeric, and mix well. Add 2 cups water and heat the mixture to boiling. Lower the heat, cover, and simmer for 30 minutes or until the flavor has developed. Serve hot over rice, sprinkled with ground peanuts.

Serves 6

Kilocalories 235 Kc • Protein 16 gm • Fat 14 gm • Percent of calories from fat 48% • Cholesterol 0 mg • Dietary fiber 6 gm • Sodium 252 mg • Calcium 83 mg

African Yam Salad

Yams are indigenous to Africa. The soft-fleshed orange sweet potatoes found in American supermarkets are often referred to as yams, to differentiate them from the firm-fleshed yellow variety of sweet potatoes.

4 large yams or sweet potatoes
1 small onion, minced
1 cup frozen peas, thawed
1/4 cup safflower oil

3 tablespoons freshly squeezed
   lemon juice
1/8 teaspoon salt
1/8 teaspoon cayenne

Place the unpeeled yams in a saucepan and cover with water. Bring to a boil and cook until tender but firm enough to slice, about 25 minutes. Cool the yams, then peel and cut into 1/4-inch-thick slices. Combine the yams, onion, peas, oil, lemon juice, salt, and cayenne in a bowl and mix gently to combine. Chill at least 1 hour before serving.

Serves 8

Kilocalories 171 Kc • Protein 3 gm • Fat 7 gm • Percent of calories from fat 36% • Cholesterol 0 mg • Dietary fiber 4 gm • Sodium 63 mg • Calcium 32 mg

Moroccan Couscous Salad

2 cups quick-cooking couscous
1/2 cup dried currants
1 1/3 cups boiling Vegetable Stock
  (see page xxi)
2 tablespoons olive oil
1/4 cup pine nuts
1 large red bell pepper, cut into
  1/8-inch dice

2 medium zucchini, chopped
4 scallions, minced
2 large shallots, minced
1 teaspoon salt
3 tablespoons freshly squeezed
  lemon juice
3/4 teaspoon ground cumin

Place the couscous and currants in medium bowl, pour the boiling stock over them, stir with fork, and let stand 5 minutes.

Heat the oil in a large skillet over medium heat. Add the pine nuts and cook until golden, about 2 minutes. Remove the pine nuts using a slotted spoon and set aside. Add the bell pepper and cook 1 minute. Add the zucchini, scallions, shallots, and salt to the skillet. Increase the heat to medium-high and cook, stirring frequently, until the vegetables begin to soften, about 2 minutes. Add the couscous mixture, lemon juice, and cumin, and cook until heated through, about 1 minute. Remove from the heat. Mix in the pine nuts. Taste and adjust seasonings. Serve hot or chilled.

Serves 6

Kilocalories 416 Kc • Protein 13 gm • Fat 8 gm • Percent of calories from fat 18% • Cholesterol 0 mg • Dietary fiber 6 gm • Sodium 417 mg • Calcium 56 mg

Egyptian Fava Beans

This traditional Egyptian breakfast of stewed fava beans, called Ful Medames, *also makes a great high-protein lunch or dinner item. Enjoy it whenever the mood strikes!*

1 tablespoon olive oil	1/2 teaspoon salt
2 garlic cloves, chopped	1 large ripe tomato, chopped
1 teaspoon ground cumin	1 medium-sized red onion, chopped
1/8 teaspoon cayenne	3 tablespoons chopped fresh parsley
2 cups cooked fava beans	

Heat the oil in a saucepan over medium heat. Add the garlic, cumin, and cayenne, and cook, stirring, for 1 minute. Add the fava beans, salt, and enough water to simmer, about 1/2 cup. Cover and cook about 10 minutes to heat through and blend flavors. Add more water if necessary. Transfer the beans to a serving bowl and sprinkle with the chopped tomato, red onion, and parsley.

Serves 4

Kilocalories 152 Kc • Protein 7 gm • Fat 4 gm • Percent of calories from fat 23% • Cholesterol 0 mg • Dietary fiber 6 gm • Sodium 318 mg • Calcium 53 mg

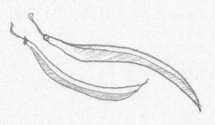

Moroccan Spiced Carrots

1 pound large carrots, cut in 1/4-inch
   julienne
Salt
1 tablespoon olive oil
1 teaspoon minced fresh garlic
1/4 teaspoon cayenne

1/4 teaspoon ground cumin
1/4 teaspoon ground cinnamon
2 tablespoons freshly squeezed
   lemon juice
2 tablespoons minced fresh parsley
1/2 teaspoon coriander seeds

Place the carrots in a saucepan, cover with water, add a pinch of salt, and bring to a boil. Cook until the carrots are just tender, about 5 minutes. While the carrots are cooking, heat the oil in a small skillet over medium heat. Add the garlic, cayenne, cumin, cinnamon, lemon juice, and salt to taste, and stir until fragrant, about 2 minutes. Drain the carrots, place in a serving bowl, and pour the sauce over them. Garnish with the parsley and coriander seeds and serve.

Serves 6

Kilocalories 56 Kc • Protein 1 gm • Fat 3 gm • Percent of calories from fat 37% •
Cholesterol 0 mg • Dietary fiber 3 gm • Sodium 28 mg • Calcium 27 mg

South African Green Beans

Seasoning green beans with curry powder is a reflection of the East Indian influence on South African cooking. This dish is also delicious without the curry, if preferred that way.

1 pound fresh green beans, trimmed	1 small hot chili, seeded and minced
1 tablespoon safflower oil	2 thin slices fresh ginger
1 large onion, chopped	1/8 teaspoon curry powder (optional)
1 garlic clove, peeled and mashed	

Steam the green beans over boiling water until just tender. Run under cold water to stop the cooking process and retain color. Set aside.

Heat the oil in a large skillet over medium heat. Add the onion and cook, stirring occasionally, until browned, about 10 minutes. Add the garlic, chili, ginger, and curry powder, if using. Mix well, then add the green beans. Continue to cook over low heat, stirring occasionally, just until the beans are heated through, about 5 minutes.

Serves 6 to 8

Kilocalories 55 Kc • Protein 1 gm • Fat 2 gm • Percent of calories from fat 40% • Cholesterol 0 mg • Dietary fiber 2 gm • Sodium 10 mg • Calcium 25 mg

Moroccan Rice with Apricots and Pine Nuts

1 tablespoon safflower oil
1/2 cup pine nuts
1/2 cup dried apricots, chopped
4 cups cooked white or brown rice

1/2 teaspoon salt
1/8 teaspoon cayenne
1/8 teaspoon ground cardamom

Heat the oil in a large skillet over medium heat. Add the pine nuts and cook, stirring, for 1 minute or until lightly browned. Add the apricots and cook for a minute longer or until warm. Add the rice, salt, cayenne, and cardamom. Toss to combine and serve.

Serves 4

Kilocalories 400 Kc • Protein 10 gm • Fat 15 gm • Percent of calories from fat 33% •
Cholesterol 0 mg • Dietary fiber 6 gm • Sodium 295 mg • Calcium 32 mg

Cameroon-Style Seitan and Spinach

This dish is traditionally made with beef and served with plantains or yams. I usually serve it over rice or couscous.

1 pound fresh spinach, washed and
   stemmed
2 tablespoons safflower oil
1 pound seitan, cut into
   1-inch cubes
1 medium onion, sliced
1/2 cup tomato sauce (commercial or
   homemade)

1 1/2 cups Vegetable Stock (see
   page xxi)
1 tablespoon smooth peanut butter
1 teaspoon low-sodium tamari
Approximately 1/8 teaspoon cayenne

Steam the spinach over boiling water for 3 minutes. Remove from the heat and allow to cool. Chop the spinach and set aside.

Heat 1 tablespoon of the oil in a large saucepan over medium heat. Add the seitan and brown on all sides, about 3 minutes. Remove the browned seitan with a slotted spoon and set aside. Cook the onion in the remaining hot oil until lightly brown, about 5 minutes, then reduce the heat and add the tomato sauce, stock, peanut butter, tamari, and cayenne to taste. Cook, stirring occasionally, until the mixture comes to a boil, then lower the heat, add the spinach, cover, and simmer for 10 minutes or until the vegetables are tender. Add the seitan and cook 5 minutes longer. Taste and adjust seasonings before serving.

Serves 6 to 8

Kilocalories 193 Kc • Protein 24 gm • Fat 6 gm • Percent of calories from fat 28% •
Cholesterol 0 mg • Dietary fiber 4 gm • Sodium 292 mg • Calcium 84 mg

Tunisian Couscous

The classic Tunisian version of couscous is made with fish, but this vegetarian adaptation is equally delicious. To be truly authentic, this dish would be prepared in a couscousière, but a saucepan works just fine.

3 large carrots, cut into ¹/₂-inch
    slices
3 small onions, cut into 1-inch dice
3 small turnips, peeled and
    quartered
4 large plum tomatoes, quartered

1 tablespoon low-sodium tamari
¹/₄ teaspoon ground turmeric
¹/₄ teaspoon cayenne
Salt and freshly ground pepper
2 cups cooked chickpeas
2¹/₂ cups quick-cooking couscous

Bring 6 cups water to a boil in a large saucepan. Add the carrots, onions, turnips, tomatoes, tamari, turmeric, cayenne, and salt and pepper to taste. Simmer, uncovered, for 45 minutes, until the vegetables are very tender. Add the chickpeas and keep warm. Cook the couscous according to the package directions. Pile the hot couscous onto a large serving dish and top with the vegetable mixture.
Serves 6

Kilocalories 524 Kc • Protein 19 gm • Fat .6 gm • Percent of calories from fat 1% •
Cholesterol 0 mg • Dietary fiber 13 gm • Sodium 176 mg • Calcium 110 mg

South African Bobotie

The classic bobotie is a curried beef with custard dish that is a favorite of my South African friends, Marianne and Matteus Swart. I've attempted many vegan versions of this dish, and we all agree that this one is the best.

1 tablespoon safflower oil
1 large onion, sliced
1 teaspoon salt
1 teaspoon sugar
1 tablespoon curry powder
1 tablespoon cider vinegar
1 thick slice white bread
1 cup soy milk

1/2 cup soft silken tofu
1 pound tempeh or other ground
    meat alternative, crumbled
1/4 teaspoon ground turmeric
1/8 teaspoon cayenne
2 tablespoons apricot preserves
Mango chutney

Preheat the oven to 350°F. Coat a shallow baking dish with nonstick vegetable cooking spray.

Heat the oil in a small skillet over medium heat. Add the onion, cover, and cook for 5 minutes. Remove the cover and cook, stirring, 2 minutes longer, until the onion is golden. In a medium bowl, combine the onion, salt, sugar, curry powder, and vinegar.

In a small bowl, soak the bread in the soy milk for 3 minutes, then squeeze the bread dry, reserving the milk. Add the bread, half the tofu, and the tempeh to the onion mixture and combine well. Pat the mixture into the prepared baking dish.

In a blender or food processor, purée the remaining tofu with the reserved soy milk, the turmeric, cayenne, and apricot preserves, and pour over the mixture in the baking dish. Place the bobotie in the oven in a larger pan with hot water halfway up side of bobotie pan and bake for 40 to 50 minutes or until the purée is set. Serve hot, with chutney on the side.

Serves 4

Kilocalories 359 Kc • Protein 25 gm • Fat 14 gm • Percent of calories from fat 33% •
Cholesterol 0 mg • Dietary fiber 10 gm • Sodium 651 mg • Calcium 158 mg

Couscous with Spiced Vegetables

2 tablespoons olive oil
1 medium onion, chopped
3 garlic cloves, chopped
1 teaspoon ground cumin
1/2 teaspoon ground cinnamon
1/2 teaspoon ground turmeric
1/2 teaspoon ground cloves
1/2 teaspoon ground coriander
1/2 teaspoon ground ginger
1/4 teaspoon cayenne
3 tomatoes, chopped
6 cups Vegetable Stock (see page xxi)

1 small sweet potato, cut into 1-inch
    chunks
2 small carrots, cut into 1/2-inch
    slices
2 small new potatoes, quartered
1/2 pound fresh green beans, cut into
    2-inch lengths
1 cup cooked chickpeas
2 cups quick-cooking couscous
1/2 cup raisins
Harissa Sauce (see page 127)

Heat the oil in a large skillet over medium heat. Add the onion, garlic, cumin, cinnamon, turmeric, cloves, coriander, ginger, and cayenne. Cover and cook for 5 minutes or until the onion softens. Add the tomatoes, stock, sweet potatoes, carrots, potatoes, and green beans, and simmer 30 minutes or until the vegetables are tender. Add the chickpeas and simmer another 10 minutes, until all of the vegetables are tender but not mushy. Remove from the heat.

In a medium saucepan heat 2 cups of the broth from the vegetables to boiling. Add the couscous and the raisins, cover, and let stand 10 minutes. Fluff up the couscous with a fork, then mound it in the center of a platter and surround with the cooked vegetables. Pass the broth from the vegetables and a bowl of Harissa Sauce separately.

Serves 6

Kilocalories 550 Kc • Protein 16 gm • Fat 5 gm • Percent of calories from fat 9% •
Cholesterol 0 mg • Dietary fiber 11 gm • Sodium 116 mg • Calcium 96 mg

Seven Vegetable Couscous

It is a Moroccan tradition to serve couscous with seven vegetables, though the vegetables can be varied according to taste. Serve accompanied by a small bowl of Harissa Sauce.

1 large onion, finely minced
2 large carrots, cut into 1-inch chunks
1 pound butternut squash, cut into 1-inch chunks
1 cup raisins
1 pound plum tomatoes, peeled and chopped
1 garlic clove, chopped
1 teaspoon salt
1 teaspoon ground cinnamon

1/2 teaspoon ground turmeric
1/2 teaspoon freshly ground pepper
1 pound small zucchini, halved lengthwise and cut into 1/2-inch pieces
1/2 cup frozen peas, thawed
2 cups cooked chickpeas
1/4 cup minced fresh parsley
2 1/2 cups quick-cooking couscous
Harissa Sauce (see page 127)

Bring 2 quarts water to a boil in a large saucepan. Add the onion, carrots, squash, raisins, tomatoes, garlic, salt, cinnamon, turmeric, and pepper. Bring to a boil, then reduce the heat, cover, and simmer for 45 minutes or until the vegetables are tender. Add the zucchini, peas, chickpeas, and parsley, and cook 5 minutes longer or until the zucchini is tender.

Meanwhile, cook the couscous according to the package directions. Mound the hot couscous onto a serving dish and, using a slotted spoon, surround with the vegetables. Taste the broth and adjust the seasonings, adding more salt if necessary. Serve the broth and the Harissa Sauce on the side.

Serves 8

Kilocalories 637 Kc • Protein 22 gm • Fat 1 gm • Percent of calories from fat 1% • Cholesterol 0 mg • Dietary fiber 17 gm • Sodium 493 mg • Calcium 167 mg

FOUR

India

India Recipe Mini-Index

Appetizers
Vegetable Pakoras *147*   Vegetable Samosas *148*

Soups and Stews
Kashmiri Vegetable Soup *149*   Mint-Flecked Curried Potato Soup *150*
Spicy Eggplant and Potato Stew *151*

Salads
Curried Rice Salad *152*   Many Bean Salad *154*   Spiced Potato Salad *153*

Sides
Braised Cabbage with Cardamom *162*   Cucumber Raita *158*
Curried Mushrooms *155*   Indian Spiced Carrots *161*   Kidney Bean Dal *157*
Spicy Indian Green Beans *159*   Spinach Saag *160*   Stir-Fried Broccoli Rabe *156*

Main Courses
Broiled East Indian Tofu *164*   Cashew Pilau with Raisins and Peas *172*
Curried No-Meat Balls *163*   Curried Vegetable Pilaf *170*
Lentils in Onion Gravy *166*   Tandoori-Style Tempeh *167*
Tofu Curry with Green Beans *165*   Tofu with Spiced Plum Sauce *168*
Vegetable Biryani *171*   Vegetable Masala *169*

Dressings, Sauces, and Condiments
Garam Masala *176*   Green Tomato and Pear Chutney *173*   Mint Chutney *174*
Pineapple-Date Chutney *175*

Fiery Bliss in India

The vast subcontinent of India is home to some of the spiciest and most flavorful dishes in the world. This is due, mainly, to the wide use of curry seasoning, which is actually a blend of many spices. In India curry mixtures are either made at home or ordered from a shop, and they can vary greatly, based on the combination of spices used. Curried dishes are always spicy but are only hot if chilies are used. Curries that contain no chilies at all derive their complex flavors from several of the more than one hundred spices used in Indian cooking, such as cumin, cardamom, cinnamon, ginger, turmeric, and cloves. The prepared curry powder we find in Western grocery stores is actually unknown in India, and was developed out of the Western desire for convenience.

In India many households make their own favorite *masalas*—or mixes of spices—and different *masalas* may be used for different dishes. I've included a recipe for a basic one in this book. However, if you don't want to mix your own spices, you will undoubtedly find high-quality blends at Indian and other specialty markets. When recipes call for curry powder, feel free to use a commercial blend or one you have mixed yourself. Curry spice mixtures are also available in the form of paste. Experiment until you find the spice mixtures you like best.

Rice and wheat are staples in India, as are lentils, kidney beans, chickpeas, split peas, and other beans that are used in the wide variety of meatless dishes enjoyed by the large vegetarian population in India. Generally, the hotter and spicier dishes of India are found in the southern regions, while the food in the northern areas tends to be milder and sweeter. While wheat predominates in the north, fragrant basmati rice is the grain of choice in the southern regions.

Indian cuisine includes a variety of delicious breads such as *naan*, *chapati*, and *papadam*. Mercifully, these breads help to absorb the fire of some of the searingly hot dishes. Indian meals often include creamy yogurt mixtures called *raitas* to help mellow the heat, plus a variety of chutneys and other condiments, some of which are hot and some of which are mild. Indian dinners usually end with sweet pudding or fresh fruit.

India

Vegetable Pakoras

Pakoras, or fritters, are a popular appetizer in India. Vary the vegetables according to your preference.

$1/2$ cup all-purpose flour
Salt
$1/4$ teaspoon cayenne
$1/8$ teaspoon dried mint
$1^1/2$ cups cooked peeled
    potatoes, diced

$1/2$ cup cooked cauliflower, chopped
$1/4$ cup cooked peas
3 tablespoons safflower oil
Mango chutney

In a large bowl combine the flour, salt to taste, cayenne, mint, and enough water to make a thick batter. Add the potatoes, cauliflower, and peas, and mix well. Shape the batter into 3-inch round fritters and set aside. Heat the oil in a large skillet over medium-high heat, add the fritters in batches, and fry until golden, about 2 minutes. Keep the cooked fritters warm in the oven until all of them are ready. Serve hot with mango chutney.
Serves 4

Kilocalories 233 Kc • Protein 5 gm • Fat 11 gm • Percent of calories from fat 40% • Cholesterol 0 mg • Dietary fiber 4 gm • Sodium 8 mg • Calcium 19 mg

Vegetable Samosas

A classic Indian appetizer, these vegetable-filled packets can also be made with packaged puff pastry dough. Although samosas are traditionally deep-fried, I use oil sparingly and finish them in the oven.

2 cups all-purpose flour
4 tablespoons margarine
1/2 teaspoon salt
2 medium white potatoes, peeled
    and diced
3 tablespoons safflower oil
1/4 cup chopped scallion
1/2 teaspoon chopped fresh
    green chili

1/2 teaspoon ground cumin
1/8 teaspoon cayenne
Salt
1/4 cup frozen peas, thawed
Chutney (pages 173–175 or
    commercial brand)

Combine the flour, margarine, and salt in a large bowl. Add enough water to make a stiff dough. Knead until smooth and elastic.

Cook the potatoes in boiling water until tender, about 15 minutes. Drain. Heat 1 tablespoon of the oil in a small skillet over medium heat. Add the scallion, green chili, cumin, cayenne, and salt to taste. Add the potatoes and peas and sauté until soft, about 5 minutes. Divide the dough into 2 pieces. Roll each piece into an 8-inch square and cut in half crosswise. Divide the potato mixture among each piece of dough, moisten the edges with water, folding one corner of dough over the filling to make a triangular packet. Seal tightly by crimping the edges with a fork. Preheat the oven to 375°F. Heat the remaining 2 tablespoons oil in a large skillet and fry the samosas until golden, about 3 minutes. Place on a lightly oiled baking sheet and bake for 10 minutes or until heated through and browned. Serve hot with your favorite chutney.

Serves 4

Kilocalories 403 Kc • Protein 8 gm • Fat 17 gm • Percent of calories from fat 37% • Cholesterol 0 mg • Dietary fiber 3 gm • Sodium 63 mg • Calcium 47 mg

Kashmiri Vegetable Soup

The people of Kashmir season their food with spices grown in the Indian lowlands, including green and black cardamom pods, cinnamon, fennel, cloves, cumin, coriander, hot chilies, and turmeric. They love strong seasonings, and often do their cooking in a kerai, *the Indian version of the wok.*

3 small white turnips, peeled and quartered
3 small boiling potatoes, peeled and quartered
2 medium onions, quartered
2 small carrots, sliced diagonally into chunks
1 cup 1-inch fresh cauliflower florets

1 teaspoon minced fresh ginger
1 teaspoon salt
1/4 teaspoon freshly ground pepper
1/2 cup chopped tomato
1 tablespoon safflower oil
1 teaspoon ground cardamom
1/2 teaspoon ground cumin

In a large saucepan, combine the turnips, potatoes, onions, carrots, cauliflower, ginger, salt, and pepper. Add 5 cups water and bring to a boil. Reduce the heat, cover, and simmer until the vegetables are tender, about 30 minutes. Add the tomato, and cook 10 minutes.

Heat the oil in a small skillet over medium-high heat. Stir in the cardamom and cumin, blending well. Turn off the heat and let the spice mixture sit for 2 minutes, then add to the soup and serve.

Serves 6

Kilocalories 90 Kc • Protein 2 gm • Fat 3 gm • Percent of calories from fat 25% • Cholesterol 0 mg • Dietary fiber 4 gm • Sodium 433 mg • Calcium 40 mg

Mint-Flecked Curried Potato Soup

The natural sweetness of mint brings out the spiciness of the curry powder in this delicate creamy soup. The sweet potatoes give the soup a lovely orange blush.

1 tablespoon safflower oil
1/2 cup chopped onion
1 teaspoon minced fresh garlic
3/4 teaspoon curry powder
1/8 teaspoon cayenne
1 pound white potatoes, peeled and
    chopped

3/4 pound sweet potatoes, peeled and
    chopped
1 teaspoon salt
1 cup soy milk
1 tablespoon finely minced fresh
    mint or 1/4 teaspoon dried

Heat the oil in a large pot over medium heat. Add the onion, garlic, curry powder, and cayenne, and stir 1 minute. Add 4 cups water, the white potatoes, sweet potatoes, and salt, and bring to a boil. Reduce the heat, cover, and simmer until the vegetables are tender, about 30 minutes.

In a food processor or blender, purée the soup in batches. Return to the pot, add the soy milk, and simmer over low heat until hot. Taste and adjust seasonings, adding more salt if necessary. Ladle into bowls, sprinkle with the mint, and serve.

Serves 6

Kilocalories 165 Kc • Protein 3 gm • Fat 3 gm • Percent of calories from fat 15% •
Cholesterol 0 mg • Dietary fiber 3 gm • Sodium 418 mg • Calcium 45 mg

Spicy Eggplant and Potato Stew

Add some cooked chickpeas for additional flavor, texture, and protein.

2 tablespoons olive oil
1 large onion, chopped
1 teaspoon minced garlic
3 cups peeled and diced white
    potatoes (about 1 pound)
4 cups diced eggplant (1 medium)
1 jalapeño, seeded and minced
1/4 teaspoon paprika
1 28-ounce can tomatoes, drained
    and chopped

1 tablespoon low-sodium tamari
1/2 teaspoon minced fresh thyme or
    1/8 teaspoon dried
1/2 teaspoon minced fresh oregano
    or 1/8 teaspoon dried
1/2 teaspoon ground fennel seeds
1/4 teaspoon ground cumin
1/4 teaspoon cayenne
Salt and freshly ground pepper

Heat the oil in a large saucepan over medium heat. Add the onion, garlic, potatoes, eggplant, and jalapeño. Sprinkle the vegetables with the paprika, cover, and cook for about 5 minutes or until the vegetables begin to soften. Reduce the heat to low. Add the tomatoes, tamari, thyme, oregano, fennel, cumin, cayenne, and 2 cups water. Season with salt and pepper to taste. Cover and cook until the vegetables are tender, about 30 minutes, adding more water if necessary.

Serves 6

Kilocalories 157 Kc • Protein 4 gm • Fat 5 gm • Percent of calories from fat 28% •
Cholesterol 0 mg • Dietary fiber 5 gm • Sodium 110 mg • Calcium 43 mg

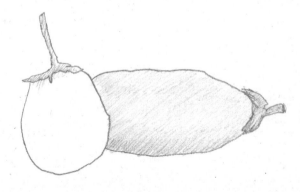

Curried Rice Salad

This colorful salad is a favorite of mine for casual buffets or potlucks, as its flavor improves when allowed to stand at room temperature.

1/4 cup safflower oil
1/2 cup mango chutney
1/4 cup freshly squeezed orange juice
2 tablespoons freshly squeezed
    lemon juice
1 tablespoon curry powder, or to
    taste
3/4 teaspoon salt
1/4 teaspoon cayenne

2 large carrots, thinly sliced on
    diagonal
1/4 cup chopped red bell pepper
1 scallion, minced
1 cup frozen peas, thawed and
    drained
4 cups cooked brown rice
2 tablespoons minced fresh parsley

In a food processor or medium bowl, blend the oil, chutney, orange juice, lemon juice, curry powder, salt, and cayenne until smooth. Set aside. Steam the carrots over a medium pot of boiling water until just tender, about 2 minutes. Drain, rinse under cold water, and pat dry. Transfer the carrots to a large bowl. Add the bell pepper, scallion, peas, rice, and parsley. Pour on the reserved dressing and toss gently to combine well. Taste and adjust seasonings. Let the salad stand at room temperature for 15 minutes before serving.

Serves 8

Kilocalories 240 Kc • Protein 4 gm • Fat 8 gm • Percent of calories from fat 29% • Cholesterol 0 mg • Dietary fiber 4 gm • Sodium 248 mg • Calcium 28 mg

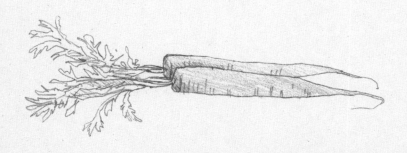

Spiced Potato Salad

This Indian variation on potato salad raises ordinary picnic food to exotic new heights.

2 pounds small red-skinned
   potatoes, quartered (skins
   left on)
3 tablespoons safflower oil
1 medium onion, chopped
3 garlic cloves
1 or 2 small fresh hot red chilies, cut
   into thin rings
$1/2$ teaspoon ground cumin

$1/2$ teaspoon ground anise seeds
1 cup soft silken tofu or low-fat
   yogurt
$1/4$ cup orange juice
$1/4$ cup minced fresh parsley
2 scallions, minced
1 tablespoon minced fresh cilantro
1 tablespoon minced fresh mint
$1/2$ teaspoon salt

Place the potatoes in a saucepan with enough water to cover and boil until just tender, about 15 to 20 minutes. Drain. Heat the oil in a large skillet over medium-high heat. Add the onion, garlic, chilies, cumin, and anise, and stir-fry until the onion is translucent but not browned, about 3 minutes. Add the potatoes and stir-fry until evenly coated with the spice mixture and lightly browned, about 5 minutes. Transfer to a serving bowl and set aside.

In a food processor, combine the tofu, orange juice, parsley, scallions, cilantro, mint, and salt. Pour the dressing over the potatoes and toss gently to combine. Chill for at least 1 hour before serving. Taste and adjust seasonings, if necessary.

Serves 4 to 6

Kilocalories 397 Kc • Protein 9 gm • Fat 12 gm • Percent of calories from fat 27% • Cholesterol 0 mg • Dietary fiber 7 gm • Sodium 319 mg • Calcium 73 mg

Many Bean Salad

Don't be put off by the long list of ingredients. This attractive and delicious salad can be put together in minutes if you use canned beans, or make the beans ahead and freeze them. This salad makes a perfect addition to an international buffet table or an Indian feast. If you don't have one of the beans, double up on another, but strive for variety, as that is an important part of the colorful presentation. This salad looks especially nice in a large shallow bowl lined with curly endive or other salad greens.

1/4 cup safflower oil

2 tablespoons cider vinegar

1/2 teaspoon sugar

3 garlic cloves, finely minced

1/2 teaspoon minced fresh ginger

1/4 teaspoon hot red pepper flakes

1/4 teaspoon dry mustard

1/8 teaspoon ground cumin

1/8 teaspoon anise seeds

2 cups cooked pinto beans

2 cups cooked chickpeas

1 cup cooked Great Northern beans

1 cup cooked black beans

1 cup cooked adzuki beans

1 cup frozen peas, thawed

4 scallions, minced

1/2 cup minced fresh parsley

1 tablespoon minced fresh cilantro

1 small fresh hot chili, minced

Salt and freshly ground pepper

In a small bowl, combine the oil, vinegar, sugar, garlic, ginger, hot red pepper flakes, dry mustard, cumin, and anise seeds, and set aside. In a large bowl, combine the pinto beans, chickpeas, Great Northern beans, black beans, adzuki beans, and peas. Add the scallions, parsley, cilantro, and hot chili, and toss gently to combine. Pour the dressing over the salad and season to taste with salt and pepper. Allow the salad to marinate in the refrigerator for at least 1 hour before serving.

Serves 8

Kilocalories 301 Kc • Protein 14 gm • Fat 8 gm • Percent of calories from fat 22% • Cholesterol 0 mg • Dietary fiber 12 gm • Sodium 27 mg • Calcium 87 mg

Curried Mushrooms

Sometimes I make this dish with zucchini instead of mushrooms.

2 cups low-fat coconut milk
1 teaspoon chopped fresh ginger
3 garlic cloves, chopped
2 or 3 small dried hot chilies, seeded and chopped
1 teaspoon ground coriander
1 teaspoon ground cumin
1 teaspoon ground turmeric

2 tablespoons safflower oil
1 large onion, thinly sliced
1 14$\frac{1}{2}$-ounce can peeled tomatoes, drained and chopped
1 pound mushrooms, quartered
Salt
Freshly cooked basmati rice

Combine the coconut milk, ginger, garlic, chilies, coriander, cumin, turmeric, and 1 cup water in a blender and purée until smooth. In a large skillet, heat the oil over medium heat. Add the onion and cook, stirring, until golden brown, about 8 minutes. Add the puréed mixture to the onions and cook, stirring occasionally, until thickened, about 20 minutes. Add the tomatoes, mushrooms, 1 cup water and salt to taste, and cook, stirring, for 3 to 5 minutes or until the mushrooms are tender. Serve over rice.

Serves 4

Kilocalories 207 Kc • Protein 5 gm • Fat 14 gm • Percent of calories from fat 55% • Cholesterol 0 mg • Dietary fiber 4 gm • Sodium 46 mg • Calcium 30 mg

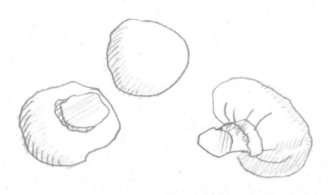

Stir-Fried Broccoli Rabe

Broccoli rabe is also known as rapini and can be found in most supermarkets. If unavailable, broccoli, spinach, or any dark green vegetable can be substituted.

2 tablespoons safflower oil	1 teaspoon salt
2 garlic cloves, minced	1/4 teaspoon hot red pepper flakes
1 pound broccoli rabe, thinly sliced	1/4 teaspoon ground turmeric

Heat the oil in a large skillet over medium-low heat. Add the garlic and stir 1 minute until fragrant. Add the broccoli rabe and stir 2 minutes until it begins to soften. Add the salt, hot red pepper flakes, turmeric, and 1 cup water. Cover and cook until the broccoli rabe is tender, about 15 minutes. Uncover and cook until almost all the liquid has evaporated.

Serves 4 to 6

Kilocalories 112 Kc • Protein 3 gm • Fat 7 gm • Percent of calories from fat 56% • Cholesterol 0 mg • Dietary fiber 1 gm • Sodium 605 mg • Calcium 208 mg

Kidney Bean Dal

One of the most basic Indian dishes, dal can be a meal in itself or a companion to a curried dish. Dals can be made with a variety of different legumes, such as lentils or peas.

2 tablespoons safflower oil
1 teaspoon garam masala (see page 176)
1 medium onion, chopped
2 garlic cloves, finely minced
1 tablespoon finely grated fresh ginger

1 cup chopped tomatoes
1/4 teaspoon cayenne
1/2 teaspoon ground coriander
1/8 teaspoon ground turmeric
Salt
2 cups cooked red kidney beans
2 tablespoons chopped fresh cilantro

Heat the oil in a small skillet over medium heat. Add the garam masala and onion and sauté until golden, about 5 minutes. Add the garlic, ginger, tomatoes, cayenne, coriander, turmeric, and salt to taste, and mix well. Place the beans in a serving dish. Stir in the onion mixture and sprinkle with the chopped cilantro.
Serves 4

Kilocalories 205 Kc • Protein 9 gm • Fat 8 gm • Percent of calories from fat 32% • Cholesterol 0 mg • Dietary fiber 7 gm • Sodium 9 mg • Calcium 46 mg

Cucumber Raita

Raita is generally served as a cooling contrast to the hot elements of an Indian meal, however this version contains a bit of pungency of its own, thanks to the black pepper and the peppery bite of the watercress. Since I don't use dairy products, I make my raita with silken tofu instead of yogurt.

1 cup silken tofu or low-fat yogurt
1 cup peeled, seeded, and chopped
   cucumber
1 teaspoon freshly squeezed
   lemon juice

1/2 teaspoon sugar
1/4 teaspoon salt
1/8 teaspoon freshly ground pepper
1/4 cup chopped watercress

In a small bowl, combine the tofu, cucumber, lemon juice, sugar, salt, and pepper. Mix to blend. Sprinkle the watercress over the top, cover, and refrigerate for at least 30 minutes before serving. Serve chilled.
Serves 4

Kilocalories 36 Kc • Protein 3 gm • Fat 2 gm • Percent of calories from fat 40% • Cholesterol 0 mg • Dietary fiber 1 gm • Sodium 150 mg • Calcium 24 mg

Spicy Indian Green Beans

Black mustard seeds are sold at Indian markets and lend a distinctive flavor to this dish. However, if you can't find any, simply omit them and the results will still be delicious.

1 pound fresh green beans, cut into 1-inch lengths

2 tablespoons safflower oil

1 teaspoon black mustard seeds

1 medium onion, chopped

1 small green hot chili, seeded and minced

1 teaspoon ground cumin

1 large tomato, peeled, seeded, and chopped

1 cup grated fresh coconut

1 tablespoon chopped fresh cilantro

2 tablespoons freshly squeezed lime juice

1 cup cooked yellow split peas

Salt and freshly ground pepper

Boil the green beans in a large saucepan of salted water for 3 to 4 minutes or until just tender. Drain the beans in a colander, refresh them under cold water, and set aside.

In a large skillet, heat the oil over medium heat. Add the mustard seeds and cook, partially covered, for 30 seconds or until they stop popping. Add the onion and cook, stirring, until softened, about 5 minutes. Add the chili, cumin, and tomato, and cook, stirring, for 2 minutes. Add the beans and cook, stirring, for 2 minutes or until the beans are soft. Add the coconut, cilantro, lime juice, split peas, and salt and pepper to taste, and cook, stirring, until heated through and combined well, about 5 minutes. Transfer the bean mixture to a bowl and serve warm or at room temperature.

Serves 6

Kilocalories 174 Kc • Protein 5 gm • Fat 10 gm • Percent of calories from fat 47% • Cholesterol 0 mg • Dietary fiber 7 gm • Sodium 87 mg • Calcium 56 mg

Spinach Saag

Saag is a popular puréed vegetable dish in India.

1 pound fresh spinach
1 tablespoon safflower oil
1/4 teaspoon hot red pepper flakes
1/4 teaspoon ground cumin
1/4 teaspoon ground coriander

1 teaspoon grated fresh ginger
1/3 cup chopped tomatoes
Salt
2 tablespoons cornstarch

Bring the spinach and 1 cup water to a boil in a large saucepan and cook until the spinach is tender, 3 to 5 minutes. Drain. Purée the spinach in a blender or food processor and set aside.

Heat the oil in a large skillet over medium heat. Add the hot red pepper flakes, cumin and coriander, and sauté for 1 minute to release flavors. Add the ginger, tomatoes, and salt to taste, and cook for 3 to 4 minutes until well combined. Stir in the spinach purée. Dissolve the cornstarch in 1/4 cup water and stir in just enough to thicken. Serve hot.

Serves 6

Kilocalories 81 Kc • Protein 2 gm • Fat 5 gm • Percent of calories from fat 51% • Cholesterol 0 mg • Dietary fiber 2 gm • Sodium 63 mg • Calcium 78 mg

Indian Spiced Carrots

The spices and the fruit juices bring out the natural sweetness of the carrots.

1 pound carrots, cut into 1/4-inch
    slices
2 tablespoons olive oil
2 garlic cloves, chopped
1/4 teaspoon salt
1/4 teaspoon ground cinnamon
1/8 teaspoon ground cumin

1/8 teaspoon cayenne
2 tablespoons minced fresh parsley
1/4 cup freshly squeezed orange juice
2 tablespoons freshly squeezed
    lemon juice
2 tablespoons finely chopped
    fresh basil

Steam the carrots until just tender and set aside. Heat the oil in a small skillet over medium heat. Add the garlic, salt, cinnamon, cumin, and cayenne, and stir until fragrant, about 1 minute. In a medium bowl, combine the carrots with the garlic mixture, parsley, orange juice, and lemon juice, and toss to combine. Serve at room temperature, garnished with the chopped basil.

Serves 4

Kilocalories 121 Kc • Protein 2 gm • Fat 7 gm • Percent of calories from fat 49% • Cholesterol 0 mg • Dietary fiber 4 gm • Sodium 187 mg • Calcium 43 mg

Braised Cabbage with Cardamom

1 tablespoon safflower oil
1 large onion, thinly sliced
2 garlic cloves, minced
1 tablespoon minced fresh ginger
1 medium head green cabbage, chopped
1 teaspoon ground cardamom

$^1\!/_2$ teaspoon salt
$^1\!/_2$ teaspoon ground turmeric
$^1\!/_4$ teaspoon hot red pepper flakes
$^1\!/_4$ teaspoon ground cinnamon
$^1\!/_8$ teaspoon freshly ground pepper
Freshly cooked basmati rice

Heat the oil in a large skillet over medium heat. Add the onion, garlic, and ginger, and cook, stirring frequently, until golden brown, about 10 minutes. Add the cabbage, cardamom, salt, turmeric, red pepper flakes, cinnamon, and pepper, and stir for 2 minutes. Add 1 cup water and bring to a boil. Reduce the heat, cover, and simmer for about 30 minutes or until the cabbage is tender. Taste and adjust seasonings. Serve with rice.

Serves 6

Kilocalories 72 Kc • Protein 1 gm • Fat 5 gm • Percent of calories from fat 56% • Cholesterol 0 mg • Dietary fiber 2 gm • Sodium 209 mg • Calcium 43 mg

Curried No-Meat Balls

1 pound ground meat alternative
1¹/4 cups silken tofu or low-fat
   yogurt
¹/4 cup chopped peanuts
¹/2 teaspoon minced fresh ginger
1 teaspoon minced fresh cilantro
Salt
¹/4 teaspoon cayenne
1 cup chopped onions

2 tablespoons safflower oil
1 teaspoon ground cinnamon
¹/2 teaspoon ground cardamom
2 cloves garlic, minced
¹/4 teaspoon ground turmeric
¹/4 teaspoon ground ginger
¹/2 teaspoon ground coriander
1 large ripe tomato, chopped
1 teaspoon chopped fresh parsley

To make the "meat" balls, in a large bowl combine the ground meat alternative, ¹/4 cup of the tofu, the peanuts, fresh ginger, cilantro, salt to taste, ¹/8 teaspoon of the cayenne, and ³/4 cup of the chopped onions. Shape into balls about 1¹/2 inches in diameter. Heat 1 tablespoon of the oil in a large skillet. Add the balls and brown on all sides, about 3 minutes. Remove from the skillet with a slotted spoon and drain on paper towels.

To make the curry sauce, heat the remaining 1 tablespoon oil in a skillet. Add the remaining ¹/4 cup onions and brown lightly. Add the cinnamon, cardamom, garlic, turmeric, ground ginger, coriander, remaining ¹/8 teaspoon cayenne, and salt to taste, and sauté 2 minutes. Add the tomato and simmer, stirring, for 2 minutes, until the flavors are blended. Remove the pan from the heat and whisk in the remaining 1 cup tofu. Add enough water to make a thick sauce. Carefully add "meat" balls to the sauce and warm over low heat without boiling. Garnish with the parsley.
Serves 8

Kilocalories 147 Kc • Protein 11 gm • Fat 7 gm • Percent of calories from fat 43% • Cholesterol 0 mg • Dietary fiber 4 gm • Sodium 184 mg • Calcium 65 mg

Broiled East Indian Tofu

This classic East Indian marinade is traditionally used on meats, but it's also a great way to serve tofu.

1 medium onion, chopped
2 garlic cloves, chopped
1 teaspoon minced fresh ginger
1 teaspoon ground cumin
1 teaspoon salt
1/4 teaspoon hot red pepper flakes

3 tablespoons freshly squeezed lemon juice
2 tablespoons safflower oil
1 pound extra-firm tofu, cut into 1/2-inch slices

In a blender or food processor, purée the onion with the garlic, ginger, cumin, salt, hot red pepper flakes, lemon juice, and oil. In a large bowl, pour the mixture over the tofu, stirring to coat the tofu well. Cover and marinate in the refrigerator for at least 1 hour.

Preheat the broiler. Oil the rack of the broiler pan. Transfer the tofu to the prepared rack, letting the excess marinade drip off. Broil the tofu, turning once, for 6 to 8 minutes or until golden brown. Serve warm or at room temperature.

Serves 4

Kilocalories 197 Kc • Protein 15 gm • Fat 13 gm • Percent of calories from fat 58% • Cholesterol 0 mg • Dietary fiber 1 gm • Sodium 597 mg • Calcium 68 mg

Tofu Curry with Green Beans

1 tablespoon safflower oil
1 tablespoon curry powder
1/2 teaspoon ground cumin
1/2 teaspoon ground cinnamon
1/8 teaspoon cayenne
2 garlic cloves, minced
1 small onion, chopped
1 yellow bell pepper, chopped

1 pound fresh green beans, cut into
    1 1/2-inch lengths
1 pound extra-firm tofu, cut into
    1/4-inch dice
1/3 cup soy milk
Salt
1 tablespoon minced fresh cilantro

Heat the oil in a large skillet over medium-high heat. Add the curry powder, cumin, cinnamon, and cayenne, and stir until fragrant, about 30 seconds. Add 1/2 cup water, the garlic, onion, and bell pepper. Cover and cook, stirring occasionally, for 5 minutes. Add the green beans and another 1/2 cup water, cover, and simmer 5 minutes longer, until tender. Add the tofu, soy milk, and salt to taste, and simmer 5 minutes. Remove from the heat and transfer to a serving bowl. Sprinkle with the cilantro and serve.

Serves 4

Kilocalories 217 Kc • Protein 17 gm • Fat 11 gm • Percent of calories from fat 41% •
Cholesterol 0 mg • Dietary fiber 5 gm • Sodium 29 mg • Calcium 137 mg

Lentils in Onion Gravy

1 cup dried lentils	1 teaspoon salt
1 medium onion, minced	1/2 teaspoon ground cardamom
2 garlic cloves, minced	1/2 teaspoon ground cinnamon
1/2 cup soft silken tofu or low-fat yogurt	1/8 teaspoon cayenne
	Freshly cooked basmati rice

Place the lentils, onion, garlic, and 2 1/2 cups water in a large saucepan and bring to a boil. Reduce the heat to low, cover, and simmer until the lentils are tender and almost all of the liquid has evaporated, about 30 minutes. Gradually stir in the tofu. Add the salt, cardamom, cinnamon, and cayenne, and stir 3 minutes to blend well. Cover and simmer until heated through, about 10 minutes, adding a little more water if the mixture is too dry. Taste and adjust seasonings. Serve over rice.

Serves 4

Kilocalories 197 Kc • Protein 15 gm • Fat 1 gm • Percent of calories from fat 6% • Cholesterol 0 mg • Dietary fiber 16 gm • Sodium 594 mg • Calcium 51 mg

Tandoori-Style Tempeh

Not as hot as curry dishes, tandoori-style cooking is a northern Indian specialty that's named for the clay oven in which the food is traditionally cooked after it has marinated in a creamy herb mixture.

3 garlic cloves, chopped
1 teaspoon minced fresh ginger
1 medium onion, chopped
1 cup silken tofu or low-fat yogurt
2 tablespoons freshly squeezed
    lemon juice
1 tablespoon olive oil
1 teaspoon ground coriander
1/2 teaspoon ground cumin
1/2 teaspoon ground turmeric

1/4 teaspoon freshly ground pepper
1/2 teaspoon salt
1/4 teaspoon ground cardamom
1/4 teaspoon ground nutmeg
1/4 teaspoon ground cinnamon
1/8 teaspoon cayenne
1 pound tempeh, cut into 8 equal
    pieces
Chopped fresh parsley
Lemon wedges

Place the garlic, ginger, and onion in a food processor and mix well. Add the tofu, lemon juice, olive oil, coriander, cumin, turmeric, pepper, salt, cardamom, nutmeg, cinnamon, and cayenne, and purée until well blended. Transfer to a large bowl. Add the tempeh to the marinade, turning to coat well. Cover, and refrigerate overnight.

Preheat the broiler. Oil a broiler pan and a large shallow baking dish. Arrange the tempeh on the broiler pan and broil until browned, about 5 minutes per side. Reduce the oven temperature to 325°F. Transfer the tempeh to the prepared baking dish. Bake until heated through, basting frequently with the marinade, about 10 minutes. Garnish with chopped parsley and lemon wedges.

Serves 4

Kilocalories 256 Kc • Protein 24 gm • Fat 10 gm • Percent of calories from fat 34% • Cholesterol 0 mg • Dietary fiber 9 gm • Sodium 10 mg • Calcium 122 mg

Tofu with Spiced Plum Sauce

4 to 6 large purple plums, about
    1¹/₂ pounds
1 tablespoon grated fresh ginger
¹/₂ teaspoon ground cinnamon
¹/₄ teaspoon ground cloves
2 tablespoons safflower oil
1 pound extra-firm tofu, cut into
    ¹/₂-inch slices

1 large onion, chopped
1 garlic clove, minced
¹/₂ teaspoon ground cumin
¹/₄ teaspoon cayenne
Freshly cooked basmati rice

Slice 1 plum and reserve for garnish. Cut the remaining plums into large chunks. Discard the pits. In a food processor, purée the plums to make a smooth sauce. Add the ginger, cinnamon, and cloves and mix well. Transfer to a small bowl and set aside.

Preheat the oven to 375°F. Heat 1 tablespoon of the oil in a large skillet over medium-high heat. Add the tofu and cook until browned on all sides, about 5 minutes. Remove the tofu with a slotted spatula to a baking pan large enough to hold all of the pieces in 1 layer. Add the remaining tablespoon oil to the skillet and reheat. Add the onion and garlic and sauté, covered, for 5 minutes or until softened. Add the cumin and cayenne and remove from the heat. Stir in the plum purée. Pour the sauce over the tofu. Cover loosely and bake for 20 minutes to blend flavors. Serve with rice, garnished with the reserved plum slices.

Serves 4

Kilocalories 288 Kc • Protein 16 gm • Fat 14 gm • Percent of calories from fat 42% • Cholesterol 0 mg • Dietary fiber 3 gm • Sodium 15 mg • Calcium 75 mg

Vegetable Masala

I like to serve this fragrant vegetable mélange over basmati rice.

2 cups peeled baby carrots
2 medium potatoes, peeled and cut
    into 1-inch chunks
1 teaspoon olive oil
4 garlic cloves, minced
1 tablespoon minced fresh ginger
3/4 teaspoon salt

1 large onion, chopped
1 green bell pepper, chopped
2 large ripe tomatoes, chopped
1 tablespoon garam masala (see
    page 176)
2 small zucchini, halved lengthwise
    and cut into 1/4-inch slices

Steam the carrots and potatoes over boiling water for 15 minutes until tender. Heat the oil in a large skillet over high heat. Add the garlic, ginger, and 1/4 teaspoon of the salt, and cook for 30 seconds, stirring constantly. Layer the onion, pepper, tomatoes, and steamed carrots and potatoes in the skillet. Add 2/3 cup water. Sprinkle the remaining 1/2 teaspoon salt and the garam masala on top of the vegetables. Cover and simmer 10 minutes until vegetables are tender. Uncover and stir the vegetables, mashing the tomatoes to create a sauce. Add the zucchini. Cover and cook 5 minutes more, until the zucchini is tender.

Serves 6

Kilocalories 134 Kc • Protein 4 gm • Fat 1 gm • Percent of calories from fat 8% •
Cholesterol 0 mg • Dietary fiber 5 gm • Sodium 327 mg • Calcium 44 mg

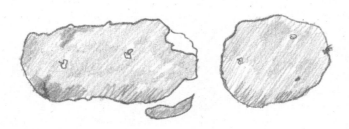

Curried Vegetable Pilaf

This Indian version of fried rice is a great way to stretch leftover rice into a delicious meal. Although the recipe calls for basmati rice, any type of white or brown rice will do.

3 cups cooked basmati rice
1 tablespoon freshly squeezed
   lemon juice
1/4 cup chopped fresh parsley
3/4 cup pineapple, chopped into
   1/2-inch cubes

1 tablespoon safflower oil
1 medium onion, chopped
1 teaspoon minced fresh ginger
2 teaspoons curry powder
2 medium zucchini, cut into
   1/2-inch cubes (about 2 cups)

Combine the rice, lemon juice, parsley, and pineapple in a large bowl. Set aside. Heat the oil in a large saucepan over medium-high heat. Add the onion and cook, stirring, for 5 minutes or until softened. Add the ginger and continue cooking for 1 minute longer. Sprinkle the curry powder over the onion and cook, stirring constantly, until fragrant, about 2 minutes. Add the zucchini and stir-fry for about 2 minutes or until the vegetables begin to soften. Cover, lower the heat, and cook for 5 minutes. Add the rice mixture, cover, and continue cooking for an additional 5 minutes or until the vegetables are cooked and the rice is heated through. Uncover, fluff the pilaf with a fork, and transfer to serving platter.
Serves 4 to 6

Kilocalories 238 Kc • Protein 5 gm • Fat 5gm • Percent of calories from fat 19% • Cholesterol 0 mg • Dietary fiber 5 gm • Sodium 8 mg • Calcium 45 mg

Vegetable Biryani

Biryani is a classic northern Mughal dish that incorporates a variety of ingredients, including vegetables, dried fruits, and nuts. Although the traditional dish is similar to a layered casserole, and can be somewhat complicated to prepare, I have adapted the basic elements into this quick and easy recipe that is an exciting way to use up leftovers. For variety, vegetables such as cauliflower, carrots, or chickpeas may be added or substituted.

1 tablespoon safflower oil
1 large onion, diced
1 red or green bell pepper, diced
1 teaspoon grated fresh ginger
2 garlic cloves, crushed
1/2 teaspoon cayenne
1/2 teaspoon ground turmeric
1/4 teaspoon ground coriander

1/4 teaspoon ground cumin
1/4 teaspoon freshly ground pepper
3 cups cooked basmati rice
1 cup cooked green beans, cut into
    1-inch pieces
1 cup frozen peas, thawed
Roasted peanuts
Raisins

Heat the oil in a saucepan over medium heat. Add the onion and bell pepper and sauté until softened, about 5 to 7 minutes. Add the ginger, garlic, cayenne, turmeric, coriander, cumin, and pepper, and cook 2 minutes longer, stirring to mix well. Add 1 cup water and cook, uncovered, until the sauce thickens, about 5 minutes. Add the rice, green beans, and peas. Cover and simmer over low heat for 10 minutes. Remove the cover and stir to heat through. Transfer to a serving plate and sprinkle with peanuts and raisins.

Serves 4

Kilocalories 309 Kc • Protein 7 gm • Fat 7 gm • Percent of calories from fat 22% • Cholesterol 0 mg • Dietary fiber 6 gm • Sodium 38 mg • Calcium 60 mg

Cashew Pilau with Raisins and Peas

1 tablespoon safflower oil
2 scallions, thinly sliced
3 cups cooked basmati rice
$1/2$ cup frozen peas, thawed
$1/4$ cup golden raisins

1 tablespoon freshly squeezed
   orange juice
$1/2$ teaspoon salt
$1/8$ teaspoon cayenne
$1/2$ cup roasted cashew pieces

Heat the oil in a large skillet over medium heat. Add the scallions, rice, peas, raisins, orange juice, salt, and cayenne, and stir to combine. Cover and cook until the rice heats through and the raisins are soft, about 5 minutes. Fluff with a fork and serve garnished with the cashews.

Serves 4

Kilocalories 359 Kc • Protein 7 gm • Fat 11 gm • Percent of calories from fat 29% • Cholesterol 0 mg • Dietary fiber 3 gm • Sodium 314 mg • Calcium 41 mg

Green Tomato and Pear Chutney

2 pounds firm green tomatoes,
   coarsely chopped
1 pound firm pears, stemmed, cored,
   and chopped
1 cup sugar
1 cup apple cider vinegar
1 medium onion, chopped

1/2 cup golden raisins
1/4 cup chopped crystallized ginger
1 tablespoon grated lemon zest
1 teaspoon ground allspice
1/2 teaspoon ground cinnamon
1/2 teaspoon salt
1/4 teaspoon cayenne

Place the tomatoes, pears, sugar, vinegar, onion, raisins, ginger, lemon zest, allspice, cinnamon, salt, and cayenne in a large saucepan and bring to a boil, stirring occasionally. Reduce the heat and simmer until the mixture is very thick, stirring frequently toward the end of the cooking time, about 1 hour. Ladle the chutney into clean glass jars. Cool to room temperature. Cover and refrigerate until ready to serve.
Serves 12

Kilocalories 144 Kc • Protein 1 gm • Fat .3 gm • Percent of calories from fat 2% • Cholesterol 0 mg • Dietary fiber 3 gm • Sodium 111 mg • Calcium 30 mg

Mint Chutney

This is one of my favorite chutneys because of its simplicity. It's also a great way to use some of the mint that likes to take over my herb garden.

1 cup fresh mint sprigs	$^1/_2$ teaspoon salt
4 scallions	$^1/_2$ teaspoon sugar
2 tablespoons freshly squeezed	$^1/_4$ teaspoon cayenne
lemon juice	$^1/_8$ teaspoon ground cumin

Combine the mint, scallions, lemon juice, salt, sugar, cayenne, and cumin in a blender or food processor. Process until smooth, adding a little water if necessary. Serve immediately or chill until needed.

Serves 4

Kilocalories 11 Kc • Protein 0 gm • Fat .1 gm • Percent of calories from fat 9% • Cholesterol 0 mg • Dietary fiber 1 gm • Sodium 293 mg • Calcium 28 mg

Pineapple-Date Chutney

The flavor of this chutney improves with time, so plan to make it several days ahead.

1 medium pineapple, peeled
   and cored
1/2 cup pitted and chopped dates
1/2 cup granulated sugar
1/4 cup light brown sugar
2 tablespoons chopped crystallized
   ginger

3 tablespoons freshly squeezed
   lemon juice
1/2 teaspoon cayenne
1/2 teaspoon freshly ground pepper
1/4 teaspoon ground cloves
1/8 teaspoon salt

Finely chop the pineapple and place in a medium saucepan over medium heat. Add the dates, sugars, ginger, and lemon juice, and cook, stirring occasionally, until thickened, about 30 minutes. Remove from the heat and stir in the cayenne, pepper, cloves, and salt. Transfer to a jar or container with a tight lid, allow to cool completely, cover, and refrigerate. This chutney will last for several weeks if kept covered and refrigerated.

Serves 8 to 10

Kilocalories 151 Kc • Protein 1 gm • Fat .4 gm • Percent of calories from fat 2% • Cholesterol 0 mg • Dietary fiber 2 gm • Sodium 42 mg • Calcium 21 mg

Garam Masala

Literally "hot mix," a garam masala is a blend of a number of spices. An electric spice grinder is a good investment if you plan to grind a lot of your own spice mixtures. This one will last for several months if you keep it tightly covered.

2 hot dried chilies
1/2 cup whole cardamom pods
1/4 cup whole black peppercorns
1/4 cup cumin seeds

1/4 cup whole cloves
1/8 cup coriander seeds
3 whole cinnamon sticks

Preheat the oven to 200°F. Spread the chilies, cardamom pods, peppercorns, cumin seeds, cloves, coriander seeds, and cinnamon sticks in a single layer on a shallow baking pan. Roast for 30 minutes, stirring occasionally. Remove the cardamom seeds from the cardamom pods and discard the pods. Break up the cinnamon sticks. Place all of the spices in a blender or electric spice grinder and pulverize at high speed until finely ground. Transfer to a container with a tight-fitting lid and shake to blend.

Makes about 1 1/2 cups

Kilocalories 29 Kc • Protein 1 gm • Fat .8 gm • Percent of calories from fat 21% • Cholesterol 0 mg • Dietary fiber 3 gm • Sodium 9 mg • Calcium 47 mg

FIVE

Asia

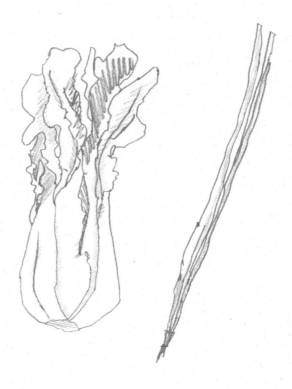

▼▼▼▼▼▼▼▼▼▼▼▼▼▼▼▼▼▼▼▼▼▼▼▼▼▼▼▼▼▼▼▼▼▼▼▼▼▼

Asia Recipe Mini-Index

Appetizers
Satays with Ginger-Peanut Sauce   217   Spicy Ginger Dumplings   183
Vegetable Spring Rolls   203

Soups and Stews
Ginger Watercress Soup   184   Hot and Sour Thai Soup   205
Hot and Spicy Corn Soup   204   Tofu Coconut Soup   206

Salads and Sides
Asparagus Daikon Salad   220   Coconut Tempeh and Papaya Salad   218
Cold Sichuan Noodle Salad   186   Five-Spice Tofu and Vegetable Salad   185
Indonesian Tempeh Salad   221   Japanese Eggplant Salad   222
Kimchi   224   Korean Bean Sprout Salad   219   Korean Cucumber Salad   223
Sichuan Cabbage   187   Spiced Coconut Vegetable Salad   207

Main Courses
Bean Curd with Hot Chili Paste   196
Cold Buckwheat Noodles with Jade Vegetables   226   Five-Spice Tempeh   189
Ginger Broccoli   188   Hot Thai Tofu   210   Hunan Fried Rice   198
Hunan Vegetable Stir-Fry   194   Indonesian Coconut Rice   228
Indonesian Tofu   225   Japanese Soba Noodles   230   Korean Rice and Millet   231
Mahogany Tempeh with Spicy Sichuan Sauce   199   Sichuan Vegetable Stir-Fry   191
Spicy Stir-Fried Tofu   193   Stir-Fried Ginger Seitan and Bok Choy   190
Stir-Fried Tempeh and Vegetables   192   Stir-Fried Thai Vegetables   213
Stir-Fried Tofu with Noodles   197   Sweet-and-Sour Bean Curd   208
Tempeh in Spicy Orange Sauce   195   Thai Tofu with Chilies and Basil   209
Tofu with Thai Peanut Sauce   211   Vegetable Pancit   229
Vietnamese Noodles with Tempeh and Peanuts   227

Sauces and Condiments
Daikon Walnut Condiment   232   Hot Mustard Dipping Sauce   201
Red Curry Paste   214   Spicy Peanut Sauce   212   Spicy Sichuan Sauce   200
Tamari Vinaigrette   234   Thai Curry Sauce   215   Thai Lime Vinaigrette   216
Vegetarian "Fish" Sauce   235   Wasabi Miso Dressing   233

▲▲▲▲▲▲▲▲▲▲▲▲▲▲▲▲▲▲▲▲▲▲▲▲▲▲▲▲▲▲▲▲▲▲▲▲▲▲

Searing Asian Appetites

Asian cooks, particularly those from China, Korea, and Thailand, have made many hot and spicy contributions to the world's cuisines. Most Asian cooks use chilies as their main heat source and a variety of other spices to create regional flavors. Japanese cuisine isn't especially spicy, but it's worth noting here for its use of the fiery green horseradish called wasabi, which is used as a condiment with sushi and sashimi.

China

The Sichuan and Hunan regions are home to China's most fiery dishes, which have become very popular in Western restaurants. Seasonings include garlic, ginger, soy sauce, and sherry, combined with hot red chilies in varying quantities. Rice and noodles are mainstays in the Chinese diet, and frequently used fresh vegetables include cabbage, bean sprouts, mushrooms, onions, and celery. Tofu, or bean curd, is a rich source of protein and provides a wonderful vehicle for the pungent Sichuan and Hunan sauces.

Thailand and Southeast Asia

Some of the most incendiary dishes of all can be found in Southeast Asia, for example, in Thailand. This is due in part to the liberal use of the Thai chili, one of the hottest chilies in the world. I don't use the Thai chili very often in recipes, as it can be too intense for many palates.

Thai food is a sensory marvel bearing Chinese and Indian influences. Many Thai dishes juxtapose the subtle flavor variances of hot, sweet, sour, bitter, and salty, all at once.

Spicy Vietnamese cuisine is similar to Chinese but features indigenous tropical ingredients such as lemongrass and citrus fruits. Although Vietnamese food can be spicy, it is not dominated by hot seasonings. Many Vietnamese dishes are accompanied by a platter of uncooked bean sprouts, fresh herbs, cucumbers, and lettuce. A popular Vietnamese seasoning is a fish sauce called *nuoc mam*, which is similar to *nam pla* in Thailand and used in much the same way soy sauce is used in China. I have included a vegetarian version of *nuoc mam* in this book for anyone who does not want to use the traditional fish sauce that is available at Asian markets and some supermarkets.

Korea

Although Korean cooking has been greatly influenced by the traditions of China, it tends to be spicier than Chinese cuisine. A liberal use of chilies, soy sauce, garlic, and the ubiquitous *kimchi* (a spicy cabbage mixture) help to rank Korean cookery among the spiciest of Asian cuisines. A traditional Korean meal will feature the colors green, white, yellow, red, and black, as well as a variety of textures and flavors. It will include rice, soup, vegetables, a main course, and *kimchi*. Like most Asian cuisines, rice is an important mainstay, as is tofu. Koreans also eat a variety of vegetables, along with barley, wheat, beans, meats, and fish.

Indonesia

Some of the Indonesian islands were once called the Spice Islands. At one time they were the only places in the world where cloves and nutmeg grew. Though the cooking of the islands of this archipelago is diverse, the most popular meals consist of rice with several savory side dishes, plus a sweet, syrupy condiment made with soy sauce and brown sugar called *ketjap manis* from which, it is believed, the word "ketchup" was derived.

Although Indonesian cuisine has been greatly influenced by China, its indigenous herbs, spices, and produce, such as lemongrass, coriander, and coconut, make it unique. Chilies as well as ginger and garlic are common flavorings. Tempeh, a meat alternative made from compressed soybeans, originated in Indonesia, where it is often prepared in coconut milk.

While meat and seafood are used throughout Asia, protein-rich meat alternatives such as tofu, tempeh, and seitan (wheat gluten) are also used in many dishes, and are easily substituted in recipes calling for meat.

China

Spicy Ginger Dumplings

These can be deep-fried or steamed to serve as an appetizer, or cooked in stock for wonton soup. I generally steam them and serve them with a tamari dipping sauce.

1 8-ounce can water chestnuts, drained
8 ounces extra-firm tofu, crumbled
2 large shiitake mushrooms
1 teaspoon minced fresh garlic
1 teaspoon minced fresh ginger
2 teaspoons low-sodium tamari
1 teaspoon cornstarch
1 teaspoon dry sherry
1/2 teaspoon salt
1/4 teaspoon hot red pepper flakes
40 wonton wrappers
2 quarts Vegetable Stock (see page xxi)

Combine the water chestnuts, tofu, mushrooms, garlic, and ginger in a food processor and mince well. Add the tamari, cornstarch, sherry, salt, and hot red pepper flakes, and blend until combined. Place 1 wonton wrapper on a dry work surface with one corner facing you. Place about 2 teaspoons of the filling mixture in the corner nearest you. Roll up wrapper from this corner to the center. Pull the left and right corners toward the center. Moisten the inside of one with water and press into the opposite corner to seal. Pull the furthest corner toward the center and press into other corners to seal. Repeat with the remaining wrappers and filling mixture. Bring the stock to a boil in a large saucepan over high heat. Reduce the heat to low, add the dumplings, and cook for 3 to 4 minutes until dumplings plump up, turn glossy, and float. Serve immediately.

Serves 12 to 15

Kilocalories 134 Kc • Protein 6 gm • Fat 2 gm • Percent of calories from fat 10% • Cholesterol 0 mg • Dietary fiber 1 gm • Sodium 342 mg • Calcium 23 mg

Ginger Watercress Soup

Ginger and cayenne give this delicate yet pungent soup its bite. Sake, a fragrant Japanese rice wine, is a flavorful seasoning in many Asian dishes. It can also be served hot or cold as a beverage.

6 ounces extra-firm tofu, cut into
  1/2-inch dice
1 tablespoon plus 1 teaspoon
  safflower oil
3/4 teaspoon cornstarch
1/8 teaspoon cayenne
1/8 teaspoon salt

4 cups Vegetable Stock (see page xxi)
2 thin slices fresh ginger
8 ounces watercress, stemmed
2 tablespoons low-sodium tamari
1 teaspoon sake or dry white wine
1 teaspoon toasted sesame oil

In a medium bowl, combine the tofu with 1 teaspoon of the safflower oil, the cornstarch, cayenne, and salt. Refrigerate for 1 hour.

Combine the stock and ginger in a medium saucepan and bring to a boil. Add the watercress and tamari. Taste and adjust seasonings. Boil for 3 minutes until watercress is just tender. Reduce the heat to low.

Heat the remaining tablespoon safflower oil in a large saucepan or wok over medium-high heat. Add the tofu and stir 1 minute. Add the wine, stock mixture, and sesame oil. Cook for 2 minutes to blend flavors. Transfer the soup to a tureen, discarding the ginger.

Serves 4

Kilocalories 146 Kc • Protein 8 gm • Fat 8 gm • Percent of calories from fat 48% • Cholesterol 0 mg • Dietary fiber 1 gm • Sodium 486 mg • Calcium 90 mg

Five-Spice Tofu and Vegetable Salad

Five-spice powder is a blend of pungent spices used in Chinese cooking. You can purchase it in Asian grocery stores or you can make your own by combining 1 teaspoon ground ginger with 1/4 teaspoon each ground allspice, anise, cinnamon, and cloves.

1/4 pound snow peas, trimmed	1 teaspoon toasted sesame oil
1/4 cup safflower oil	1 teaspoon sugar
1/2 teaspoon chili oil	1 teaspoon salt
2 large garlic cloves, minced	1/2 teaspoon five-spice powder
1 teaspoon minced fresh ginger	1 red bell pepper, cut into
1 pound extra-firm tofu, cut into	1/2-inch dice
1/2-inch cubes	1 large carrot, grated
3 tablespoons rice vinegar	4 scallions, chopped
1 tablespoon sake or dry white wine	1/2 cup dry-roasted cashews

Cook the snow peas in boiling salted water until they begin to soften, about 1 minute. Drain, rinse under cold water, and drain again. Transfer to a large bowl.

Heat the safflower and chili oils in a large skillet over medium-high heat. Add the garlic, ginger, and tofu, and cook until the tofu is lightly browned, about 2 minutes. Transfer the tofu to a plate using a slotted spoon. Add the vinegar, sake, sesame oil, sugar, salt, and five-spice powder to the liquid in the skillet and bring to a boil, scraping up any browned bits. Remove from the heat.

Add the bell pepper, carrot, and scallion to the snow peas. Add the tofu and sauce, and toss gently to combine. Cover and refrigerate at least 1 hour before serving. Just before serving, drain any liquid. Mix in the cashews. Taste and adjust seasonings.

Serves 6

Kilocalories 260 Kc • Protein 12 gm • Fat 20 gm • Percent of calories from fat 66% • Cholesterol 0 mg • Dietary fiber 2 gm • Sodium 405 mg • Calcium 55 mg

Cold Sichuan Noodle Salad

Make this salad the day before you want to serve it to give the flavors some time to mingle.

3 tablespoons rice vinegar
2 tablespoons low-sodium tamari
2 tablespoons minced fresh ginger
2 tablespoons toasted sesame oil
1 tablespoon sugar
1 teaspoon hot chili paste
3 cups fresh bean sprouts

12 ounces thin fresh Chinese noodles
1 teaspoon safflower oil
1 red bell pepper, cut into 2 × 1/4-inch strips
4 scallions, minced
2 tablespoons minced fresh parsley

Stir together the vinegar, tamari, ginger, sesame oil, sugar, and chili paste in a small bowl until well blended. Let stand, covered, at room temperature for at least 1 hour.

Blanch the bean sprouts in boiling unsalted water to cover for 1 minute. Drain immediately in a colander, rinse under cold water until chilled; drain again, and set aside.

Bring 2 quarts salted water to a boil in a large saucepan over high heat. Cook the noodles, uncovered, stirring gently to keep the strands separate, until firm but tender, 1 to 3 minutes. Drain the noodles immediately, rinse under cold water until cool, then drain again. Toss the noodles with the safflower oil to coat all of the strands. Toss again in the serving bowl with the bean sprouts, bell pepper, scallions, parsley, and reserved sauce. Cover and chill in the refrigerator until ready to serve.

Serves 4

Kilocalories 257 Kc • Protein 8 gm • Fat 14 gm • Percent of calories from fat 46% • Cholesterol 0 mg • Dietary fiber 1 gm • Sodium 315 mg • Calcium 55 mg

Sichuan Cabbage

Although the people of China do include some meat in their diets, they often prefer vegetable dishes and salads during the hot summer months.

3 medium carrots, shredded
4 cups shredded Napa cabbage
   (about 1/2 medium head)
1/4 cup plus 2 tablespoons rice
   vinegar

1 tablespoon sugar
2 tablespoons minced fresh ginger
1 teaspoon chili oil
2 teaspoons toasted sesame oil

Bring a large pot of salted water to a boil. Add the carrots and cook until almost tender, about 2 minutes. Add the cabbage and continue cooking for 3 minutes until just tender. Drain the vegetables and cool completely. Transfer to a large bowl and set aside.

In a small saucepan, combine the vinegar, sugar, ginger, chili oil, and sesame oil. Bring to a boil, stirring constantly. Reduce the heat and simmer 2 minutes. Cool completely. Pour the dressing over the vegetables and toss well.

Serves 4

Kilocalories 72 Kc • Protein 2 gm • Fat 1 gm • Percent of calories from fat 12% •
Cholesterol 0 mg • Dietary fiber 4 gm • Sodium 45 mg • Calcium 44 mg

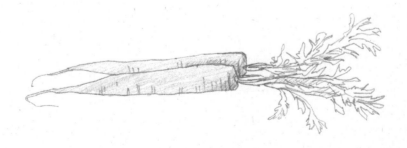

Ginger Broccoli

Although this recipe calls for broccoli, tofu will also work well, as will any favorite vegetable combinations. If you like your vegetable soft, cover the skillet with a lid during the cooking time to keep the steam in and hasten the cooking process.

2 tablespoons safflower oil
1 head broccoli, cut into 1-inch
    florets, stems reserved for
    another use
2 tablespoons low-sodium tamari
1 teaspoon sugar
1½ tablespoons minced fresh ginger

1 scallion, chopped
1 garlic clove, minced
1 tablespoon toasted sesame oil
1 teaspoon rice vinegar
¼ teaspoon hot red pepper flakes
Freshly cooked white or brown rice

Heat the oil in a large skillet or wok over medium-high heat. Add the broccoli and stir-fry about 20 seconds or until bright green. Sprinkle the broccoli with the tamari and sugar. Add the ginger, scallion, and garlic, and stir-fry 1 minute until fragrant. Stir in the sesame oil, vinegar, and hot red pepper flakes, and continue to stir-fry until the broccoli is crisp-tender, about 2 minutes. Serve immediately with freshly cooked rice.

Serves 4

Kilocalories 130 Kc • Protein 4 gm • Fat 11 gm • Percent of calories from fat 68% • Cholesterol 0 mg • Dietary fiber 3 gm • Sodium 328 mg • Calcium 48 mg

Five-Spice Tempeh

1 pound tempeh, cut into 1-inch
    slices
1 tablespoon five-spice powder
1/4 teaspoon cayenne
2 tablespoons safflower oil
2 cups Vegetable Stock (see page xxi)

Salt and freshly ground pepper
2 tablespoons grated orange zest
2 tablespoons sake or dry
    white wine
1 tablespoon chopped fresh cilantro
Freshly cooked white or brown rice

Poach the tempeh in a pan of simmering water for 10 minutes. Pat the tempeh dry. Combine the five-spice powder and cayenne, then coat the tempeh pieces with the spice mixture. Heat the oil in a large skillet over medium heat. Add the tempeh and cook until browned on all sides, about 8 minutes total. Keep warm.

Place the stock in a saucepan over high heat and simmer until reduced to 1 cup, about 5 minutes. Season the stock with salt and pepper to taste. Add the orange zest and sake to the stock and bring to a simmer. Pour the sauce over the reserved tempeh, sprinkle with cilantro, and serve over rice.

Serves 4 to 6

Kilocalories 317 Kc • Protein 22 gm • Fat 16 gm • Percent of calories from fat 42% • Cholesterol 0 mg • Dietary fiber 9 gm • Sodium 49 mg • Calcium 113 mg

Stir-Fried Ginger Seitan and Bok Choy

With its pale ribs and dark green leaves, bok choy, or Chinese cabbage, looks like a cross between celery and Swiss chard. It is a common ingredient in Chinese stir-fries and has a more subtle flavor than head cabbage.

2 tablespoons safflower oil
1 pound seitan, cut into $1/2 \times 2$-inch strips
4 garlic cloves, minced
1 tablespoon minced fresh ginger
1 large onion, thinly sliced
4 small thin, fresh hot chilies, blanched
2 tablespoons low-sodium tamari
$1/4$ teaspoon five-spice powder
$1/4$ teaspoon freshly ground pepper
$1/2$ teaspoon sugar
1 tablespoon dry sherry
1 pound bok choy, cut crosswise into $1/2$-inch strips
1 teaspoon cornstarch dissolved in 1 tablespoon water
Freshly cooked white or brown rice

Heat the oil in a large skillet or wok over high heat. Add the seitan and stir-fry until browned on all sides, about 5 minutes. Remove from the pan with a slotted spoon and set aside. Add the garlic and ginger to the pan and stir-fry for about 1 minute. Add the onion and blanched chilies and stir-fry until the onion is limp. Add the tamari, 2 tablespoons water, the five-spice powder, pepper, sugar, and sherry, and toss together. Add the bok choy and stir-fry until the greens are wilted. Return the seitan to the pan. Add the cornstarch mixture and continue stirring until the sauce thickens. Serve over cooked rice.
Serves 6

Kilocalories 173 Kc • Protein 23 gm • Fat 5 gm • Percent of calories from fat 24% • Cholesterol 0 mg • Dietary fiber 2 gm • Sodium 376 mg • Calcium 75 mg

Sichuan Vegetable Stir-Fry

Shiitake mushrooms are among the few mushrooms that grow on logs instead of in soil. Aromatic and chewy with a subtly woodsy flavor, shiitakes absorb the taste of the ingredients with which they are cooked. Once only common in their dried form, most supermarkets now carry them fresh.

1 teaspoon safflower oil
1 tablespoon grated fresh ginger
2 scallions, minced
2 garlic cloves, minced
1/2 cup grated carrot
1/4 cup dry sherry
1/2 cup chopped red bell pepper
1 cup thinly sliced fresh shiitake or
   domestic mushrooms

2 cups thinly sliced Napa cabbage
1/2 teaspoon chili paste
2 tablespoons toasted sesame oil
1 tablespoon sugar
2 tablespoons low-sodium tamari
Freshly cooked white or brown rice

Heat the oil in a large skillet or wok over medium-high heat. Add the ginger, scallions, and garlic, and stir-fry 2 minutes or until fragrant. Add the carrot, sherry, bell pepper, mushrooms, and cabbage, and stir-fry 2 to 3 minutes or until the vegetables soften. In a small bowl, combine the chili paste, sesame oil, sugar, and tamari. Add to the vegetables and serve over rice.

Serves 4

Kilocalories 155 Kc • Protein 3 gm • Fat 8 gm • Percent of calories from fat 44% • Cholesterol 0 mg • Dietary fiber 3 gm • Sodium 321 mg • Calcium 28 mg

Stir-Fried Tempeh and Vegetables

Hoisin sauce, often referred to as Chinese ketchup, is available in the gourmet section of most supermarkets. Tsing Tsao or one of the other excellent Chinese beers available in this country will help put out the fire of this tantalizing stir-fry.

1/4 cup rice vinegar
2 tablespoons light brown sugar
1/4 cup low-sodium tamari
1 1/2 teaspoons tomato paste
2 tablespoons minced fresh garlic
1 tablespoon grated fresh ginger
1/2 teaspoon dry mustard
1/2 teaspoon hot red pepper flakes
2 tablespoons hoisin sauce
1 teaspoon cornstarch dissolved in 1 tablespoon water

2 tablespoons safflower oil
1 large onion, thinly sliced
1/2 pound broccoli florets, blanched
1 green bell pepper, cut into thin strips
1 red bell pepper, cut into thin strips
1/2 cup canned water chestnuts, drained
8 ounces tempeh, crumbled
Freshly cooked white or brown rice

In a food processor or blender, combine 1/2 cup water, the vinegar, sugar, tamari, tomato paste, garlic, ginger, mustard, hot red pepper flakes, and hoisin sauce, and purée until well blended. Pour the purée into a small saucepan and bring to a boil. Reduce the heat to a simmer and cook for 10 minutes, stirring occasionally to prevent sticking. Add the cornstarch mixture and simmer, stirring, until the sauce is thickened and translucent. Set aside.

In a large skillet or wok, heat the oil over medium-high heat. Add the onion and stir-fry for about 1 minute. Add broccoli and stir-fry until heated through but still crisp, about 2 minutes. Add the bell peppers, water chestnuts, and tempeh, and stir-fry until the tempeh is golden brown, about 3 minutes. Add the sauce and stir-fry to coat all of the vegetables. Serve with freshly cooked rice.

Serves 6

Kilocalories 206 Kc • Protein 11 gm • Fat 8 gm • Percent of calories from fat 34% • Cholesterol 0 mg • Dietary fiber 5 gm • Sodium 591 mg • Calcium 75 mg

Spicy Stir-Fried Tofu

2 tablespoons safflower oil
2 tablespoons chopped scallion
2 teaspoons minced fresh ginger
2 garlic cloves, minced
1 teaspoon minced fresh hot
  green chili

1 pound extra-firm tofu, cut into
  1/2-inch strips
1 tablespoon toasted sesame oil
2 tablespoons low-sodium tamari
1 teaspoon hot chili paste
Freshly cooked white or brown rice

Heat the safflower oil in a large skillet or wok over medium-high heat. Add the scallion, ginger, garlic, and chili, and stir-fry until the garlic is fragrant, about 1 minute. Add the tofu, sesame oil, tamari, and chili paste. Cook, stirring constantly, until tofu is heated through and coated with sauce, about 3 minutes. Serve over rice.

Serves 6

Kilocalories 109 Kc • Protein 8 gm • Fat 8 gm • Percent of calories from fat 67% •
Cholesterol 0 mg • Dietary fiber 0 gm • Sodium 181 mg • Calcium 31 mg

Hunan Vegetable Stir-Fry

For a mild yet flavorful version of this stir-fry, omit the hot red pepper flakes and red wine vinegar.

1 teaspoon hot red pepper flakes	1 tablespoon grated fresh ginger
1 1/2 teaspoons red wine vinegar	4 garlic cloves, minced
1/2 cup tomato purée	1 pound bok choy, thinly sliced
1/4 cup dry sherry	1 large carrot, shredded
1/4 cup low-sodium tamari	1/2 pound snow peas, trimmed
1 tablespoon toasted sesame oil	1/2 pound mushrooms, sliced
1 tablespoon sugar	Freshly cooked white or brown rice
2 tablespoons safflower oil	

Soak the hot red pepper flakes in the wine vinegar in a small bowl for 30 minutes. In another small bowl, combine the tomato purée, sherry, tamari, sesame oil, and sugar, and set aside. Heat the safflower oil in a large skillet over medium-high heat. Add the ginger, garlic, bok choy, carrot, and undrained red pepper flakes, and stir-fry for 2 minutes until just tender. Add the snow peas and mushrooms and stir-fry for 2 minutes longer until just tender. Add the tomato-sherry sauce and cook until heated through. Serve over rice.

Serves 6

Kilocalories 110 Kc • Protein 4 gm • Fat 5 gm • Percent of calories from fat 42% • Cholesterol 0 mg • Dietary fiber 2 gm • Sodium 327 mg • Calcium 70 mg

Tempeh in Spicy Orange Sauce

2 tablespoons safflower oil
1 pound tempeh, cut into 1/2-inch
   strips
1 teaspoon minced fresh garlic
1 tablespoon hot pepper sauce
1 tablespoon light brown sugar

1 tablespoon low-sodium tamari
1 1/2 cups freshly squeezed
   orange juice
1 tablespoon cornstarch dissolved in
   1 tablespoon cold water
Freshly cooked white or brown rice

Heat the oil in a large skillet or wok over medium-high heat. Add the tempeh and stir-fry until golden brown, about 1 minute. Add the garlic and cook 1 minute. Stir in the hot pepper sauce, brown sugar, and tamari. Add the orange juice and bring to a boil. Cook 2 minutes to blend flavors. Stir in the dissolved cornstarch and continue cooking until the sauce thickens, about 2 minutes. Serve over freshly cooked rice.

Serves 6

Kilocalories 177 Kc • Protein 11 gm • Fat 8 gm • Percent of calories from fat 38% • Cholesterol 0 mg • Dietary fiber 4 gm • Sodium 97 mg • Calcium 61 mg

Bean Curd with Hot Chili Paste

Bean curd and tofu are two different terms for the same ingredient.

2 tablespoons tomato paste
1 tablespoon low-sodium tamari
2 teaspoons sake or dry white wine
3/4 teaspoon sugar
1/2 teaspoon salt
1 pound extra-firm tofu, cut into
   1/2-inch strips

1/4 cup cornstarch
1/8 teaspoon freshly ground pepper
3 tablespoons safflower oil
1/4 cup minced scallions
1 teaspoon hot chili paste
1 teaspoon minced fresh garlic
1 teaspoon minced fresh ginger

Combine the tomato paste, 4 teaspoons water, tamari, sake, sugar, and 1/4 teaspoon of the salt in a small bowl. Pat the tofu dry. Combine the cornstarch, remaining 1/4 teaspoon salt, and the pepper in another small bowl. Dredge the tofu in the cornstarch mixture, shaking off the excess. Heat 2 tablespoons of the oil in a large skillet or wok over medium-high heat. Add the tofu in batches and cook 20 seconds on each side. Drain on paper towels.

Heat the remaining tablespoon oil in a clean skillet or wok over high heat. Add the scallions, chili paste, garlic, and ginger, and stir for 15 seconds. Add the tomato paste mixture and stir until well blended. Add the tofu, toss gently to coat with the sauce, and cook until heated through, about 2 minutes. Transfer the tofu to a platter and serve immediately.

Serves 4

Kilocalories 263 Kc • Protein 15 gm • Fat 17 gm • Percent of calories from fat 56% • Cholesterol 0 mg • Dietary fiber 1 gm • Sodium 505 mg • Calcium 74 mg

Stir-Fried Tofu with Noodles

Substitute linguine if Asian noodles are unavailable for this hearty one-dish meal.

1 pound extra-firm tofu, cut into
    1/4-inch strips
1 tablespoon plus 1 teaspoon dry
    sherry
1 teaspoon cornstarch
12 ounces udon or lo mein noodles
2 teaspoons toasted sesame oil
1/2 cup Vegetable Stock (see
    page xxi)

3 tablespoons low-sodium tamari
1/2 teaspoon chili paste
2 tablespoons safflower oil
4 scallions, thinly sliced
1 tablespoon minced fresh ginger
6 shiitake mushrooms, trimmed and
    sliced
1 small head bok choy, trimmed
    and cut into 1/4-inch slices

Combine the tofu, 1 teaspoon of the sherry, and the cornstarch in a small bowl and mix until well blended. Set aside.

Cook the noodles in a large pot of boiling salted water until just tender but still firm to bite. Drain, rinse under cold water until cool, and drain again. Combine the noodles and sesame oil in a medium bowl. Combine the stock, tamari, the remaining tablespoon sherry, and the chili paste in a small bowl.

Heat safflower oil in a wok or large skillet over high heat. Add the scallions, ginger, and mushrooms, and stir-fry for 30 seconds. Add the tofu and stir-fry for about 2 minutes until lightly browned. Remove from the wok. Add the bok choy and stir-fry until it begins to soften, about 2 minutes. Add the noodles and stir-fry until heated through, about 30 seconds. Return the tofu mixture to the wok and stir for 30 seconds. Add the stock mixture and stir until absorbed by the noodles, about 1 minute. Transfer to a shallow bowl or platter and serve.

Serves 4

Kilocalories 567 Kc • Protein 31 gm • Fat 19 gm • Percent of calories from fat 29% •
Cholesterol 0 mg • Dietary fiber 6 gm • Sodium 645 mg • Calcium 187 mg

Hunan Fried Rice

This is a relatively mild yet flavorful version of fried rice from the Hunan region of south-western China, a region known for its spicy cuisine.

2 tablespoons light brown sugar
3 tablespoons low-sodium tamari
2 tablespoons dry sherry
1 tablespoon toasted sesame oil
1 teaspoon minced fresh ginger
1 garlic clove, minced
1/4 teaspoon cayenne
1 pound extra-firm tofu, cut into
    1/4-inch dice

2 teaspoons cornstarch
1 red bell pepper, chopped
1 cup shredded green cabbage
1/4 cup minced scallion
3 cups cold cooked white or
    brown rice
2 tablespoons sesame seeds

Combine the brown sugar, tamari, sherry, sesame oil, ginger, garlic, and cayenne in a shallow bowl. Add the tofu and marinate for 30 minutes in the refrigerator. Drain the tofu, reserving 1/4 cup of the marinade.

Combine the reserved marinade and the cornstarch. Toss with the tofu. Heat the oil in a large skillet or wok. Add the bell pepper, cabbage, and scallion, and stir-fry for 1 minute. Add the tofu and reserved 1/4 cup marinade and stir-fry until the liquid is nearly absorbed, about 2 minutes. Add the rice and stir-fry until heated through and well combined, about 3 to 5 minutes. Serve garnished with sesame seeds.

Serves 4

Kilocalories 405 Kc • Protein 20 gm • Fat 11 gm • Percent of calories from fat 24% •
Cholesterol 0 mg • Dietary fiber 2 gm • Sodium 335 mg • Calcium 102 mg

Mahogany Tempeh with Spicy Sichuan Sauce

Brown rice syrup is a natural sweetener available in natural food stores, but honey may be used, if you prefer.

1 pound tempeh, cut into 2-inch-wide pieces
1/2 cup low-sodium tamari
2 tablespoons brown rice syrup or honey
2 garlic cloves

1/2 teaspoon chopped fresh ginger
1/4 teaspoon ground coriander
1/8 teaspoon cayenne
Grated zest of 1 orange
Spicy Sichuan Sauce (see page 200)

Place the tempeh in a shallow baking dish. Combine the tamari, brown rice syrup, garlic, ginger, coriander, cayenne, and orange zest in a blender and purée until smooth. Pour the mixture over the tempeh and marinate, basting often, at room temperature for 1 hour.

Preheat the oven to 450°F. Bake the tempeh, basting often with the marinade, until golden brown, about 15 minutes. Top with Spicy Sichuan Sauce and serve hot.
Serves 4

Kilocalories 225 Kc • Protein 22 gm • Fat 9 gm • Percent of calories from fat 32% • Cholesterol 0 mg • Dietary fiber 8 gm • Sodium 7 mg • Calcium 105 mg

Spicy Sichuan Sauce

2 teaspoons safflower oil
1 teaspoon minced fresh garlic
1 teaspoon minced fresh ginger
1 tablespoon minced scallion
1/4 teaspoon hot red pepper flakes

1 tablespoon low-sodium tamari
1 tablespoon light brown sugar
1 teaspoon rice vinegar
1 tablespoon toasted sesame oil

Heat the safflower oil in a small saucepan over medium heat. Add the garlic, ginger, scallion, and hot red pepper flakes, and cook for 2 minutes or until fragrant. Add tamari, brown sugar, 1 tablespoon water, and the vinegar, and cook for 1 minute to blend flavors. Strain the sauce into a small bowl and stir in the sesame oil. Sauce will thicken slightly.

Serves 4

Kilocalories 69 Kc • Protein 1 gm • Fat 6 gm • Percent of calories from fat 72% • Cholesterol 0 mg • Dietary fiber 0 gm • Sodium 154 mg • Calcium 7 mg

Hot Mustard Dipping Sauce

This sauce can be made a day ahead of time if covered tightly and refrigerated. Serve with egg rolls or tempura vegetables.

1 tablespoon chopped fresh ginger
2 garlic cloves
1 tablespoon sugar
3 tablespoons low-sodium tamari

1 tablespoon cider vinegar
2 tablespoons dry mustard
1/4 teaspoon toasted sesame oil

In a food processor, combine the ginger, garlic, and sugar until finely minced. Add the tamari, vinegar, 4 tablespoons water, mustard, and sesame oil, and blend for 30 seconds, stopping once to scrape down the sides of the work bowl. Transfer the dipping sauce to a small serving bowl.

Serves 6 to 8

Kilocalories 18 Kc • Protein 0 gm • Fat .2 gm • Percent of calories from fat 10% • Cholesterol 0 mg • Dietary fiber 0 gm • Sodium 269 mg • Calcium 6 mg

Thailand

Vegetable Spring Rolls

These spring rolls are delicious, so make plenty. Serve with Spicy Peanut Sauce (page 212) or Hot Mustard Dipping Sauce (page 201).

6 shiitake mushrooms, chopped
1 cup chopped bok choy
1/4 cup canned bamboo shoots, chopped
1/4 cup grated carrot
1/4 teaspoon salt
1/8 teaspoon cayenne

1 tablespoon safflower oil
1 tablespoon cornstarch
12 store-bought spring roll wrappers
1 tablespoon all-purpose flour
Safflower oil, for frying

Combine the mushrooms, bok choy, bamboo shoots, carrot, salt, and cayenne in a medium bowl and let stand for 30 minutes.

Heat 1 tablespoon safflower oil in a wok or skillet. Add the vegetable mixture and stir-fry for 2 minutes or until tender. Combine the cornstarch with 2 tablespoons cold water, add to the vegetables in the wok, and cook until thickened. Cool. Divide the filling into 12 portions and place a portion on a short end of each wrapper. Fold the top edge over. Fold in both ends and roll up lengthwise into a tight cylinder. Combine the flour with 2 tablespoons cold water and use this paste to seal the ends.

Heat 1/4-inch depth of oil in a large saucepan until very hot. Fry the spring rolls, a few at a time, turning until golden brown all over, about 2 minutes. Drain on a paper towel.

Serves 12

Kilocalories 87 Kc • Protein 1 gm • Fat 6 gm • Percent of calories from fat 59% • Cholesterol 0 mg • Dietary fiber 1 gm • Sodium 97 mg • Calcium 13 mg

Hot and Spicy Corn Soup

The natural sweetness of the corn is complemented by the fragrant lemongrass and ginger. A swirl of chili paste added just prior to serving provides a touch of heat.

1 tablespoon safflower oil	2 cups Vegetable Stock (see page xxi)
1/2 cup minced fresh onion	1 cup soy milk
1 1/2 tablespoons minced fresh lemongrass	2 teaspoons sugar
1 tablespoon minced fresh ginger	Salt and freshly ground pepper
3 cups fresh corn kernels	1 teaspoon hot chili paste, or more
	2 tablespoons minced fresh cilantro

Heat the oil in a medium saucepan over low heat. Add the onion, lemongrass, and ginger, and stir for 2 minutes. Add the corn and stir for 1 minute. Add the stock and simmer until the corn is tender but still firm to bite, about 5 minutes. Add the soy milk and sugar. Season with salt and pepper to taste. Cool completely. Purée the soup (in batches if necessary) in a blender. Return to the saucepan and bring to a simmer. Transfer to serving bowls. Swirl chili paste into the center of each one. Garnish with the cilantro. Serve immediately.

Serves 4 to 6

Kilocalories 198 Kc • Protein 4 gm • Fat 8 gm • Percent of calories from fat 32% • Cholesterol 0 mg • Dietary fiber 2 gm • Sodium 134 mg • Calcium 30 mg

Hot and Sour Thai Soup

Delicate pieces of bean curd replace the traditional shrimp in this well-known Thai soup. The rich broth is spiced with chilies and made tangy with lemongrass and lime juice.

6 cups Vegetable Stock (see page xxi)
1 teaspoon salt
3 stalks lemongrass, cut into 1-inch
   lengths
1 teaspoon lime zest, slivered
2 green serrano chilies, slivered

1 pound extra-firm tofu, cut into
   1/4-inch dice
1 tablespoon low-sodium tamari
Juice of 2 limes
2 tablespoons chopped fresh cilantro
3 scallions, chopped

In a large saucepan, combine the stock, salt, lemongrass, lime zest, and chilies. Bring to a boil, cover, reduce the heat, and simmer for 20 minutes. Strain through a sieve, return the liquid to the saucepan, bring to a boil, and cook for 2 to 3 minutes to blend flavors. Reduce the heat to a simmer and add the tofu, tamari, and lime juice. Stir gently and simmer 1 minute to heat through. Serve hot, garnished with the cilantro and scallions.

Serves 6 to 8

Kilocalories 131 Kc • Protein 11 gm • Fat 4 gm • Percent of calories from fat 29% • Cholesterol 0 mg • Dietary fiber 1 gm • Sodium 581 mg • Calcium 46 mg

Tofu Coconut Soup

Usually made with chicken, this Thai favorite is just as tasty made with tofu.

1/3 cup chopped fresh cilantro
1/4 cup chopped fresh garlic
1/4 cup thinly sliced lemongrass
1 teaspoon freshly ground white
    pepper
1 tablespoon safflower oil
3 1/2 cups canned unsweetened
    coconut milk

1 pound extra-firm tofu, cut into
    1/2-inch dice
1/4 cup thin strips red bell pepper
4 tablespoons freshly squeezed
    lime juice
3 tablespoons low-sodium tamari
1/8 teaspoon sugar

In a food processor, purée the cilantro, garlic, lemongrass, white pepper, and oil to a fine paste and set aside. In a large saucepan, bring the coconut milk and 1 1/2 cups water to a simmer. Stir in 5 tablespoons of the reserved paste and simmer 10 minutes. Remove the pan from the heat and cool the mixture to warm. Strain the mixture through a fine sieve into a bowl, pressing on the solids with the back of a spoon. Discard the solids and transfer the liquid back to the saucepan. Stir in the remaining paste, the tofu, bell pepper, lime juice, tamari, and sugar, and cook until heated through, about 5 minutes.

Serves 6

Kilocalories 244 Kc • Protein 12 gm • Fat 18 gm • Percent of calories from fat 67% • Cholesterol 0 mg • Dietary fiber 3 gm • Sodium 330 mg • Calcium 103 mg

Spiced Coconut Vegetable Salad

¹/₄ pound fresh green beans, cut into
   1-inch pieces
¹/₄ pound fresh spinach, stemmed
1 red bell pepper, chopped
³/₄ teaspoon salt
¹/₄ teaspoon cayenne
2 tablespoons safflower oil

¹/₄ cup thinly sliced shallot
1 garlic clove, minced
¹/₂ cup shredded unsweetened
   coconut
2 tablespoons freshly squeezed
   lime juice

Blanch the green beans in boiling salted water until just tender, about 4 minutes. Drain, rinse under cold water, and drain again. Blanch the spinach in boiling salted water until wilted, about 1 minute. Drain, rinse under cold water, and drain again. Squeeze the spinach dry and set aside.

Purée the bell pepper with the salt and cayenne in a blender. Heat the oil in a medium skillet over medium heat. Add the shallot and garlic and stir until softened, about 5 minutes. Transfer to a medium bowl. Add the bell pepper purée to the skillet and stir just until fragrant, about 2 minutes. Add the hot purée to the bowl with the shallot and garlic. Add the beans, spinach, coconut, and lime juice to the bowl and toss well. Taste and add more salt if necessary. Serve at room temperature.

Serves 4

Kilocalories 128 Kc • Protein 2 gm • Fat 10 gm • Percent of calories from fat 66% •
Cholesterol 0 mg • Dietary fiber 3 gm • Sodium 462 mg • Calcium 47 mg

Sweet-and-Sour Bean Curd

As with many Thai recipes, this sweet-and-sour dish is much spicier than the Chinese version.

1 tablespoon safflower oil
1 pound extra-firm tofu, cubed
1 large cucumber, peeled, halved
    lengthwise, and seeded
1 large onion, cut into 1-inch dice
1 garlic clove, minced
4 small green chilies, seeded and
    sliced into thin strips

4 medium tomatoes, each cut into
    8 pieces
2 tablespoons light brown sugar
2 tablespoons white vinegar
1 tablespoon low-sodium tamari

Heat the oil over medium heat in a large skillet or wok. Add the tofu and cook, stirring occasionally, until lightly browned, about 3 minutes. Transfer to a platter and set aside.

Cut the cucumber halves into 1/4-inch slices. Reheat the skillet over medium heat. Add the cucumbers and cook until lightly browned, about 2 minutes. Add to the tofu on the platter.

Add the onion to the skillet and sauté until tender and lightly brown, about 5 minutes. Transfer to the platter. Add the garlic and chilies to the skillet and cook until softened, about 3 minutes. Add the tomatoes and brown the entire mixture quickly, about 2 minutes. Add the brown sugar, vinegar, tamari, and 1/2 cup water. Heat to boiling, then add all the reserved ingredients from the platter. Stir well and heat thoroughly, about 3 to 5 minutes.

Serves 6

Kilocalories 154 Kc • Protein 11 gm • Fat 7 gm • Percent of calories from fat 38% • Cholesterol 0 mg • Dietary fiber 2 gm • Sodium 122 mg • Calcium 58 mg

Thai Tofu with Chilies and Basil

Hot chilies and pungent basil are frequently paired in Thai dishes. Holy basil, an especially minty basil, can be found in Asian grocery stores. If unavailable, substitute another variety of basil or fresh mint. This dish is delicious with jasmine rice.

1 pound extra-firm tofu	2 tablespoons minced fresh garlic
1 tablespoon safflower oil	3 tablespoons low-sodium tamari
1 small onion, thinly sliced	1 teaspoon light brown sugar
1/2 red bell pepper, cut into 1/4-inch strips	1 teaspoon cider vinegar
2 small serrano chilies, thinly sliced	1 cup loosely packed holy basil

Drain the tofu and cut into 1/2-inch slices. Place the tofu slices on a baking sheet lined with paper towels. Cover the tofu with another layer of paper towels and press on the slices to expel excess water. Cut the pressed tofu slices into 1/2-inch strips and set aside.

Heat the oil in a large sauté pan over medium-high heat. Add the onion, bell pepper, chilies, and garlic, and stir-fry for 2 minutes or until the onion begins to soften. Add the tamari, sugar, vinegar, and tofu, and continue to stir-fry for 2 minutes or until the tofu is heated through. Add the basil and cook a few seconds longer before serving.

Serves 4 to 6

Kilocalories 182 Kc • Protein 16 gm • Fat 10 gm • Percent of calories from fat 47% • Cholesterol 0 mg • Dietary fiber 1 gm • Sodium 471 mg • Calcium 83 mg

Hot Thai Tofu

1 pound extra-firm tofu
1 tablespoon dry white wine
2 tablespoons low-sodium tamari
1 tablespoon cornstarch
1/4 teaspoon cayenne
1 teaspoon toasted sesame oil
1 head broccoli, peeled and cut into
    1-inch pieces

2 medium carrots, peeled and cut
    into 1/8-inch-thick slices
2 tablespoons safflower oil
1 garlic clove, minced
Salt

Drain the tofu and cut into 1/2-inch slices. Place the tofu slices on a baking sheet lined with paper towels. Cover the tofu with another layer of paper towels and press on the slices to expel excess water. Cut the pressed tofu slices into 1/2-inch strips and set aside.

In a bowl, combine the wine, 1 tablespoon water, the tamari, cornstarch, cayenne, and sesame oil, and set aside. Boil the broccoli and carrots in a large pot of salted water until almost tender, about 2 minutes. Drain well. Heat 1 tablespoon of the safflower oil in a large skillet or wok over high heat. Add the broccoli and carrots and stir-fry 1 minute. Season lightly with salt and transfer to a plate. Wipe the skillet clean. Heat the remaining tablespoon safflower oil over high heat and add the tofu, garlic, and salt to taste. Return the broccoli and carrots to the skillet. Stir until heated through, about 10 seconds Add the tamari mixture and stir 20 seconds. Transfer to a platter and serve.

Serves 4

Kilocalories 244 Kc • Protein 18 gm • Fat 15 gm • Percent of calories from fat 51% •
Cholesterol 0 mg • Dietary fiber 4 gm • Sodium 353 mg • Calcium 109 mg

Tofu with Thai Peanut Sauce

1 tablespoon safflower oil
1 pound extra-firm tofu, cut into 1/2-inch strips
1 tablespoon minced fresh garlic
1 small hot chili, minced
1/2 cup chopped scallions
1 tablespoon chopped fresh ginger
1 tablespoon low-sodium tamari
1 tablespoon dry sherry
1 teaspoon sugar
1 8-ounce can sliced bamboo shoots, drained
1/4 cup unsalted peanuts, chopped
Spicy Peanut Sauce (see page 212)
Freshly cooked jasmine rice

Heat the oil in a large skillet over medium-high heat. Add the tofu, garlic, chili, scallions, and ginger, and cook for 5 minutes or until tofu is lightly browned. Add the tamari, sherry, sugar, bamboo shoots, and peanuts, and mix well. Add the Peanut Sauce and stir until well combined. Cook for 2 minutes or until all of the ingredients are hot. Serve at once over freshly cooked jasmine rice.

Serves 4

Kilocalories 226 Kc • Protein 17 gm • Fat 14 gm • Percent of calories from fat 54% • Cholesterol 0 mg • Dietary fiber 2 gm • Sodium 169 mg • Calcium 75 mg

Spicy Peanut Sauce

This makes a good dipping sauce for steamed vegetables, spring rolls, or just about anything.

4 tablespoons creamy peanut butter   2 teaspoons white vinegar
2 tablespoons low-sodium tamari $1^1/_2$ teaspoons chili paste
2 teaspoons sugar

In a small bowl or food processor, blend the peanut butter, 2 tablespoons water, the tamari, sugar, vinegar, and chili paste. Taste and adjust seasonings. Use at once or cover and refrigerate until ready to use.
Serves 4

Kilocalories 112 Kc • Protein 5 gm • Fat 6 gm • Percent of calories from fat 47% • Cholesterol 0 mg • Dietary fiber 1 gm • Sodium 493 mg • Calcium 8 mg

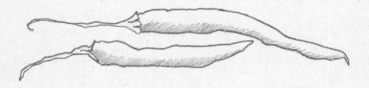

Stir-Fried Thai Vegetables

Although commercially prepared Thai curry pastes are available at Asian markets, making your own is simple and allows you to customize the flavor to suit your own taste.

2 tablespoons safflower oil
1 medium onion, halved lengthwise
  and thinly sliced
1 red bell pepper, cut into thin strips
1 green bell pepper, cut into thin
  strips
2 cups fresh broccoli florets,
  blanched

1 small hot chili, minced (optional)
2 tablespoons Red Curry Paste (see
  page 214) or commercial Thai
  red curry paste
2 tablespoons low-sodium tamari
1 teaspoon light brown sugar
1 cup fresh Thai basil leaves
Fresh cooked jasmine rice

Heat the oil in a large skillet or wok over high heat. Add the onion and stir-fry two minutes until it begins to soften. Add the bell peppers and stir-fry until almost tender, 2 minutes. Add the broccoli and chili, if using, and stir-fry 2 minutes until just tender. Add the curry paste, tamari, and sugar, and stir-fry 30 seconds or until well combined. Remove the skillet from the heat and add the basil, tossing to combine well. Transfer the mixture to a platter and serve with rice.
Serves 4

Kilocalories 122 Kc • Protein 3 gm • Fat 8 gm • Percent of calories from fat 54% • Cholesterol 0 mg • Dietary fiber 3 gm • Sodium 319 mg • Calcium 57 mg

Red Curry Paste

This curry paste can be used as a base for Thai red curries and as an addition to sauces, stir-fries, marinades, soups, and stews. Refrigerated and tightly covered, this curry paste will keep for 2 weeks.

12 dried red Thai chilies
2 teaspoons coriander seeds
1 teaspoon cumin seeds
1/2 cup chopped onion
4 garlic cloves, chopped
1/4 cup thinly sliced fresh lemongrass
2 tablespoons chopped fresh cilantro

1 tablespoon chopped fresh ginger
2 teaspoons finely grated lime zest
1/2 tablespoon sweet paprika
1 teaspoon nutmeg
1/2 teaspoon salt
1 1/2 tablespoons safflower oil

Wearing rubber gloves, stem and seed the chilies and cut them into 1/2-inch pieces. Soak for 20 minutes in a small bowl with enough warm water to cover. Drain the chilies, reserving 1 tablespoon of the soaking liquid.

Place the coriander and cumin seeds in a small skillet over medium heat and stir until fragrant, about 45 seconds, being careful not to burn them. Cool the spices, then finely grind in a blender or an electric spice grinder. In a food processor, purée the chilies to a paste with the reserved soaking liquid, the ground spices, and the onion, garlic, lemongrass, cilantro, ginger, lime zest, paprika, nutmeg, salt, and oil. Keep the curry paste tightly covered in the refrigerator until ready to use.

Serves 8 to 10 (makes about 1 cup)

Kilocalories 47 Kc • Protein 1 gm • Fat 3 gm • Percent of calories from fat 56% • Cholesterol 0 mg • Dietary fiber 2 gm • Sodium 3 mg • Calcium 24 mg

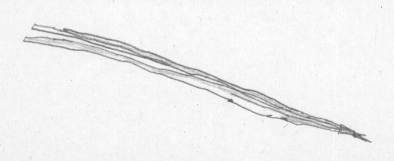

Thai Curry Sauce

This recipe is quick and easy because it uses prepared Madras curry powder rather than numerous individual spices. The use of lime and coconut make it distinctly different from an Indian curry sauce. Use it to transform stir-fried vegetables into an exotic feast.

2 tablespoons crushed dried hot
    chilies
6 garlic cloves, minced
2 tablespoons grated fresh ginger
1 tablespoon paprika
1 teaspoon grated lime zest
1 tablespoon Madras-style curry
    powder

2 tablespoons sugar
2 tablespoons freshly squeezed
    lime juice
2 tablespoons safflower oil
1/2 cup freshly grated coconut

In a blender, combine the chilies, garlic, ginger, paprika, lime zest, curry powder, sugar, lime juice, 2 cups water, the safflower oil, and coconut and purée. Pour the mixture into a saucepan and bring to a boil. Reduce the heat and simmer for about 15 minutes to blend flavors, stirring frequently to prevent scorching. Remove from the heat and set aside until ready to use.

Serves 6 to 8

Kilocalories 142 Kc • Protein 1 gm • Fat 12 gm • Percent of calories from fat 71% • Cholesterol 0 mg • Dietary fiber 2 gm • Sodium 13 mg • Calcium 20 mg

Thai Lime Vinaigrette

The basic vinaigrette of Southeast Asia is perfect as a dipping sauce and for salads or marinated vegetables.

¹/₂ cup freshly squeezed lime juice (from about 4 limes)

2 tablespoons low-sodium tamari

3 tablespoons light brown sugar

2 small dried red Thai chilies

1 large garlic clove, crushed

Combine the lime juice, tamari, sugar, chilies, and garlic in a bowl and whisk until well blended. Allow to stand at least 15 minutes at room temperature. Before serving, discard chilies and garlic.

Serves 4 to 6 (makes 1 cup)

Kilocalories 60 Kc • Protein 1 gm • Fat .1 gm • Percent of calories from fat 2% • Cholesterol 0 mg • Dietary fiber 0 gm • Sodium 312 mg • Calcium 19 mg

Pan-Asia

Satays with Ginger-Peanut Sauce

These Asian kebabs are traditionally made with chicken on the island of Bali, but seitan is a delicious alternative. Serve alone as an appetizer or over rice as an entrée.

1 pound seitan, cut into ¹/₄ × 6-inch strips

4 10-inch bamboo skewers, soaked in cold water for 30 minutes

3 tablespoons low-sodium tamari

1 tablespoon plus 1 teaspoon light brown sugar

2 garlic cloves, minced

1 cup Vegetable Stock (see page xxi)

¹/₄ cup roasted peanuts

1 tablespoon freshly squeezed lemon juice

1 tablespoon minced fresh ginger

¹/₄ teaspoon cayenne

Salt

Orange slices

Thread the seitan strips on the skewers, pushing down firmly. Blend ¹/₂ cup water, the tamari, 1 tablespoon of the brown sugar, and half the garlic in a shallow pan. Add the seitan and marinate for 30 minutes at room temperature, turning frequently.

Meanwhile, combine the stock, peanuts, lemon juice, remaining 1 teaspoon brown sugar, ginger, remaining garlic, and cayenne in a blender and purée until smooth. Transfer to a small saucepan over medium heat and simmer, stirring constantly, until thick enough to coat a spoon, about 10 minutes. Season with salt to taste.

Preheat the broiler. Place the satays 4 inches from the heat source and broil until well browned, about 3 minutes per side. Set 1 satay on each plate. Garnish with orange slices. Pass the sauce separately for dipping.

Serves 4

Kilocalories 204 Kc • Protein 33 gm • Fat 5 gm • Percent of calories from fat 20% • Cholesterol 0 mg • Dietary fiber 2 gm • Sodium 335 mg • Calcium 7 mg

Coconut Tempeh and Papaya Salad

The coconut milk and papaya add a hint of sweetness to this tangy Indonesian salad.

2 cups canned unsweetened
   coconut milk
1 pound tempeh
1/4 cup freshly squeezed lime juice
2 tablespoons low-sodium tamari
1 1/2 teaspoons sugar
2 small fresh serrano chilies, seeded
   and minced

1/3 cup finely chopped red onion
1/2 ripe papaya, cut into 1/4-inch dice
2 tablespoons finely chopped red
   bell pepper
2 tablespoons minced fresh cilantro
1 bunch watercress, trimmed

In a saucepan, bring the coconut milk to a simmer. Add the tempeh and poach for 5 minutes. Using a slotted spoon, transfer the tempeh to a large bowl. Add the lime juice, tamari, sugar, chilies, onion, papaya, bell pepper, and cilantro, and combine gently. Cover the salad mixture and refrigerate at least 2 hours or overnight. To serve, divide the watercress among salad plates and, using a slotted spoon, top with the marinated tempeh mixture.

Serves 4 to 6

Kilocalories 358 Kc • Protein 24 gm • Fat 15 gm • Percent of calories from fat 35% •
Cholesterol 0 mg • Dietary fiber 10 gm • Sodium 360 mg • Calcium 172 mg

Korean Bean Sprout Salad

This refreshing and crunchy salad is a traditional accompaniment to the Korean barbecue, but I find it complements most Asian meals. It's best to add the dressing at the last minute to keep the bean sprouts as crisp as possible.

3 tablespoons toasted sesame oil
3 tablespoons rice wine vinegar
1/8 teaspoon salt
1/8 teaspoon hot red pepper flakes

2 cups fresh bean sprouts
3 scallions, minced
1 tablespoon toasted sesame seeds

In a small bowl, combine the oil, vinegar, salt, and hot red pepper flakes until well blended. Place the bean sprouts in a medium bowl. Add the scallions and the dressing and toss lightly to combine. Spoon the salad into small individual bowls and sprinkle the sesame seeds on top.

Serves 4

Kilocalories 131 Kc • Protein 3 gm • Fat 12 gm • Percent of calories from fat 74% • Cholesterol 0 mg • Dietary fiber 2 gm • Sodium 79 mg • Calcium 39 mg

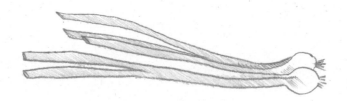

Asparagus Daikon Salad

Daikon is a large carrot-shaped white radish with a mild flavor. It is popular throughout Asia, where it is served raw and cooked. If asparagus are not in season, substitute broccoli or cauliflower florets.

1 pound fresh asparagus, tough ends trimmed	1/2 teaspoon salt
1 cup daikon, cut into matchstick julienne	1/2 teaspoon sugar
	2 tablespoons low-sodium tamari
3 garlic cloves, minced	2 teaspoons toasted sesame oil
1 tablespoon grated fresh ginger	1 tablespoon rice vinegar
	1/4 teaspoon cayenne

Slice the asparagus into matchsticks by cutting each stalk into 3-inch lengths, then slivering the lengths into thin strips with a sharp paring knife. Steam the asparagus for 3 to 5 minutes or until crisp tender. Combine the daikon, garlic, ginger, salt, sugar, tamari, sesame oil, vinegar, and cayenne in a large bowl. Add the warm asparagus and marinate for 10 minutes at room temperature before serving.

Serves 4

Kilocalories 69 Kc • Protein 4 gm • Fat 3 gm • Percent of calories from fat 32% • Cholesterol 0 mg • Dietary fiber 3 gm • Sodium 612 mg • Calcium 38 mg

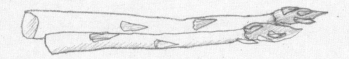

Indonesian Tempeh Salad

3 tablespoons rice vinegar
1 tablespoon toasted sesame oil
1/4 teaspoon hot chili sauce
1 teaspoon low-sodium tamari
2 cups crumbled poached tempeh
4 cups shredded iceberg lettuce
1 cup snow peas, blanched 1 minute
    in boiling salted water

1 cup bean sprouts
1 8-ounce can sliced water
    chestnuts, drained
1/2 cup grated carrot
3 scallions, chopped
2 tablespoons chopped walnuts

Combine the vinegar, sesame oil, chili sauce, and tamari in a shallow bowl. Add the tempeh and toss to coat well. Cover and refrigerate overnight. In a large bowl, combine the lettuce, snow peas, bean sprouts, water chestnuts, carrot, scallions, and walnuts. Add the marinated tempeh and the dressing and toss well. Serve immediately.
Serves 6

Kilocalories 190 Kc • Protein 13 gm • Fat 8 gm • Percent of calories from fat 37% • Cholesterol 0 mg • Dietary fiber 8 gm • Sodium 52 mg • Calcium 76 mg

Japanese Eggplant Salad

Japanese eggplants are smaller than those grown in the West. The most common variety is also drier and sweeter than Western eggplants, and can be found in most Asian grocery stores and many supermarkets.

2 tablespoons safflower oil
1 tablespoon toasted sesame oil
4 Japanese eggplants, trimmed and
    quartered lengthwise
1/2 teaspoon hot red pepper flakes
1 cup Vegetable Stock (see page xxi)
2 tablespoons low-sodium tamari
2 tablespoons dry sherry
1 tablespoon sugar
1/4 teaspoon cornstarch mixed with
    1 tablespoon water

1 teaspoon grated fresh ginger
4 tablespoons rice vinegar
1/8 teaspoon minced fresh garlic
8 ounces romaine lettuce, rinsed,
    dried, and cut crosswise into
    1-inch strips (about 6 cups)
6 ounces fresh snow peas, blanched
    1 minute in boiling salted water
1/4 cup thinly sliced red bell pepper
1/4 cup thinly sliced daikon

Heat the safflower and sesame oils in a large skillet over medium-high heat. Add the eggplant and hot red pepper flakes and stir-fry about 5 minutes, until the eggplant slices are lightly browned on both sides. Add the stock, tamari, sherry, and sugar. Reduce the heat to medium, cover, and cook until the eggplant is tender but still holds its shape, about 6 to 8 minutes. Transfer the eggplant to a large plate with a slotted spoon.

Strain the cooking liquid, reserving 3/4 cup. Boil the reserved liquid in the skillet until reduced to 1/2 cup, about 3 to 5 minutes. Stir in the cornstarch mixture and cook, stirring constantly, until the sauce is thickened, about 15 seconds. Pour the sauce into a small bowl along with any liquid from the eggplant. Add the ginger, rice vinegar, and garlic to the sauce. Taste and adjust seasonings. Set aside and allow to come to room temperature.

Divide the lettuce evenly among 4 dinner plates. In a small bowl, toss 3 tablespoons of the sauce with the snow peas, red bell pepper, and daikon. Place one quarter of the salad mixture in the center of each bed of romaine. Divide the eggplant slices among the plates, arranging the slices in a spoke pattern on each salad. Spoon the remaining sauce over the eggplant.

Serves 4

Kilocalories 182 Kc • Protein 4 gm • Fat 11 gm • Percent of calories from fat 50% • Cholesterol 0 mg • Dietary fiber 5 gm • Sodium 337 mg • Calcium 49 mg

Korean Cucumber Salad

This salad is best served within a few days. Otherwise, the cucumbers may lose their crispness.

3 medium cucumbers	$1/2$ teaspoon chopped fresh ginger
$3/4$ teaspoon salt	1 large scallion, chopped
$1/8$ teaspoon cayenne	1 small garlic clove, minced

Peel the cucumbers and slice lengthwise into halves, then cut each half into pieces $1/2$ inch wide. Place the cucumber pieces in a medium bowl and sprinkle with $1/4$ teaspoon of the salt. Stir gently to spread the salt. Wait 10 minutes, then wash the cucumber pieces well and drain. In a medium bowl, combine the cucumbers, cayenne, ginger, scallion, garlic, remaining $1/2$ teaspoon salt, and $1/3$ cup water. Mix well, cover the bowl with plastic wrap, and set in a warm place. Marinate 48 hours, stirring occasionally. Transfer the salad to a deep container, cover with water, cover the container, and then refrigerate. Drain and serve cold.

Serves 6 to 8

Kilocalories 21 Kc • Protein 1 gm • Fat .2 gm • Percent of calories from fat 8% • Cholesterol 0 mg • Dietary fiber 1 gm • Sodium 294 mg • Calcium 23 mg

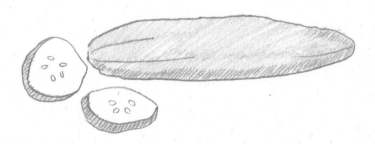

Kimchi

A classic Korean condiment, these sweet, sour, and spicy pickled vegetables will keep about 2 weeks if stored properly.

1 cup red wine vinegar
1 cup sugar
1/3 cup dry sherry
1/2 teaspoon salt
1/2 tablespoon minced fresh ginger
1 dried hot red chili, split, seeds removed
1/2 head Napa cabbage, chopped

1 large rib celery, cut in 1/4-inch diagonal slices
1 medium carrot, cut in 1/4-inch diagonal slices
1/2 red bell pepper, cut in 1/4-inch dice
2 large scallions, chopped

Combine 1 cup water, the vinegar, sugar, sherry, and salt in a medium saucepan over medium-high heat and bring to a boil. Reduce the heat to low and simmer 5 minutes. Remove the saucepan from the heat and let the mixture cool to room temperature. Stir the ginger and chili into the cooled vinegar mixture. Place the cabbage, celery, carrot, bell pepper, and scallions in a 1-quart glass jar or bowl with a tight-fitting lid. Ladle the vinegar mixture into the jar, seal tightly, and refrigerate at least 2 days before serving.

Serves 8 to 12

Kilocalories 124 Kc • Protein 1 gm • Fat .1 gm • Percent of calories from fat 1% • Cholesterol 0 mg • Dietary fiber 1 gm • Sodium 164 mg • Calcium 15 mg

Indonesian Tofu

The Indonesian rijsttafel, or "rice table," is a style of dining known the world over in which as many as thirty dishes, many vegetarian, are placed on a large buffet table. Indonesian cooking is known for its use of pungent spices, varying textures, and bright colors.

2 tablespoons olive oil
1/2 medium onion, diced
3 large garlic cloves, minced
1 fresh jalapeño, thinly sliced
6 large tomatoes, peeled and quartered
1 pound extra firm tofu, drained on paper towels

6 ounces canned unsweetened coconut milk
1 tablespoon freshly squeezed lime juice
3 cups freshly cooked white or brown rice
1 lime, quartered

Heat the oil in a large saucepan over medium heat. Add the onion, garlic, and jalapeño, and stir until the onion is lightly browned, about 5 minutes. Add all but 4 of the tomato quarters, cover, and cook, stirring occasionally, until the tomatoes are soft, about 15 minutes. Uncover and cook, stirring occasionally, until the sauce thickens, about 10 minutes. Increase the heat to medium-high. Add the tofu and stir until heated through, about 5 minutes. Reduce the heat to low. Blend in the coconut milk and lime juice. Remove from the heat. Spoon the rice into shallow bowls. Top with the tofu and sauce. Garnish with the lime and the remaining 4 tomato quarters and serve.

Serves 4

Kilocalories 251 Kc • Protein 16 gm • Fat 16 gm • Percent of calories from fat 54% • Cholesterol 0 mg • Dietary fiber 3 gm • Sodium 41 mg • Calcium 69 mg

Cold Buckwheat Noodles
with Jade Vegetables

Buckwheat noodles, or soba, are popular in Japan where they are used in soups, sautéed with vegetables, and served cold as in this recipe.

2 teaspoons minced fresh garlic
2 teaspoons minced fresh ginger
2 teaspoons grated orange zest
6 tablespoons safflower oil
6 tablespoons seasoned rice vinegar
    (sushi vinegar)
1 teaspoon dry mustard
1 teaspoon toasted sesame oil
1/4 teaspoon hot red pepper flakes
Approximately 1/4 teaspoon salt

1 medium head bok choy, cut into
    1/2-inch strips
1/4 cup chopped scallion
1 green bell pepper, cut into 1/8-inch
    julienne strips
2 medium zucchini, cut into
    1/2-inch dice
6 ounces buckwheat soba noodles
1 head romaine lettuce, cut
    crosswise into 1/4-inch strips

In a food processor, combine the garlic, ginger, and orange zest, and pulse to combine. With the machine running, add the safflower oil, vinegar, mustard, sesame oil, hot red pepper flakes, and salt to taste, and mix until well combined. Set aside. Heat a large skillet or wok over high heat, add the bok choy, scallion, bell pepper, zucchini, and sauce mixture, and stir until the vegetables are slightly softened, about 3 minutes. Remove from the heat. Taste and adjust seasonings.

Cook the noodles in large pot of boiling salted water, stirring occasionally, until just tender, about 10 minutes. Drain, rinse under cold water, and drain again. Add the noodles to the vegetable mixture, tossing gently to combine. Transfer to a large bowl. Cover and refrigerate until chilled.

Serves 4

Kilocalories 432 Kc • Protein 9 gm • Fat 24 gm • Percent of calories from fat 49% • Cholesterol 0 mg • Dietary fiber 6 gm • Sodium 558 mg • Calcium 143 mg

Vietnamese Noodles with Tempeh and Peanuts

Vietnamese cuisine is similar to Thai, but is generally less spicy. The hottest Vietnamese dishes will be found in the South, where cooks are more liberal with chilies than their Northern counterparts.

2 tablespoons safflower oil

8 ounces tempeh, sliced 1/4 inch thick and cut into 1-inch-wide strips

1/4 cup low-sodium tamari or Vegetarian "Fish" Sauce (see page 235)

3 tablespoons rice vinegar

2 tablespoons sugar

1 tablespoon hoisin sauce

2 teaspoons hot chili oil

6 ounces linguine

1 cup shredded carrot

4 scallions, minced

2 tablespoons minced fresh cilantro leaves

1/2 cup chopped unsalted dry-roasted peanuts

Heat the oil in a large skillet or wok over medium-high heat. Add the tempeh and cook until browned, about 5 minutes. Transfer to a large bowl. Blend the tamari, vinegar, sugar, hoisin sauce, and chili oil in a small bowl, then add the mixture to the tempeh in the bowl.

Cook the noodles in a large pot of boiling salted water, stirring occasionally, until almost tender, about 5 minutes. Add the carrot and continue cooking until both are just tender, about 2 minutes. Drain well, then add the noodles and carrots to the tempeh mixture. Add the scallions, cilantro, and peanuts to the tempeh and noodle mixture, tossing gently to combine. Taste and adjust seasonings. Serve warm or at room temperature.

Serves 4

Kilocalories 529 Kc • Protein 23 gm • Fat 24 gm • Percent of calories from fat 39% • Cholesterol 0 mg • Dietary fiber 6 gm • Sodium 750 mg • Calcium 87 mg

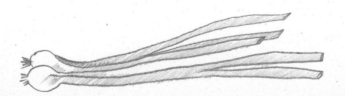

Indonesian Coconut Rice

Coconut-flavored rice is a one-dish feast. For special occasions in Indonesia it is molded into a tower and garnished with vegetables, peanuts, or toasted coconut.

2 tablespoons safflower oil
1 large onion, minced
4 garlic cloves, minced
4 scallions, minced
1 tablespoon grated fresh ginger
1 teaspoon ground turmeric
1 teaspoon hot red pepper flakes
1 teaspoon ground cinnamon

1/4 teaspoon ground cloves
1 teaspoon dry mustard
1 tablespoon sugar
4 cups cooked long-grain rice
1 cup unsweetened shredded
    coconut
Salt and freshly ground pepper

Heat the oil in a large skillet over medium-high heat. Add the onion and garlic, cover, and cook until the onion is softened, about 5 minutes. Remove cover, add the scallions, ginger, turmeric, hot red pepper flakes, cinnamon, cloves, mustard, and sugar, and cook over medium-high heat, stirring constantly, for 2 minutes until fragrant. Add the rice and stir to mix evenly. Remove from heat and gently stir in the shredded coconut. Season to taste with salt and pepper, cover, and leave for 5 minutes before serving.

Serves 6

Kilocalories 236 Kc • Protein 3 gm • Fat 8 gm • Percent of calories from fat 31% • Cholesterol 0 mg • Dietary fiber 2 gm • Sodium 34 mg • Calcium 22 mg

Vegetable Pancit

Pancit *is the Filipino word for noodle. If Filipino-style* pancit *noodles are unavailable, substitute angel hair pasta.*

2 tablespoons safflower oil
1 small onion, thinly sliced
2 garlic cloves, minced
2 cups shredded green cabbage
$^1/_2$ cup shredded carrot
$^1/_4$ cup Vegetable Stock (see
    page xxi)
2 tablespoons low-sodium tamari

8 ounces pancit noodles or angel
    hair pasta, cooked according to
    package directions
$^1/_4$ teaspoon freshly ground pepper
2 scallions, minced
Additional tamari (optional)

Heat the oil in a large skillet or wok over medium-high heat. Add the onion, garlic, cabbage, and carrot, and stir-fry for 2 minutes until slightly softened. Add the stock and tamari, cover, and cook 2 minutes longer or until tender. Remove the cover and add the cooked noodles, tossing well to combine. Season with pepper and additional tamari, if desired. Transfer to a serving platter and garnish with the minced scallions.

Serves 4

Kilocalories 310 Kc • Protein 9 gm • Fat 8 gm • Percent of calories from fat 23% •
Cholesterol 0 mg • Dietary fiber 3 gm • Sodium 325 mg • Calcium 45 mg

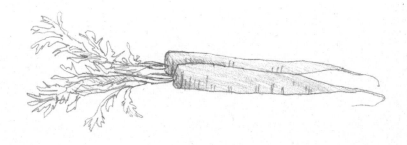

Japanese Soba Noodles

This Japanese dish of hearty buckwheat noodles and crisp stir-fried vegetables in a spicy-sweet sauce is one of my husband's favorites.

1 tablespoon light brown sugar

1/4 cup low-sodium tamari

2 tablespoons dry sherry

2 tablespoons toasted sesame oil

1 tablespoon rice vinegar

1 teaspoon minced fresh ginger

1 garlic clove, minced

1/4 teaspoon cayenne

2 teaspoons cornstarch

1 tablespoon safflower oil

1 red bell pepper, cut into thin strips

1/4 cup sliced scallions

1 cup shredded green cabbage

8 ounces buckwheat soba noodles, cooked

2 tablespoons sesame seeds

2 tablespoons minced fresh parsley

In a shallow bowl, combine the sugar, tamari, sherry, sesame oil, vinegar, ginger, garlic, and cayenne. Stir in the cornstarch and set aside. Heat the safflower oil in a large skillet over medium-high heat. Add the bell pepper, scallions, and cabbage, and cook 3 minutes to soften. Add the sauce and cook 2 minutes longer, stirring to thicken sauce. Add the cooked soba noodles, tossing to coat. Serve garnished with the sesame seeds and parsley.

Serves 4

Kilocalories 258 Kc • Protein 6 gm • Fat 10 gm • Percent of calories from fat 33% • Cholesterol 0 mg • Dietary fiber 3 gm • Sodium 438 mg • Calcium 34 mg

Korean Rice and Millet

Koreans serve rice at every meal, either alone or combined with beans or another grain, such as millet, which has a delicate, nutty flavor. This dish can be made spicier by increasing the amount of black pepper.

1 1/2 cups white or brown rice
1/2 cup millet
3 cups Vegetable Stock (see page xxi)
1 teaspoon toasted sesame oil

Salt and freshly ground pepper
1 tablespoon chopped fresh cilantro
   or parsley
1 tablespoon toasted sesame seeds

In a large saucepan, bring the rice, millet, and stock to a boil. Reduce the heat to low, cover the saucepan, and simmer for 25 minutes or until the water has been absorbed. Remove the pan from the heat, add the sesame oil and salt and pepper to taste, fluff with fork, and cover for 5 minutes longer. Transfer to a bowl, fluff again with a fork, and garnish with the cilantro and toasted sesame seeds.

Serves 4

Kilocalories 403 Kc • Protein 9 gm • Fat 5 gm • Percent of calories from fat 12% • Cholesterol 0 mg • Dietary fiber 5 gm • Sodium 66 mg • Calcium 52 mg

Daikon Walnut Condiment

I like to serve this deliciously spicy Indonesian condiment with rice or noodle dishes.

¹/₂ cup walnuts
1 cup peeled and thinly sliced daikon
1 small fresh hot green chili, halved
   and seeded

¹/₂ teaspoon salt
1 teaspoon cider vinegar

Preheat the oven to 350°F. Spread the walnuts on a baking sheet. Bake until lightly toasted, about 10 minutes. Turn the oven off. Leave the walnuts in the oven for 5 minutes. In a food processor, chop the daikon and chili in short on and off bursts. Add the walnuts and salt and coarsely purée. Blend in the vinegar. Transfer to a jar or bowl with a tight-fitting lid and refrigerate until ready to serve.

Serves 4 to 6

Kilocalories 103 Kc • Protein 4 gm • Fat 9 gm • Percent of calories from fat 72% •
Cholesterol 0 mg • Dietary fiber 1 gm • Sodium 296 mg • Calcium 16 mg

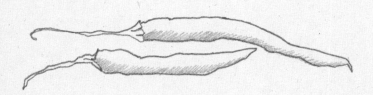

Wasabi Miso Dressing

This Japanese-inspired dressing features wasabi, the fiery green horseradish served with sushi, and miso paste, a nutritious fermented soybean paste available at natural food stores and Asian grocery stores.

1 tablespoon miso paste
1/4 cup sake or dry white wine
1 teaspoon sugar
3/4 teaspoon wasabi powder

2 garlic cloves, finely minced
1/2 teaspoon finely grated fresh
   ginger

Combine the miso, sake, sugar, wasabi, garlic, ginger, and 1/2 cup water in a small bowl and stir until well blended. Taste and adjust seasonings.

Serves 4 (makes about 1 cup)

Kilocalories 37 Kc • Protein 1 gm • Fat .3 gm • Percent of calories from fat 7% • Cholesterol 0 mg • Dietary fiber 0 gm • Sodium 158 mg • Calcium 7 mg

Tamari Vinaigrette

Use this dressing on salads and as a light dipping sauce for Japanese tempura.

^{1}/3 cup safflower oil
2 tablespoons low-sodium tamari
2 tablespoons rice vinegar
1 tablespoon toasted sesame oil

^{1}/4 teaspoon minced fresh garlic
^{1}/4 teaspoon sugar
^{1}/8 teaspoon hot red pepper flakes

Combine the safflower oil, tamari, vinegar, sesame oil, garlic, sugar, and hot red pepper flakes in a food processor or small bowl until well blended. Store tightly covered in a small bowl or jar in the refrigerator.

Serves 4 (makes about ^{1}/2 cup)

Kilocalories 205 Kc • Protein 1 gm • Fat 21 gm • Percent of calories from fat 92% • Cholesterol 0 mg • Dietary fiber 0 gm • Sodium 374 mg • Calcium 3 mg

Vegetarian "Fish" Sauce

Known as nuoc mam *in Vietnam and* nam pla *in Thailand, this sauce is traditionally used in much the same way as soy sauce and tamari in China and Japan. I like the extra dimension it gives to a recipe, although, in a pinch, tamari can be substituted. Bottles of traditional* nuoc mam *and* nam pla *are available at most Asian markets.*

3/4 cup low-sodium tamari
1 garlic clove, minced
1/8 teaspoon hot red pepper flakes

1 tablespoon freshly squeezed
  lemon juice
1 tablespoon sugar

Combine the tamari, garlic, hot red pepper flakes, lemon juice, sugar, and 1/4 cup water in a small jar with a tight-fitting lid. Shake until well blended. Store the jar in the refrigerator to use as needed in recipes.

Serves 8 (makes about 1 cup)

Kilocalories 16 Kc • Protein 1 gm • Fat 0 gm • Percent of calories from fat 0% • Cholesterol 0 mg • Dietary fiber 0 gm • Sodium 456 mg • Calcium 5 mg

INDEX

Adzuki beans for Many Bean Salad, 154
African cuisine, 99–100, 121–40
   see also individual recipes
African Yam Salad, 130
Alioli, Chili, 73
Almonds:
   Gazpacho, White, 75
   Pilaf, Persian, with Golden Raisins and, 115
Aluminum pans, xxi
Anaheim (or California) chilies, xiii
Anchos, xiii
Appetizers:
   Alioli, Chili, 73
   Baba Ghanouj, 102
   Caviar, Texas, 7
   Cherry Peppers, Stuffed, 57
   Chickpeas:
      Hummus, Red Chili, 101
      Patties, Egyptian, 121
   Dumplings, Spicy Ginger, 183
   Guacamole, Smooth and Sassy, 17
   Hummus, Red Chili, 101
   Jerk-Spiced Nuggets, Jamaican, 38
   Pakoras, Vegetable, 147
   Peperonata, 58
   Plantain Fritters, Spicy, 37
   Samosas, Vegetable, 148
   Satays with Ginger-Peanut Sauce, 217
   Spring Rolls, Vegetable, 203
   Tapenade on French Bread Rounds, 83
Apricots:
   Rice, Moroccan, with Pine Nuts and, 135
   Vegetable Tagine, Moroccan, with, 128
Argentinian-Inspired Seitan Cutlets, 47

Arugula Potato Salad, 65
Asian cuisine, 180–235
Asparagus Daikon Salad, 220
Avocado(s):
   Guacamole, Smooth and Sassy, 17
   Quinoa-Stuffed, 46
   Salad with Lime Dressing, Jicama and, 23
   Soup, Chilled, 19

Baba Ghanouj, 102
Barbados-Style Grilled Kebabs, 42
Barbecue Sauce, Texas, 15
Basil:
   about, xv
   Thai Tofu with Chilies and, 209
Basmati Rice:
   Biryani, Vegetable, 171
   Cashew Pilau with Raisins and Peas, 172
   Curried Vegetable Pilaf, 170
   Persian Pilaf with Almonds and Golden
      Raisins, 115
Basque Chickpea Stew, 85
Basque Chicory Salad, 88
Basque cuisine, 55
Basque Eggplant Salad, 87
Bean curd, *see* Tofu
Bean(s):
   about, xviii–xix
   cooking times, xix
   Salad, Many, 154
   soaking, xviii–xix
   see also specific types of beans
Bean Sprout(s):
   Salad, Korean, 219

Bean Sprouts *(cont.)*
  Sichuan Noodle Salad, Cold, 186
  Tempeh Salad, Indonesian, 221
Beet(s):
  Salad, Syrian, 104
  Svikla, 91
Bell Pepper(s):
  Bulgur-Stuffed, Middle Eastern, 117
  Catalan-Style Vegetables, Roasted, 79
  Chilean Stuffed, 49
  Farfalle Salad with Roasted, 63
  Kebabs, Spicy Skewered Vegetable, 108
  Majorcan Baked Vegetables, 89
  Peperonata, 58
  Potatoes and, Roasted, 67
  Red, and Mushroom Salad with Walnuts, 76
  Stir-fried Thai Vegetables, 213
Beverages for cooling down, xxii
Biryani, Vegetable, 171
Black beans for Many Bean Salad, 154
Black-eyed peas for Texas Caviar, 7
Blender, xxii
Bobotie, South African, 138
Bok Choy:
  Buckwheat Noodles with Jade Vegetables,
    Cold, 226
  Seitan, Stir-Fried Ginger, and, 190
  Spring Rolls, Vegetable, 203
Borracha Sauce, 35
Brazilian Lemon-Chili Sauce, 50
British cuisine, 55
Broccoli:
  Ginger, 188
  Stir-fried Thai Vegetables, 213
  Tofu, Hot Thai, 210
Broccoli Rabe, Stir-Fried, 156
Brown Rice:
  with Apricots and Pine Nuts, Moroccan, 135
  and Bean Salad with Cumin Vinaigrette,
    Mexican, 22
  Casserole, Red beans and, 31
  with Creole Sauce, 12
  Fried, Hunan, 198
  with Lentils and Onions, 110
  and Millet, Korean, 231
  Persian Orange, with Pistachios, 113
  Salad:
    with Cumin Vinaigrette, Mexican Bean and,
      22

Curried, 152
  Island, 40
  Middle Eastern, 106
Buckwheat Noodles:
  with Jade Vegetables, Cold, 226
  Japanese Soba, 230
Bulgur:
  Chickpea Patties, Egyptian, 121
  Pilaf, Turkish, 114
  -Stuffed Peppers, Middle Eastern, 117
Burritos, Spicy Bean Curd and Spinach, 27

Cabbage:
  Braised, with Cardamom, 162
  Coleslaw, Cajun, 9
  Kimchi, 224
  Pancit, Vegetable, 229
  Sichuan, 187
    Vegetable Stir-fry, 191
  Soba Noodles, Japanese, 230
Cajun Coleslaw, 9
Cameroon-Style Seitan and Spinach, 136
Cannellini beans:
  Chili, Red-Hot White Bean, 10
  Escarole Soup, 59
Capers:
  Pasta alla Puttanesca, 72
  Tapenade on French Bread Rounds, 83
Cardamom:
  Braised Cabbage with, 162
  Garam Masala, 176
Caribbean cuisine, 6, 37–44
  see also individual recipes
Caribbean Vegetable Stew, 39
Carrots:
  Indian Spiced, 161
  Masala, Vegetable, 169
  Moroccan Spiced, 133
  Tofu, Hot Thai, 210
Cashew Pilau with Raisins and Peas, 172
Cauliflower:
  with Mustard-Dill Sauce, 90
  Pakoras, Vegetable, 147
  Soup, Kashmiri Vegetable, 149
Cavatelli Primavera, Spicy, 64
Caviar, Texas, 7
Cayenne chilies, about, xiii
Cherry Peppers, Stuffed, 57

Chickpea(s):
  Couscous, Tunisian, 137
  Hummus, Red Chili, 101
  Patties, Egyptian, 121
  Salad, Many Bean, 154
  Soup:
    and Lentil, Moroccan, 126
    Middle Eastern, 103
  Stew, Basque, 85
  and Sweet Potatoes, 107
  Vegetable Tagine with Apricots, Moroccan, 128
Chicory Salad, Basque, 88
Chilean Stuffed Peppers, 49
Chili, Red-Hot White Bean, 10
Chili(es):
  about, xii–xiii
  Alioli, 73
  experimenting with, xii–xiii
  handling, xiii
  Harissa Sauce, 127
  hot, xiii
  mild, xiii
  Pesto, Cilantro-, 14
  Red Chili Hummus, 101
  Red Curry Paste, 214
  Rice with Tomatillos and, 34
  Sauce, Brazilian Lemon-, 50
  substitutions, xiii–xiv
  suggestions for mild and hot, xiii
  Thai Tofu with Basil and, 209
China, cuisine of, 181, 183–200
  see also individual recipes
Chocolate for Mole Poblano, 36
Chutney:
  Green Tomato and Pear, 173
  Island Rice Salad, 40
  Mint, 174
  Pear and Green Tomato, 173
  Pineapple Date, 175
Cilantro:
  about, xv
  Pesto, Chili-, 14
Coconut:
  Rice, Indonesian, 228
  Soup, Tofu, 206
  Tempeh and Papaya Salad, 218
  Thai Curry Sauce, 215
  Tofu, Indonesian, 225
  Vegetable Salad, Spiced, 207

Condiments, *see* Sauces, dressings, and
  condiments
Cooking spray, nonstick vegetable, xviii
Cooling down after eating spicy food, xxii
Coriander (seeds), about, xvi
Corn:
  Peppers, Chilean Stuffed, 49
  Soup:
    Hot and Spicy, 204
    Spicy, 20
Couscous:
  about, xvi
  Salad, Moroccan, 131
  Seven Vegetable, 140
  with Spiced Vegetables, 139
  Tunisian, 137
Cucumber:
  Raita, 158
  Salad, Korean, 223
Cumin:
  about, xiv
  Vinaigrette, Mexican Rice and Bean Salad
    with, 22
Currants:
  Couscous Salad, Moroccan, 131
  Tomatoes Stuffed with Pine Nuts and, 111
Curry(ied):
  Mushrooms, 155
  No-Meat Balls, 163
  Paste, Red, 214
  Potato Soup, Mint-Flecked, 150
  Rice Salad, 152
  Sauce, Thai, 215
  Tofu, with Green Beans, 165
  Vegetable Pilaf, 170
Curry (powder or paste), about, xiv, 144

Daikon:
  Salad, Asparagus, 220
  Walnut Condiment, 232
Dairy product substitutions, xviii
Dal, Kidney Bean, 158
Dates for Pineapple Chutney, 175
Dill-Mustard Sauce, Cauliflower with, 90
Dressing, *see* Sauces, dressings, and condiments
Dumplings, Spicy Ginger, 183

Eastern European cuisine, 55
East Indian Tofu, Broiled, 164

Eggplant:
  Baba Ghanouj, 102
  Catalan-Style Vegetables, Roasted, 79
  Majorcan Baked Vegetables, 89
  and Potato Stew, Spicy, 151
  Ratatouille, 86
  Salad:
    Basque, 87
    Japanese, 222
  Turkish Stuffed, 109
Egyptian Chickpea Patties, 121
Egyptian Fava Beans, 132
Enchiladas, Baked Tempeh, 32
Equipment, xxi–xxii
Escarole Soup, 59
Ethiopian Wat, 129
Europe, Mediterranean, cuisine of, 55–93
  see also individual recipes

Fajitas, Grilled Vegetable, 29
Falafel, Egyptian, 121
Farcia Intchauspe, 92
Farfalle Salad with Roasted Peppers, 63
Fat intake, tips for lowering, xviii
Fava Beans:
  Egyptian, 132
  Ragout, Italian Vegetable, 61
  Rice and, with Vegetables, 81
"Fish" Sauce, Vegetarian, 235
Five-Spice:
  Tempeh, 189
  Tofu and Vegetable Salad, 185
Food processor, xxii
French cuisine, 55
Fried Rice, Hunan, 198
Fritters:
  Pakoras, Vegetable, 147
  Plantain, Spicy, 37
Fruit:
  Salad, Mexican, 24
  see also specific types of fruit

Garam Masala, 176
Garlic:
  about, xvi
  -Mint Sauce, Middle Eastern, 118
  Soup, 74
Gazpacho, White, 75

Ginger:
  about, xiv
  Broccoli, 188
  Dumplings, Spicy, 183
  Orange Dressing, 119
  -Peanut Sauce, Satays with, 217
  Seitan and Bok Choy, Stir-Fried, 190
  Watercress Soup, 184
Grains:
  about, xix–xx
  cooking whole grains, xix–xx
  see also specific grains, e.g., Bulgur; Millet
Grapes for White Gazpacho, 75
Great Northern bean(s):
  Salad, Many Bean, 154
  Soup, Tuscan White Bean, 60
Greek cuisine, 56
Green Beans:
  Biryani, Vegetable, 171
  Coconut Vegetable Salad, Spiced, 207
  South African, 134
  Spicy Indian, 159
  Tofu Curry with, 165
Green Bell Peppers, see Bell Peppers
Green Tomato and Pear Chutney, 173
Guacamole, Smooth and Sassy, 17

Harissa Sauce, 127
Horseradish:
  about, xiv
  Svikla, 91
  Wasabi Miso Dressing, 233
Hot and Sour Thai Soup, 205
Hot and Spicy Corn Soup, 204
Hot Chili Paste, Bean Curd with, 196
Hot Mustard Dipping Sauce, 201
Hotness of recipe, symbols indicating, xvii
Hummus, Red Chili, 101
Hunan Fried Rice, 198
Hunan Vegetable Stir-fry, 194

India, cuisine of, 145–76
  see also individual recipes
Indian Spiced Carrots, 161
Indonesia, cuisine of, 182
  see also individual recipes
Indonesian Coconut Rice, 228
Indonesian Tempeh Salad, 221
Indonesian Tofu, 225

Island Rice Salad, 40
Italian Vegetable Ragout, 61
Italy, cuisine of, 55–72
   see also individual recipes

Jalapeño(s):
   about, xiii
   Sauce, Penne Pasta with, 13
   Soup with Tortilla Triangles, Holy, 21
Jamaican Baked Vegetables, 43
Jamaican Jerk Sauce, 44
Jamaican Jerk-Spiced Tempeh Nuggets, 38
Jambalaya, Jumpin', 11
Japanese Soba Noodles, 230
Jerk-Spice(d):
   Sauce, Jamaican, 44
   Tempeh Nuggets, Jamaican, 38
Jicama Salad:
   Fruit, Mexican, 24
   with Lime Dressing, Avocado and, 23

Kale Soup, Portuguese Spicy, 84
Kashmiri Vegetable Soup, 149
Kebabs:
   Barbados-Style Grilled, 42
   Spicy Skewered Vegetable, 108
Kidney Bean(s):
   Dal, 158
   Pumpkin Stew, North African, 124
   Rice Casserole, Red Beans and, 31
Kimchi, 224
Knives, xxi–xxii
Korea, cuisine of, 182
   see also individual recipes
Korean Bean Sprout Salad, 219
Korean Rice and Millet, 231

Lemon:
   Chili-Sauce, Brazilian, 50
   Tempeh with Sweet Potatoes, Citrus-
      Marinated, 48
Lemongrass, about, xvi
Lentil(s):
   in Onion Gravy, 166
   Rice with Onions and, 110
   Soup, Moroccan Chickpea and, 126
   Spanish, 77
Lime:
   Dressing, Avocado and Jicama Salad with, 23

-Marinated White Bean Salad, 45
   Sweet Potato(es), Rum and Lime-Laced, 41
   Thai Curry Sauce, 215
   Vinaigrette, Thai, 216
Lo mein noodles, Stir-Fried Tofu with, 197

Main courses
   Bean Curd with Hot Chili Paste, 196
   Biryani, Vegetable, 171
   Bobotie, South African, 138
   Broccoli, Ginger, 188
   Brown Rice:
      with Apricots and Pine Nuts, Moroccan,
         135
      with Creole Sauce, 12
      Fried, Hunan, 198
      with Lentils and Onions, 110
      with Millet, Korean, 231
      Persian Orange, with Pistachios, 113
      Red Beans and, Casserole, 31
   Buckwheat Noodles:
      with Jade Vegetables, Cold, 226
      Japanese Soba, 230
   Bulgur:
      Pilaf, Turkish, 114
      -Stuffed Peppers, Middle Eastern, 117
   Burritos, Spicy Bean and Spinach, 27
   Cashew Pilau with Raisins and Peas, 172
   Couscous:
      Seven Vegetable, 140
      with Spiced Vegetables, 139
      Tunisian, 137
   Easter Pie, Italian, 69
   Eggplant, Turkish Stuffed, 109
   Enchiladas, Baked Tempeh, 32
   Fajitas, Grilled Vegetable, 29
   Hunan Vegetable Stir-fry, 194
   Jambalaya, Jumpin', 11
   Kebabs:
      Barbados-Style Grilled, 42
      Spicy Skewered Vegetable, 108
   Lentils in Onion Gravy, 166
   Majorcan Baked Vegetables, 89
   Masala, Vegetable, 169
   No-Meat Balls, Curried, 163
   Noodles:
      Cold Buckwheat, with Jade Vegetables, 226
      Stir-fried Tofu with, 197
      Vegetable Pancit, 229

Main courses *(cont.)*
  Vietnamese, with Tempeh and Peanuts, 227
Paella, Vegetarian, 80
Pasta alla Puttanesca, 72
Penne:
  Pasta with Jalapeño Sauce, 13
  with Uncooked Tomato Sauce and Olives,
    70
Peppers, Chilean Stuffed, 49
Pilaf with Almonds and Golden Raisin,
    Persian, 115
Quesadillas, Veggie, 30
Red Beans and Rice Casserole, 31
Rice:
  with Apricots and Pine Nuts, Moroccan,
    135
  and Fava Beans with Vegetables, 81
  Fried, Hunan, 198
  Indonesian Coconut, 228
  with Lentils and Onions, 110
  and Millet, Korean, 231
  with Tomatillos and Chilies, 34
Seitan:
  and Bok Choy, Stir-Fried Ginger, 190
  Cutlets, Argentinian-Inspired, 47
  Jambalaya, Jumpin', 11
  and Spinach, Cameroon-Style, 136
  with Tomato-Orange Sauce, Mexican, 33
Tacos with Salsa Fresca, 25
Tahini Vegetables with Pita Bread, 116
Tandoori-Style Tempeh, 167
Tempeh:
  Cacciatore, 68
  Five-Spice, 189
  and Peanuts, Vietnamese Noodles with, 227
  in Spicy Orange Sauce, 195
  with Spicy Sichuan Sauce, Mahogany, 199
  with Sweet Potatoes, Citrus-Marinated, 48
  and Vegetables, Stir-Fried, 192
Tofu:
  Broiled East Indian, 164
  with Chilies and Basil, Thai, 209
  Curry with Green Beans, 165
  Farcia Intchauspe, 92
  Fried Rice, Hunan, 198
  Hot Thai, 210
  Indonesian, 225
  with Noodles, Stir-fried, 197
  Piperade, 93

  with Romesco Sauce, 82
  with Spiced Plum Sauce, 168
  Spicy Stir-Fried, 193
  Sweet-and-Sour Bean Curd, 208
  with Thai Peanut Sauce, 211
Tomatoes Stuffed with Currants and Pine
    Nuts, 111
Vegetable(s):
  Jamaican Baked, 43
  Pilaf, Curried, 170
  Seven Vegetable Couscous, 140
  Stir-fried Thai, 213
  Stir-fry, Sichuan, 191
  Tagine with Apricots, Moroccan, 128
  Tekka, Broiled, 112
  White Bean Chili, Red-Hot, 10
  Ziti with Spicy Tomato Sauce, 71
Majorcan Baked Vegetables, 89
Masalas, 144
  Garam Masala, 176
  Vegetable, 169
Mediterranean Europe, cuisine of, 55–93
  see also individual recipes
Mexican cuisine, 6, 17–36
  see also individual recipes
Mexican Fruit Salad, 24
Mexican Seitan and Tomato-Orange Sauce, 33
Middle Eastern Bulgur-Stuffed Peppers, 117
Middle Eastern Chickpea Soup, 103
Middle Eastern Cuisine, 99, 101–19
  see also individual recipes
Middle Eastern Garlic-Mint Sauce, 118
Middle Eastern Rice Salad, 106
Millet, Korean Rice and, 231
Mint:
  Chutney, 174
  -Flecked Curried Potato Soup, 150
  -Garlic Sauce, Middle Eastern, 118
Mole Poblano, 36
Moroccan Chickpea and Lentil Soup, 126
Moroccan Couscous Salad, 131
Moroccan Rice with Apricots and Pine Nuts,
    135
Moroccan Spiced Carrots, 133
Moroccan Vegetable Tagine with Apricots, 128
Mushroom(s):
  Curried, 155
  Hunan Vegetable Stir-fry, 194
  Kebabs, Spicy Skewered Vegetable, 108

Portobello:
    Broiled Vegetables Tekka, 112
    Fajitas, Grilled Vegetable, 29
    Salad with Walnuts, Red Pepper and, 76
    Shiitake:
        Sichuan Vegetable Stir-fry, 191
        Spring Rolls, Vegetable, 203
    Sichuan Vegetable Stir-fry, 191
Mustard:
    about, xiv
    -Dill Sauce, Cauliflower with, 90
    Dipping Sauce, Hot, 201

Nigerian Peanut Soup, 122
No-Meat Balls, Curried, 163
Noodle(s):
    Buckwheat:
        with Jade Vegetables, Cold, 226
        Japanese, 230
    Salad, Cold Sichuan, 186
    Stir-fried Tofu with, 197
    Vegetable Pancit, 229
North African Pumpkin Stew, 124

Oat milk, xviii
Okra:
    Gumbo, Spicy, 8
    Peanut Soup, Nigerian, 122
Olive oil, xvi, xviii
Olives:
    Orange and Onion Salad, Turkish Spiced,
        105
    Pasta alla Puttanesca, 72
    Penne with Uncooked Tomato Sauce and, 70
    Tapenade on French Bread Rounds, 83
    Vegetable Stew, Caribbean, 39
Onion(s):
    Catalan-Style Vegetables, Roasted, 79
    Gravy, Lentils in, 166
    Rice with Lentils and, 110
    Salad, Turkish Spiced Orange and, 105
    Sweet and Sour Zucchini and, 66
Orange(s):
    Ginger Dressing, 119
    Rice with Pistachios, Persian, 113
    Salad:
        Middle Eastern Rice, 106
        Onion and, Turkish Spiced, 105
        Sicilian, 2

Sauce, Spicy, Tempeh in, 195
Oregano, about, xvi
Organic produce, xviii

Paella, Vegetarian, 80
Pans and pots, xxi
Pantry, international, xv–xvii
Papaya Salad, Coconut Tempeh and, 218
Parsley, Cilantro-Chili Pesto with, 14
Pasta:
    Cavatelli Primavera, Spicy, 64
    Noodles with Tempeh and Peanuts,
        Vietnamese, 227
    Pancit, Vegetable, 229
    Penne:
        with Jalapeño Sauce, 13
        with Uncooked Tomato Sauce and Olives, 70
    Spaghetti alla Puttanesca, 72
    Ziti with Spicy Tomato Sauce, 71
Peanut(s):
    Biryani, Vegetable, 171
    No-Meat Balls, Curried, 163
    Sauce:
        Ginger-peanut, Satays with , 217
        Spicy, 212
        Thai, with Tofu, 211
    Soup, Nigerian, 122
    Vietnamese Noodles with Tempeh and, 227
    Yam and Groundnut Stew, West African, 123
Pear Chutney, Green Tomato and, 173
Peas:
    black-eyed, for Texas Caviar, 7
    Cashew Pilau with Raisins and, 172
    Pakoras, Vegetable, 147
    Rice Salad, Curried, 152
    Salad, Many Bean, 154
    Samosas, Vegetable, 148
    Split, for Spicy Indian Green Beans, 159
Penne:
    Pasta with Jalapeño Sauce, 13
    with Uncooked Tomato Sauce and Olives, 70
Peppercorns, about, xv
Peppers:
    Bell, see Bell Peppers
    Cherry, Stuffed, 57
Persian Orange Rice with Pistachios, 113
Persian Pilaf with Almonds and Golden Raisins,
    115
Pesto, Cilantro-Chili, 14

Pilaf:
    with Almonds and Golden Raisins, Persian, 115
    Curried Vegetable, 170
    Turkish, 114
Pineapple:
    Chutney, Date, 175
    Vegetable Pilaf, Curried, 170
    Vegetable Stew, Caribbean, 39
Pine Nuts:
    Cilantro-Chili Pesto, 14
    Rice, Moroccan, with Apricots and, 135
    Tomatoes Stuffed with Currants and, 111
Pinto Bean(s):
    Burritos, Spicy Bean and Spinach, 27
    Salad:
        Many Bean, 154
        Mexican Rice and Bean, with Cumin
            Vinaigrette, 22
    Tacos with Salsa Fresca, 25
    Vegetable Stew, Caribbean, 39
Pistachios, Persian Orange Rice with, 113
Pita Bread, Tahini Vegetables with, 116
Plantain Fritters, Spicy, 37
Plum Sauce, Spiced, Tofu with, 168
Pomegranate for Mexican Fruit Salad, 24
Portobello mushrooms:
    Broiled Vegetables Tekka, 112
    Fajitas, Grilled Vegetable, 29
Portuguese Spicy Kale Soup, 84
Potato(es):
    Majorcan Baked Vegetables, 89
    Masala, Vegetable, 169
    Pakoras, Vegetable, 147
    Roasted, and Peppers, 67
    Salad:
        Arugula, 65
        Spiced, 153
    Samosas, Vegetable, 148
    Soup:
        Kashmiri Vegetable, 149
        Mint-Flecked Curried, 150
        Yucatán, 18
    Spanish, Spicy, 78
    Stew, Spicy Eggplant and, 151
Pots and pans, xxi
Pumpkin Stew, North African, 124

Quesadillas, Veggie, 30
Quinoa-Stuffed Avocados, 46

Ragout, Italian Vegetable, 61
Raisins:
    Biryani, Vegetable, 171
    Cashew Pilau with Peas and, 172
    Golden, Persian Pilaf with Almonds and,
        115
Raita, Cucumber, 158
Rataouille, 86
Red Bell Peppers, see Bell Peppers
Red Curry Paste, 214
Rice:
    with Apricots and Pine Nuts, Moroccan,
        135
    Basmati:
        Biryani, Vegetable, 171
        Cashew Pilau with Raisins and Peas, 172
        Curried Vegetable Pilaf, 170
        Persian Pilaf with Almonds and Golden
            Raisins, 115
    Brown, see Brown Rice
    Coconut, Indonesian, 228
    Curried Vegetable Pilaf, 170
    Fried, Hunan, 198
    Jambalaya, Jumpin', 11
    with Lentils and Onions, 110
    and Millet, Korean, 231
    Paella, Vegetarian, 80
    with Tomatillos and Chilies, 34
Rice milk, xviii
Romesco Sauce, Tofu with, 82
Rum and Lime-Laced Sweet Potatoes, 41

Safflower oil, saturated fat content, xviii
Saag, Spinach, 160
Salads:
    Asparagus Daikon, 220
    Avocado and Jicama, with Lime Dressing,
        23
    Bean, Many, 154
    Bean Sprout, Korean, 219
    Beet, Syrian, 104
    Brown Rice:
        and Bean with Cumin Vinaigrette, Mexican,
            22
        Curried, 152
        Island, 40
        Middle Eastern, 106
    Cavatelli Primavera, 64
    Chicory, Basque, 88

Coconut:
  Tempeh and Papaya, 218
  Vegetable, Spiced, 207
Couscous, Moroccan, 131
Cucumber, Korean, 223
Eggplant:
  Basque, 87
  Japanese, 222
Farfalle, with Roasted Peppers, 63
Fruit, Mexican, 24
Orange:
  Middle Eastern Rice, 106
  and Onion, Turkish Spiced, 105
  Sicilian, 62
Potato:
  Arugula, 65
  Spiced, 153
Red Pepper and Mushroom, with Walnuts, 76
Rice, brown, *see this entry under* Brown Rice
Sichuan Noodle, Cold, 186
Tempeh, Indonesian, 221
Tofu and Vegetable, Five-Spice, 185
White Bean, Lime-Marinated, 45
Yam, African, 130
Salsa Fresca, 26
  Tacos with, 25
Salsa Picante, 28
Samosas, Vegetable, 148
Satays with Ginger-Peanut Sauce, 217
Sauces, dressings, and condiments:
  Barbecue Sauce, Texas, 15
  Borracha, 35
  Chutney:
    Green Tomato and Pear, 173
    Mint, 174
    Pineapple Date, 175
  Daikon Walnut Condiment, 232
  "Fish" Sauce, Vegetarian, 235
  Garam Masala, 176
  Garlic-Mint Sauce, Middle Eastern, 118
  Harissa Sauce, 127
  Jerk Sauce, Jamaican, 44
  Lemon-Chili Sauce, Brazilian, 50
  Lime Vinaigrette, Thai, 216
  Mole Poblano, 36
  Mustard Dipping Sauce, Hot, 201
  Orange Ginger Dressing, 119
  Peanut Sauce:
    Satays with Ginger-, 217

    Spicy, 212
    Tofu with Thai, 211
  Pesto, Cilantro-Chili, 14
  Red Curry Paste, 214
  Salsa Fresca, 26
  Salsa Picante, 28
  Spicy Sichuan Sauce, 200
  Thai Curry Sauce, 215
  Vinaigrette:
    Tamari, 234
    Thai Lime, 216
  Wasabi Miso Dressing, 233
Sausages, vegetarian:
  Easter Pie, Italian, 69
  Jambalaya, Jumpin', 11
  Paella, Vegetarian, 80
Seitan:
  about, xvi
  and Bok Choy, Stir-Fried Ginger, 190
  Cutlets, Argentinian-Inspired, 47
  Jambalaya, Jumpin', 11
  Kebabs, Barbados-Style Grilled, 42
  Paella, Vegetarian, 80
  Satays with Ginger-Peanut Sauce, 217
  and Spinach, Cameroon-Style, 136
  with Tomato-Orange Sauce, Mexican, 33
Senegalese Soup, 125
Serrano chilies, about, xiii
Sesame oil, xvi, xviii
Shiitake mushrooms:
  Sichuan Vegetable Stir-fry, 191
  Spring Rolls, Vegetable, 203
Sichuan Cabbage, 187
Sichuan Noodle Salad, Cold, 186
Sichuan Sauce, Spicy, 200
  Mahogany Tempeh with, 199
Sichuan Vegetable Stir-fry, 191
Sicilian Orange Salad, 62
Side dishes:
  Broccoli Rabe, Stir-Fried, 156
  Cabbage with Cardamom, Braised, 162
  Carrots:
    Indian Spiced, 161
    Moroccan Spiced, 133
  Catalan-Style Vegetables, Roasted, 79
  Cauliflower with Mustard-Dill Sauce, 90
  Chickpeas and Sweet Potatoes, 107
  Coleslaw, Cajun, 9
  Cucumber Raita, 158

Side dishes *(cont.)*
  Fava Beans, Egyptian, 132
  Green Beans:
    South African, 134
    Spicy Indian, 159
  Kidney Bean Dal, 158
  Kimchi, 224
  Lentils, Spanish, 77
  Mushrooms, Curried, 155
  Potatoes:
    Roasted, and Peppers, 67
    Spicy Spanish, 78
  Quinoa-Stuffed Avocados, 46
  Sichuan Cabbage, 187
  Spinach Saag, 160
  Svikla, 91
  Sweet and Sour Onions and Zucchini, 66
  Sweet Potatoes, Rum and Lime-Laced, 41
Snow Peas:
  Five-Spice Tofu and Vegetable Salad, 185
  Hunan Vegetable Stir-fry, 194
  Japanese Eggplant Salad, 222
  Tempeh Salad, Indonesian, 221
Soups:
  Avocado, Chilled, 19
  Chickpea:
    and Lentil, Moroccan, 126
    Middle Eastern, 103
  Corn:
    Hot and Spicy, 204
    Spicy, 20
  Escarole, 59
  Garlic, 74
  Gazpacho, White, 75
  Hot and Sour Thai, 205
  Jalapeño with Tortilla Triangles, Holy, 21
  Kale, Portuguese Spicy, 84
  Lentil and Chickpea, Moroccan, 126
  Okra Gumbo, Spicy, 8
  Peanut, Nigerian, 122
  Potato:
    Mint-Flecked Curried, 150
    Yucatán, 18
  Senegalese, 125
  Tofu:
    Coconut, 206
    Hot and Sour Thai, 205
  Vegetable, Kashmiri, 149
  Watercress, Ginger, 184

  White Bean, Tuscan, 60
South African Bobotie, 138
South African Green Beans, 134
South American cuisine, 6, 45–50
  see also individual recipes
Southeast Asian Cuisine, 180–81
  see also individual recipes
Soy cheese for Veggie Quesadillas, 30
Soy milk, xviii
Soy sausages, *see* Sausages, vegetarian
Spaghetti alla Puttanesca, 72
Spain, cuisine of, 56, 73–82
  see also individual recipes
Spanish Lentils, 77
Spice mill, xxii
Spiciness of recipe, symbols indicating, xvii
Spicy Sichuan Sauce, 200
  Mahogany Tempeh with, 199
Spinach:
  Burritos, Spicy Bean and, 27
  Coconut Vegetable Salad, Spiced, 207
  Saag, 160
  and Seitan, Cameroon-Style, 136
Spring Rolls, Vegetable, 203
Stews:
  Chickpea, Basque, 85
  Eggplant and Potato, Spicy, 151
  Pumpkin, North African, 124
  Ragout, Italian Vegetable, 61
  Ratatouille, 86
  Vegetable, Caribbean, 39
  Vegetable Tagine with Apricots, Moroccan, 128
  Wat, Ethiopian, 129
  Yam and Groundnut, West African, 123
Stir-fry(ied):
  Broccoli Rabe, 156
  Ginger Seitan and Bok Choy, 190
  Hunan Vegetable, 194
  Sichuan Vegetable, 191
  Tempeh and Vegetables, 192
  Thai Vegetables, 213
  Tofu:
    with Noodles, 197
    Spicy, 193
Stock, Vegetable:
  about, xx
  Basic, xxi
Svikla, 91

Sweet-and-Sour Bean Curd, 208
Sweet Potato(es):
  Baked Vegetables, Jamaican, 43
  Chickpeas and, 107
  Citrus-Marinated, Tempeh with, 48
  Rum and Lime-Laced, 41
  Soup, Mint-Flecked Curried Potato, 150
  Vegetable Stew, Caribbean, 39
  see also Yams
Syrian Beet Salad, 104

Tabasco, about, xiii
Tacos with Salsa Fresca, 25
Tagine, Moroccan Vegetable with Apricots,
  128
Tahini:
  about, xvi
  Vegetables with Pita Bread, 116
Tamari:
  "Fish" Sauce, Vegetarian, 235
  Vinaigrette, 234
Tandoori-Style Tempeh, 167
Tapenade on French Bread Rounds, 83
Tekka, Broiled Vegetables, 112
Tempeh:
  about, xvi
  Bobotie, South African, 138
  Cacciatore, 68
  Coconut, and Papaya Salad, 218
  Enchiladas, Baked, 32
  Five-Spice, 189
  Jerk-Spiced Nuggets, Jamaican, 38
  Paella, Vegetarian, 80
  and Peanuts, Vietnamese Noodles with, 227
  Salad, Indonesian, 221
  in Spicy Orange Sauce, 195
  with Spicy Sichuan Sauce, Mahogany, 199
  with Sweet Potatoes, Citrus-Marinated, 48
  Tandoori-Style, 167
  and Vegetables, Stir-Fried, 192
  Wat, Ethiopian, 129
Tequila for Borracha Sauce, 35
Texas Barbecue Sauce, 15
Texas Caviar, 7
Thai chilies, about, xiii
Thai Curry Sauce, 215
Thailand, cuisine of, 181–82, 203–16
  see also individual recipes
Thai Lime Vinaigrette, 216

Thai Soup, Hot and Sour, 205
Thai Tofu with Chilies and Basil, 209
Tofu:
  about, xvi–xvii
  Bean Curd with Hot Chili Paste, 196
  Broiled East Indian, 164
  with Chilies and Basil, Thai, 209
  Cucumber Raita, 158
  Curry with Green Beans, 165
  as dairy substitute, xviii
  Dumplings, Spicy Ginger, 183
  Easter Pie, Italian, 69
  Farcia Intchauspe, 92
  Five-Spice, and Vegetable Salad, 185
  Fried Rice, Hunan, 198
  Hot and Sour Thai Soup, 205
  Hot Thai, 210
  Indonesian, 225
  No-Meat Balls, Curried, 163
  Penne Pasta with Jalapeño Sauce, 13
  Piperade, 93
  with Romesco Sauce, 82
  Soup:
    Coconut, Thai, 206
    Hot and Sour Thai, 205
  with Spiced Plum Sauce, 168
  Stir-Fried:
    with Noodles, 197
    Spicy, 193
  Sweet-and-Sour Bean Curd, 208
  with Thai Peanut Sauce, 211
Tomatillos, Rice with Chilies and, 34
Tomato(es):
  Bean Curd, Sweet-and-Sour, 208
  Jambalaya, Jumpin', 11
  Okra Gumbo, Spicy, 8
  -Orange Sauce, Mexican Seitan with, 33
  Pasta alla Puttanesca, 72
  Peppers, Chilean Stuffed, 49
  Ragout, Italian Vegetable, 61
  Ratatouille, 86
  Salsa Fresca, 26
  Salsa Picante, 28
  Sauce, Spicy, Ziti with, 71
  Sauce, Uncooked, and Olives, Penne with, 70
  Stuffed with Currants and Pine Nuts, 111
  Tempeh Cacciatore, 68
  Tofu, Indonesian, 225

Tortilla(s):
Fajitas, Grilled Vegetable, 29
Quesadillas, Veggie, 30
Triangles, Holy Jalapeño Soup with, 21
Tunisian Couscous, 137
Turkish Bulgur Pilaf, 114
Turkish Spiced Orange and Onion Salad, 105
Turkish Stuffed Eggplant, 109
Turmeric, about, xvii
Turnips for Kashmiri Vegetable Soup, 149
Tuscan White Bean Soup, 60

United States, cuisine of, 5, 7–15
see also individual recipes

Vegetable Stock, *see* Stock, Vegetable
Vietnamese Noodles with Tempeh and Peanuts,
227
Vinaigrette:
Tamari, 234
Thai Lime, 216

Walnut(s):
Condiment, Daikon, 232
Red Pepper and Mushroom Salad with,
76
Wasabi:
about, xv
Miso Dressing, 233
Wat, Ethiopian, 129

Water chestnut(s):
Dumplings, Spicy Ginger, 183
Tempeh Salad, Indonesian, 221
Watercress Soup, Ginger, 184
West African Yam and Groundnut Stew, 123
White Bean(s):
Chili, Red-Hot, 10
Escarole Soup, 59
Salad, Lime-Marinated, 45
Soup, Tuscan, 60
Wonton wrappers for Spicy Ginger Dumplings,
183

Yam(s):
Baked Vegetables, Jamaican, 43
and Groundnut Stew, West African, 123
Salad, African, 130
see also Sweet Potato(es)
Yogurt for Cucumber Raita, 158
Yucatán Potato Soup, 18

Ziti with Spicy Tomato Sauce, 71
Zucchini:
Buckwheat Noodles with Jade Vegetables,
Cold, 226
Kebabs, Spicy Skewered Vegetable, 108
Ragout, Italian Vegetable, 61
Ratatouille, 86
Sweet and Sour Onions and, 66
Vegetable Pilaf, Curried, 170